Key Concepts in
Human Resource
Management

Recent volumes include:

Fifty Key Concepts in Gender Studies
Jane Pilcher and Imelda Whelehan

Key Concepts in Medical Sociology
Jonathan Gabe, Mike Bury and Mary
Ann Elston

Key Concepts in Leisure Studies
David Harris

**Key Concepts in Critical Social
Theory**
Nick Crossley

Key Concepts in Urban Studies
Mark Gottdiener and Leslie Budd

Key Concepts in Mental Health
David Pilgrim

**Key Concepts in Journalism
Studies**
Bob Franklin, Martin Hamer, Mark
Hanna, Marie Kinsey and John
Richardson

**Key Concepts in Political
Communication**
Darren G. Lilleker

**Key Concepts in Teaching Primary
Mathematics**
Derek Haylock

Key Concepts in Work
Paul Blyton and Jean Jenkins

Key Concepts in Nursing
Edited by Elizabeth
Mason-Whitehead, Annette
McIntosh, Ann Bryan and
Tom Mason

**Key Concepts in Childhood
Studies**
Allison James and Adrian James

**Key Concepts in Public
Relations**
Bob Franklin, Mike Hogan,
Quentin Langley, Nick Mosdell
and Elliot Pill

The SAGE Key Concepts series provides students with accessible and authoritative knowledge of the essential topics in a variety of disciplines. Cross-referenced throughout, the format encourages critical evaluation through understanding. Written by experienced and respected academics, the books are indispensable study aids and guides to comprehension.

JOHN MARTIN

Key Concepts in
Human Resource
Management

Los Angeles | London | New Delhi
Singapore | Washington DC

First published 2010

SAGE Publications Ltd
1 Oliver's Yard
55 City Road
London EC1Y 1SP

SAGE Publications Inc.
2455 Teller Road
Thousand Oaks, California 91320

SAGE Publications India Pvt Ltd
B 1/I 1 Mohan Cooperative Industrial Area
Mathura Road
New Delhi 110 044

SAGE Publications Asia-Pacific Pte Ltd
33 Pekin Street #02-01
Far East Square
Singapore 048763

Library of Congress Control Number: 2009938116

British Library Cataloguing in Publication data

A catalogue record for this book is available from the British Library

ISBN 978-1-84787-330-9
ISBN 978-1-84787-331-6 (pbk)

Typeset by C&M Digitals (P) Ltd, Chennai, India
Printed and bound in Great Britain by
CPI Antony Rowe, Chippenham, Wiltshire
Printed on paper from sustainable resources

FSC
www.fsc.org
MIX
Paper from
responsible sources
FSC® C013604

Dedicated to Val, Orla, Lily, Phoebe, Jake and Nathan

contents

key concepts in
human resource management

Introduction

Key Concepts in Human Resource Management offers an important guide to making the most of, and extending your understanding of the key concepts in your human resource management (HRM) course. It will provide you with essential help designed to enhance your understanding in line with your course requirements.

The book should be used as a supplement to your HRM textbook and lecture notes. You should read the relevant entries in parallel with your course lectures and wider reading and note where each topic is covered in both the syllabus and this book. Ideally, you should buy this book at the beginning of your HRM course – it will provide you with a brief explanation of any topics you are having trouble with, and of course its value in revising for assignments and exams should not be underestimated!

This *Key Concepts* book is intended to:

- Provide you with a summary of key concepts that will facilitate your understanding of them when they are encountered in lectures and tutorials.
- Provide you with a summary of key concepts that will facilitate your understanding of textbooks and the associated wider reading.
- Identify which key concepts are primarily associated with each other through the 'See also' feature.
- Identify significant recommended reading and references for each key concept discussed.
- Save you time when you are preparing for seminars and tutorials by providing key information on the main terms that you would be expected to know and use.
- Save you time when you are preparing coursework by providing summary information on key terms that you would be expected to know and use.
- Save you time when you are revising for exams by providing a ready source of material in relation to HRM key concepts.
- Provide a framework to organise the most important HRM points from textbooks, lecture notes, and other learning materials.

Whichever HRM textbook you are using you should read this *Key Concepts* book in parallel with it to identify where specific topics are covered because some topics will appear in more than one location in a textbook. For example, performance appraisal has relevance in reward management, training and career development and might be covered in each of those chapters in a textbook. Each entry or key concept that follows is intended to summarise that topic and some of the debates surrounding it. The approach adopted by the book does not automatically assume a managerial perspective in that managers will sometimes have an agenda or perspective which would be different from that of employees, the owners of a business or academics that study HRM. It is therefore intended that each key concept discussed provides an insight into more than one perspective on the topic discussed. As a student of HRM, you need to be aware of how practitioners think about the key issues that face them as professionals seeking to provide a business with the best people management advice and guidance. But you also need to be aware of some of the other points of view and interpretations in relation to the key concepts in HRM. For example, the UK is a predominantly capitalist-based economy and that carries with it certain expectations in relation to the nature of organisations; the role of work; and the relative rights and obligations of employees, managers, owners, politicians, and society at large. HR managers must work within these 'givens' as the behaviour of employees is strongly grounded in the social structures that shape society. The strongest and most able HR managers are aware of the socially determined nature of work and much of what they do, and can work with the degree of ambiguity and uncertainty implied by such perspectives.

One difficulty in defining what HRM means arises because the term 'human resource management' is used in two different ways. Firstly it can refer to the department within an organisation that has the responsibility for policy and practice in relation to 'people management' within the business. The primary activities embraced within such a department would typically be those covered by most HRM textbooks. Used in the second way, HRM seeks to reflect a particular approach to the management of people as distinct from the earlier approach adopted under the umbrella term 'personnel management'. Because the practices associated with the organisational need to manage people are subject to constant adaptation as a consequence of fashion, legislative, social, educational, organisational, economic and labour market changes, it has been argued that personnel management had become outdated and that the philosophy, focus and approach to people management offered by HRM more effectively meet the needs of modern organisations.

It is against that background and on the following criteria that the HRM key concepts were selected for inclusion:

- *Concepts of significance in the HR discipline*   There is a vast range of topics, concepts and perspectives that have significance for the theory and practice of HRM. Every HRM concept is ultimately related to every other concept in a complex web of interactions, dependencies and consequential chains of events. For example, performance appraisal occurs in many areas of HR practice including resourcing, performance management, career development, promotion, discipline and redundancy decisions. Consequently a way had to be found to provide a comprehensive, meaningful and accessible listing of key concepts. Some compromise was inevitable.
- *Concepts that have some durability*   In HRM new ideas and approaches emerge on a frequent basis and some practices will disappear or change just as quickly as they emerge. Only a few will display durability and consequently in selecting the concepts to include here the decision was taken to adopt a 'topics' rather than 'practices' approach. The topics included were selected to provide the best focus on appropriate concepts with scope for a discussion of actual practices within each as appropriate.
- *Concepts that were neither too small or too large*   This was the most difficult decision criteria to achieve in that some concepts had of necessity to be broken down into a number of separate entries whilst others were not so easily dealt with and so some degree of compromise had to be made between the relative magnitude and the number of concepts to be included.
- *Concepts that could provide a basis for discussion*   The purpose of this book is to explore the key concepts in some degree of depth. As a result, although some degree of description is necessary it is not intended to be a practitioner handbook or a recipe book based on 'How to do HRM'. Consequently, the number and range of concepts cover the most significant issues and so provide an opportunity to discuss the academic perspectives on each.

introduction

3

Absence Management

> *Absence refers to an individual not being at work at a time when they would normally be expected to be present. This can be for many reasons both acceptable and unacceptable. Absence management refers to the processes and procedures adopted by management to identify and wherever possible control and minimise avoidable absence.*

The levels of attendance at work can be viewed as a reflection of the general wellbeing of an organisation as well as the individuals that work within it. That is because it can be viewed as having causes beyond the immediate health issues of the employees concerned and therefore as a reflection of what goes on within the organisation. For example, people may stay away from work because they are being bullied, or they are under too much pressure, or their boss has an aggressive management style. It is also possible that stress at work can cause physical or psychological problems for employees and in turn this will make it impossible for employees to attend work. It is a significant problem for UK employers. For example, it has been suggested that the cost to UK employers in 2002 was £11.6 billion. The employee reactions might include a lowering of morale among workers having to cover for absent colleagues and management's loss of credibility by not dealing effectively with people considered to be 'pulling a fast one'. It has been suggested that approximately 26 million requests are made each year for medical sick-notes, of which about 9 million are perhaps not genuine.

The CIPD (2008) annual survey of absence found that during the previous 12 months the levels of absence in both the public and private sectors had reduced. In the public sector it was reported as 9.8 days per employee and in the private sector as 8.4 days per employee. The average cost of absence was reported as being £666 per employee per year, up by about £7 on the previous year. The survey also found that the main causes of short-term absence for all employees were minor illnesses such as colds, flu and stomach upsets. Among all workers these were followed by back pain, musculoskeletal injuries, and stress together with home and family responsibilities. The main causes of long-term absence reported among manual workers were acute medical conditions, back pain, musculoskeletal conditions, stress and mental health problems. Among non-manual workers stress was reported as the major cause of long-term absence, followed by acute medical conditions, mental health problems (anxiety and depression), musculoskeletal conditions and back pain.

A number of sources suggest that absence from work can result from a number of factors that can be categorised under the following headings:

1 *Job content and context*   This can include factors such as the design of the job; work output pressures; the stress levels associated with work; work group dynamics; management style; company procedures and policies; nature and type of employment contract (permanent or fixed/short-term); and group/organisational norms with regard to attendance.

2 *Employee values*   The level of responsibility that the individual feels towards the job; customers; the work group; management; and the organisation. The personal values that an individual holds in relation to regular attendance under particular conditions (their personal work ethic).

3 *Employee characteristics*   Factors such as age; education; family circumstances and background; and personality.

4 *Pressure to attend work*   Factors such as economic and market conditions; company wage policies and incentive arrangements; company disciplinary and other absence management policies and practice; work group norms and dynamics; and level of organisational commitment.

5 *Ability to attend work*   Factors such as illness (short- or long-term); accidents (at work or outside); family responsibilities and commitments; and transport difficulties.

Each of the first four categories will impact on the motivation (or likelihood) that the individual will attend work on a regular basis, whilst the fifth will impact on the ability of an individual to actually do so.

There are a number of statistics that can be calculated to measure absence rates, including the following:

1 *The Lost Time Rate*   This reflects the percentage of total working time (hours or days) available in a given period (week, month, quarter or annual) which has been lost due to absence. It can be calculated

for the company, department, team or individuals to identify relative absence rates:

$$\frac{\text{Total absence (hours or days) in the period} \times 100}{\text{Possible total (hours or days) in the period}}$$

2   *The Frequency Rate*   This reflects the number of absences on average taken by employees, expressed as a percentage of the total number of employees:

$$\frac{\text{Number of spells of absence in the period} \times 100}{\text{Number of employees}}$$

So, for example, where an organisation employs 250 workers, and during this time there was a total of 25 occurrences of absence, the frequency rate would be:

$$\frac{25}{250} \times 100 = 10\%$$

Replacing the total number of occurrences of absence with the number of employees having at least one spell of absence in the period, this calculation produces an individual level frequency rate. So, for example, by using the same organisation from the example above which employed 250 workers, and calculating that during the review period there was a total of 18 employees who each had at least one occurrence of absence, the frequency rate would be:

$$\frac{18}{250} \times 100 = 7.2\%$$

3   *The Bradford Factor*   The Bradford Factor identifies frequent short-term absences by individuals, by measuring the number of spells of absence. The formula is:

Absence score = (Spells of absence × Spells of absence) × Total duration of absence

This measure considers both the number and duration of absences, but gives a heavier weighting to the number of spells of absence. It is also usually calculated over a one year time period. For example:

- 15 one-day absences: $(15 \times 15) \times 15 = 3375$
- 5 two-day absences: $(5 \times 5) \times 10 = 250$
- 2 five-day absences and 4 three-day absences: $(6 \times 6) \times 22 = 792$

The issue common to each of these measures of absence is that the results in themselves don't provide an absolute indication of the existence of a problem; they simply provide a measure of the magnitude of the occurrence. It is for each organisation to decide for itself what 'level' of absence is acceptable and at what point some form of action will become necessary to deal with the implications that such figures indicate. In that sense the results of these calculations provide a comparative measure – one that gains significance from a comparison with the same results obtained from somewhere else or at another time: for example, the same data from a previous year (or years); the same data from a benchmark company; the same data from the same industry or locality. Each of these comparisons provides a basis for decision making in relation to the absence data collected.

Traditionally, absence will have been dealt with through the disciplinary processes that an organisation has available to it. The underlying logic here is that the contract of employment requires absolute attendance unless a serious issue prevents it. From the discussion above it should be clear that there are many reasons for absence and that a more sophisticated approach is required that would take account of the wide variety of potential causes. One approach to guiding the development of an absence strategy involves the following stages:

- *Assess the absence problem* Use appropriate and accurate records (perhaps by adopting the measures outlined above) to monitor general and specific incidences of absence. Also engage in benchmarking absence levels against other organisations and industries.
- *Locate specific absence problems, areas or individuals* Not everyone or every department will have significant absence problems and so it is necessary first to identify where high absence levels exist and who takes the most time off work, and more importantly for what reason.
- *Identify and prioritise absence causes* This process does not automatically indicate that everyone so identified will be subjected to disciplinary action. It might identify sections in which the stress levels are very high due to work pressures or other factors; it might identify areas of work activity with particular safety problems; it might also identify areas of poor job design. There are many possible reasons for absence and it is necessary to begin to find out what lies behind this before deciding on appropriate courses of action.
- *Evaluate current absence control methods.*

- *Redesign (if necessary) the absence control procedures* Set targets for absence levels and absence reduction and determine action levels. Establish procedures and guidelines for return to work interviews and 'during absence'/progress reviews. Consider the impact of absence on performance management; career development; and incentive payment practices.

- *Implement the absence control policy and procedures* Form clear procedural links between the disciplinary procedure and its appropriate application for instances of absence. Disciplining for absence (including dismissal) can be a potentially fair action but only if it is undertaken in an appropriate manner and based on sound information.

- *Monitor the effectiveness of the procedure* Monitor absence levels and take appropriate action within the established procedures.

- *Provide training and support for line managers.*

- *Consider health promotion and occupational health involvement in work design and employee support.*

- *Consider various support issues* These could include flexible working; job sharing; part-time working; tele-working; and medical insurance as ways of minimising the disruptive effects (for employees and employers) of some forms of absence.

The CIPD (2009) suggest that absence policies should clearly set out employees' rights and obligations when taking time off from work due to sickness by:

- Providing details of contractual sick pay terms and its relationship with statutory sick pay.

- Outlining the process employees must follow if taking time off sick, covering when and whom employees should notify if they are not able to attend work.

- Including when (after how many days) employees will need a self-certificate form.

- Containing information on when they will require a medical certificate (sick-note) from their doctor to certify their absence.

- Mentioning that the organisation reserves the right to require employees to attend an examination by a company doctor and (with the employee's consent) to request a report from the employee's doctor.

- Outlining the role of any occupational health department or provision (if such exists) in developing proactive measures to support staff health and wellbeing.

- Including a provision for return to work interviews (identified as one of the most effective interventions to manage short-term absence).
- Including an indication of company intentions with regard to maintaining contact with sick employees and also to facilitating effective return to work strategies.

When seeking to manage absence levels care should be taken to avoid presenteeism, which refers to situations where individuals will feel pressured to attend work when they should not do so and to stay at work beyond their normal working hours. Common difficulties with effective return to work arrangements include a lack of consultation with employees, their trade union, HR staff and line managers; a lack of training in making work/job adjustments possible; and little or no budget allocations for such adaptations or return to work processes. It is often difficult to persuade other departments to absorb workers for whom special provision might be necessary or who have been out of the workforce for some considerable time. Wellness management is a topic beginning to emerge in organisations which includes a range of services, processes and facilities to promote good health. Benefits can result in resourcing, the psychological contract, duty of care and productivity aspects of HR activity.

See also: behaviour management; counselling, coaching and mentoring; discipline and grievance; employee empowerment and engagement; incentive schemes; organisational culture; quality of working life and the psychological contract

BIBLIOGRAPHY

ACAS (2009) 'Managing attendance and employee turnover'. Advisory booklet. London: ACAS. Available at http://www.acas.org.uk/
CIPD (2008) 'Absence management'. Annual Survey Report. Available at http://www.cipd.co.uk/NR/rdonlyres/6D0CC654-1622-4445-8178-4A5E071B63EF/0/absencemanagementsurveyreport2008.pdf (last accessed July 2009).
CIPD (2009) 'Absence measurement and management'. *Factsheet*. Available at www.cipd.co.uk (last accessed July 2009).
Incomes Data Services (2009) *Absence Management*. HR Studies, No. 889. London: IDS.

absence management

9

Assessment/ Development Centre

> *A recruitment or development process using a series of tests, interviews, group and individual exercises that are scored by a team of assessors in order to evaluate candidates.*

The origins of assessment centres go back to the 1940s in the UK when they were used by War Office Selection Boards. They were developed because the then current officer selection system had resulted in a significant proportion of officers being subsequently rejected as unsuitable. The officer selection system at the time was based on interviews incorporating factors such as social and educational background, achievement in the "other ranks"' (if candidates were already serving in the military), and exceptional smartness in appearance and presentation. The revised selection process involving the development of what would now be recognised as an assessment centre was based on the types of behaviour that a successful officer was considered to display. The tasks included leaderless group exercises, selection tests and individual interviews carried out by a senior officer, junior officer, and a psychiatrist. The proportion of officers being subsequently defined as unfit for duty dropped significantly as a result of the revised selection process.

The major strength of an assessment or development centre is that it allows for a broader range of relevant methods to be used in the recruitment or development process. It is claimed in the CIPD (2009) factsheet that assessment centres used as part of the recruitment and selection process allow the potential employee to experience a microcosm of the actual job that they have applied for; and that from the employer's perspective these allow job behaviours to be displayed by candidates working both individually and in groups and to be assessed by a range of assessors. Interviews could also be used to assess existing performance and predict future job performance. Of course that implies that the assessment centre is designed to include such opportunities. It also implies that assessment centres would be specific to each job for which they are to be used. As a development tool, such centres can be specifically designed to explore delicate behaviours in a range of job situations and to identify development needs as a consequence. The design of an assessment centre should reflect (according to the same CIPD factsheet):

- The ethos of the organisation.
- The actual skills required to carry out the job.
- Potential sources of recruits
- The extent to which recruitment is devolved to line managers.
- The HR strategy.

It is also suggested that organisations undergoing significant change should seek to assess the learning capability in candidates (to deal with the consequences of the change process), whereas those organisations in a 'steady state' situation should assess existing skills and abilities (as these are of more immediate use and value). Centres which look for potential should also be designed and developed differently from those which are looking for current knowledge and skills. The essential design criteria of any assessment/development centre should include a consideration of issues such as:

- Duration of the centre (for example, one day might be insufficient for more senior posts).
- Content and mix of activities to be included in the particular centre.
- Location (for example, a real work environment or conference room-type surroundings, accessibility for any candidates with disabilities).
- Facilities available during the running of the centre (for example, the need for hotel accommodation and provision of meals).
- Number of candidates brought together (for example, five may be too few for comfort under observation and more than eight gives problems in sharing the assessed time).
- Candidate background and comparability of past experience.
- Number, mix, training and experience of assessors.

There will inevitably be two levels of desirable characteristics, competencies, and job behaviours that would be sought within any centre. These could be classified as either 'essential' or 'desirable' depending on their importance to the achievement of job performance and effectiveness. These should then be matched to techniques and tasks which can test them. Depending on the nature of the job and the purpose of the centre, the tasks might include (either as individual or group activities): being able to act upon written and/or oral instructions; being able to produce written and/or oral reports of case-study recommendations/ solutions; being able to undertake in-tray exercises, the analysis of (sometimes) complex financial, market or operational data, individual problem solving; leading or participating in group discussions and/or problem solving exercises; engaging in tasks which reflect actual business or job activities; and participating in personal and/or functional role-play exercises. Exercises should be as realistic as possible, should identify clear outcomes or objectives, and also have a specified time-limit. Reasonable preparation time before exercises should be allowed. The exercises might be designed to encourage competitiveness or co-operation, and to test for creativity or building the building of consensus or building on the ideas of others in a productive manner.

Bradley and Povah (2006) identified four broad categories into which the most popular tools used within an assessment centre will fall:

- Interview-based processes and techniques.
- The use of application or nomination forms.
- Questionnaires, such as psychometric tests or 360-degree or self-perception appraisal-based forms.
- Assessment centre exercises or simulations, providing high face validity as they are designed to replicate the tasks involved in daily work relevant to the assessment centre. That might involve meetings, decision making, report writing, presentations, prioritising emails and other tasks, performance reviews, meetings with external clients, etc. The scoring of such tasks would need to be standardised and based on objective (behavioural) evidence of candidate capability – the assumption being that such measures provide a good indication of future potential.

It is often suggested that one assessor is necessary for every two candidates in order to ensure that adequate and effective candidate concentration, focus and scoring can be undertaken. It is also necessary to have relevant checklists of the competencies being sought through each activity to serve as score and/or comment sheets so that adequate records can be produced which, when completed by assessors, can form the basis of decision making and feedback. The scheduling of candidates through the various activities is also necessary to ensure that everyone knows where they should be at a certain time and what will be happening at every stage of the process. Candidates also need to be carefully briefed before attending the assessment centre so that they know what is going to happen and for what reason and when they might expect to hear the outcome of the process.

After the completion of the assessment centre tasks, assessors will need to combine their findings and marks into a final assessment for each candidate and possibly into a rank order of candidates running from the most successful at demonstrating the necessary competencies to the candidate demonstrating the least number/level of competencies. Although there exists a high face validity with such processes related to recruitment decisions – they appear to intuitively offer a fairer, more balanced way of selecting people – the actual correlation with subsequent job performance is not perfect. Anderson and Shackleton (1993), for example, indicated that the correlation for an assessment centre intended for promotion decisions was 0.68, compared to that for structured interviews at 0.62. Torrington et al. (2005) went on to suggest how some organisations have improved the performance of assessment centres by using fewer, longer scenarios and simulations that reflect real job experience events and possibly separating the testing from activity-based exercises. The same source (ibid., p. 4223) suggests that in relation to development centres less emphasis is given to the pass/fail type of assessment to focus more on identifying strengths and weaknesses in relation to career development planning intended to encourage the individual candidates to make the most of their potential in the various ways and directions that suit them.

The CIPD (2009) suggest that depending on the nature (or level) of the job forming the rationale for the assessment centre, the tasks included in it might involve individual and/or group work; written and/or oral input in relation to the activities being used; written and/or oral output as the conclusion to the exercises involved; in-tray tasks involving prioritising work, taking decisions and drafting responses; analysing work situations and data; individual problem solving; group discussions; group problem solving; engaging with tasks which match business activities; personal role-play; and functional role-play and providing reasoned arguments and participating in discussions about particular events.

The CIPD also suggest that group exercises should be as real as possible, should set goals and have a specified time, should require candidates to share information and reach decisions, and should require the candidates to read the brief very carefully. In addition assessors should assist in a role-play if they are trained to facilitate discussion and assist in group decision making. Reasonable preparation times before exercises begin should be allowed, as should the opportunity to ask questions or clarify aspects of the process or requirements. Tasks in assessment centres will usually be designed to encourage competitiveness and/or co-operation, to test for creativity and/or for building on the ideas of others in a productive manner. However, this must be carefully thought about in the assessment centre's design process, as the opportunity to compete with others will assist some candidates in performing better but may hinder others from maximising their contribution. It is important to ensure that the assessment centre is designed in a way that it can deliver appropriate outcomes in relation to the objective and intentions set for it. For example, in organisations wishing to widen their level of diversity, the approach to assessment centre design might actively reduce the level of competition in favour of increasing those activities that can provide opportunities for co-operation, as these competencies are likely to encourage the wider participation implicit in diversity. Presentation activities can also provide a valuable insight if the job requires such tasks to be undertaken as part of the normal duties. Consequently allowing considerable preparation time for an exercise should be built into the assessment centre in order to provide candidates with the time to refine their approach to it.

See also: *career management; competency; employee development; expatriation and international management; management development; psychometric and other tests; resourcing/retention; succession planning and talent management*

BIBLIOGRAPHY

Anderson, N. and Shackleton, V. (1993) *Successful Selection Interviewing*. Oxford: Blackwell.

Bradley, H. and Povah, N. (2006) 'How to choose the right assessment tools', in *The Guide to Assessment* (October 2007), People Management Supplement. London: CIPD.

CIPD (2009) 'Assessment centres for recruitment and selection', *Factsheet*. Available at www.cipd.co.uk (last accessed July 2009).

Incomes Data Services (2005) *Assessment Centres*. HR Study 800. London: IDS.

Torrington, D., Hall, L. and Taylor, S. (2005) *Human Resource Management* (6th edition). Harlow: Prentice Hall.

Balanced Business Scorecard

Developed by Kaplan and Norton (1996) as the means by which to measure the performance of an organisation using material from four distinct areas of activity – financial; innovation and learning; internal processes; and customers.

Developed in the early 1990s by Robert Kaplan and David Norton, the balanced scorecard is a management and measurement system which enables organisations to clarify their vision and strategy and then translate these into action. The goal of the balanced scorecard is to tie business performance to organisational strategy by measuring results in four areas: financial performance, customer knowledge, internal business processes, and learning and growth. The model has also been used to assess and reward the performance of senior managers. The four areas of activity that form the focus of the balanced scorecard are:

- *Financial perspectives* This reflects issues associated with how the organisation appears to the financial world. It might include measures of return on capital employed, cash flow, sales backlog and profit forecast reliability.
- *Innovation and learning perspectives* This reflects how the organisation and its employees learn and innovate in creating the future. It might include measures of the proportion of revenue from new products or services; staff attitudes; level of employee contribution and engagement; and revenue growth per employee.
- *Internal business perspectives* This reflects what the organisation must do very well in order to succeed. It might include measures of order success rate, frequency of contact with customers; order, delivery, invoice times; error rates; quality and rework levels.
- *Customer perspectives* This reflects how customers regard the organisation. It might include measures of customer satisfaction and competitor ranking by customers and market share.

The balanced scorecard provides feedback around both the internal business processes and the external outcomes in order to continuously improve the strategic performance and results. When fully utilised, it transforms strategic planning from an academic and sterile paper exercise into the central driving force of an enterprise. The balanced scorecard methodology builds on some key concepts of earlier management ideas such as Total Quality Management (TQM), which includes an emphasis on customer-defined quality, continuous improvement, employee empowerment, and measurement-based management and feedback.

Many sources identify the following reasons to implement, and benefits arising from, the use of the balanced scorecard:

- Focusing the whole organisation on the few key things needed to create a breakthrough performance. In practice this demands an increased focus on strategy and results.
- Helping to integrate various corporate programmes, such as quality, re-engineering, and customer service initiatives.
- Breaking down strategic measures to local unit levels so that unit managers, operators, and employees can see what is required at their level and how that will contribute to an excellent performance overall. In practice this requires aligning an organisation strategy with the work that people do on a day-to-day basis.
- Improving organisational performance by measuring what matters.
- Focusing on the drivers of future performance.
- Improving communication of the organisation's vision and strategy.
- Helping to prioritise projects/and other initiatives.

Using the balanced scorecard at its simplest level involves the following six steps:

1 An evaluation of the basis of the organisation, its core beliefs and values; market opportunities, competition; financial position; short-and long-term goals; and an understanding of what satisfies customers.
2 Development of a business strategy; for example to grow the business, to develop new products, to improve operational efficiency.
3 Conversion of this strategy into objectives that can be measured.
4 Mapping of the identified strategy using the balanced scorecard classification to link the identified objectives and chains of actions.

5 Development of performance measures to track objectives and strategy achievement in the organisational dynamic.
6 Identify new initiatives that need to be funded and implemented if the strategic objectives are to be achieved.

In practice, for each of the four headings used in the balanced scorecard four activity headings will be identified as a consequence of the six stage process just described. These are:

- *Objectives* What strategy must be achieved and what is critical to its success?
- *Measure* How will success be measured and tracked?
- *Target* The performance expectations for each objective (and element within the objective) if these are to be achieved.
- *Initiatives* A list of the key actions necessary if the objectives are to be achieved.

Anthony and Govindarajan (1998) suggested that there were a number of potential problems that if not dealt with effectively could limit the value potentially available through the use of the balanced scorecard model. These are:

- *A poor correlation between non-financial measures and results* There is no guarantee that achieving targets for non-financial objectives will result in additional profitability. In simple terms, everyone in an organisation might work much harder in one year than in the previous but that does not automatically result in additional revenue or profits for the organisation.
- *Becoming fixated with financial results alone* Most managers will concentrate on financial results for the reasons outlined above. Equally bonus payments and promotions are often linked to the achievement of financial results. However, that tends to undervalue the potential contribution over the long term from the non-financial aspects of the organisation.
- *Not having any mechanisms for improvement in place* If an organisation cannot innovate effectively it will be at a disadvantage relative to the wider environment and competitors in the long run. Innovating means bringing about change and improvement, not just tinkering with refinements to the basic product, service or operating processes.

- *Not updating the measures used*   Unless the measures used by an organisation reflect the current strategy being followed they will tend to become outdated and unhelpful in directing actions in support of what is being sought.
- *Measurements becoming overloaded*   How many targets or measures can a manager seek to achieve without losing overall control? People will seek to deliver what their performance will be measured against and the use of too many measures can encourage individuals to lose sight of what is actually important.
- *Difficulty in establishing trade-offs*   This is about deciding the relative importance of measures. Faced with a number of targets to achieve how should a manager determine which are the most significant? This becomes particularly difficult when faced with both financial and non-financial measures at the same time.

The Balanced Scorecard Institute (2009) has identified what they see as the main success factors for the implementation of the balanced business scorecard. These are:

- Obtaining senior management sponsorship and commitment.
- Involving a wide range of leaders, managers and employees in the scorecard development.
- Agreeing on the terminology to be used and the meaning of key terms.
- Choosing an appropriate balanced business scorecard development and implementation project leader and champion.
- Beginning the project with extensive two-way communication at all levels of the organisation.
- Working through the organisation's mission, vision, strategic results, and strategy mapping processes first in order to avoid rushing to make a judgement on the basis of a measurement or the specific software to be used.
- Viewing the balanced business scorecard project as a long-term journey rather than a short-term project.
- Planning for and managing change as part of the implementation process and in relation to follow up action based on the results of the analysis.
- Applying a disciplined implementation framework.
- Getting outside help if necessary.

Barr (2009) has suggested that in trying to identify what should be measured it is necessary to follow a five-step process:

Step 1: Begin with the end in mind
Performance measures should be an objective basis for comparisons in relation to significant performance outcomes. It is important to decide which outcomes are the most significant and therefore worthy of tracking.

Step 2: Be sensory specific
Once the end is clearer, it should be possible to identify specifically what will be measured. Hence the need for precision and care in the choice of words used to describe the outcome as clearly as possible.

Step 3: Check the bigger picture
Check the bigger picture for what might happen when the outcome is measured. What level of control exists for achieving it? What might be the unintended consequences of measuring the outcome (both positive and negative)? What behaviour would the measures drive? Which other areas of performance might be undermined or limited as a result of focusing on the particular measure identified? At this stage some of the measures identified might need to be changed in order to positively impact on the entire business activity – some measures might improve aspects of the business but also have a negative effect on others.

Step 4: What's the evidence?
This stage involves being highly specific about what potential measures can best inform everyone that the outcome is being achieved and to what extent this is being achieved.

Step 5: Name the measure
This final step of naming (or announcing) the performance measures marks the point at which everyone will know exactly what will be measured and why. It is necessary to continually and easily identify each measure as it becomes active in the balanced business scorecard process and decision making.

In relation to HR activity, the balanced business scorecard has several implications: the following extracts from Mind Tools (2009) suggest the

balanced business scorecard

idea of the balanced business scorecard is an important one for managing people because:

- Balance (in effect success in business) follows on from the alignment of financial activity with that related to customers, internal business processes, and innovation and learning. Financial measures alone will not ensure success nor will any of the other performance measures taken in isolation.
- The balanced business scorecard will not measure the correctness of a business strategy. It will however help monitor and measure progress towards achieving the identified strategy across all areas of the business.
- Leadership is a key aspect of strategy (and its achievement). It is often suggested that 'management is about doing things right, while leadership is about doing the right things'. Leadership and management are therefore different (but complementary) processes for ensuring success.
- The balanced business scorecard is about managing the achievement of a desired strategy, while leadership is about motivating people to give of their best in order to achieve a worthwhile goal. These two aspects integrate and effectively work together in high performance organisations.

See also: benchmarking; downsizing, reorganisation, outsourcing and redundancy; flexibility; high performance working; human resource planning; job, job analysis and job design; organisational development (OD) and change; organisational structure; strategic HRM; succession planning and talent management

BIBLIOGRAPHY

Anthony, R.N. and Govindarajan, V. (1998) *Management Control Systems* (9th edition) Boston, MA: McGraw-Hill. pp. 463–471.

Balanced Scorecard Institute (2009) *What are the Primary Implementation Success Factors?* Available at http://www.balancedscorecard.org/BSCResources/AbouttheBalancedScorecard/tabid/55/Default.aspx (last accessed July 2009).

Barr, S. (2009) *5 Steps to Find the Right Measures.* Available at http://www.balancedscorecard.org/BSCResources/PerformanceMeasurement/5StepstoMeasurement/tabid/379/Default.aspx (last accessed July 2009).

Kaplan, R.S. and Norton, D.P. (1996) *The Balanced Scorecard: Translating Strategy into Action.* Boston: Harvard Business School Press.

Mind Tools (2009) *The Balanced Scorecard: Motivating Employees to Deliver Your Strategy.* Available at http://www.mindtools.com/pages/article/newLDR_85.htm (last accessed July 2009).

Behaviour Management

> *The encouragement of particular behaviours in employees through the application of the principles of conditioning to achieve and maintain the desired (as defined by controller) behaviour patterns.*

Any organisation with more than one employee has to direct and channel the behaviour of employees in order to capture the benefit available from human labour. Control and direction of human behaviour are achieved in many ways within an organisational setting: for example, the use of structure to compartmentalise work into task areas such as accounting, transport and sales. The use of job descriptions to describe in written form what each job consists of in terms of tasks and responsibilities is another form of 'procedure' that effectively directs the behaviour of the people doing each job. In addition there are the supervisory levels of managerial responsibilities that are charged with ensuring that day-to-day activity is directed at the achievement of the operational objectives and meeting customer needs. That might involve giving instructions to subordinates, issuing orders to do certain jobs at a particular point in time, and ensuring that training is provided so that employees are capable of undertaking the allocated tasks expected of them. In some instances it might also involve the application of disciplinary procedures when something happens that should not have done and an individual is held to account for their failings. There is also the dynamic and social interaction that takes place between individual employees in a work setting – usually referred to as group dynamics and which control to a significant extent the behaviour of individual group members. Such interaction also includes the daily and frequent contact and communication between managers and subordinates in ensuring that instructions are passed down the chain of command and acted upon and that progress, direction and difficulties are communicated back to management.

However, psychology also has much to offer by way of the control of human behaviour. The most obvious (and oldest) application of psychological thinking to controlling the behaviour of a subject (another living organism) by an experimenter is the work of Skinner and instrumental conditioning. Instrumental in this context refers to behaviour being 'instrumental' in producing an outcome. For example, a hungry rat can be conditioned to press a lever to obtain food. Pressing the lever (behaviour) releases the food and allows feeding (the effect). Pressing the lever is therefore instrumental in obtaining food. Conditioning in this context simply means being trained to do something. There is an enormous range of variations that can be introduced to this basic process and it has been used on a wide range of animals. Pigeons have been taught to recognise colours and play table tennis, whales and dolphins have been trained for wildlife shows and dolphins have also been trained to hunt for underwater mines in a military context.

The process of reinforcement is used to shape the behaviour pattern desired. Over many cycles of repetition only behaviours closer and closer to the desired outcome will be rewarded until the actual behaviour presented matches that desired by the trainer. Once established, it is not necessary to reinforce every occurrence (or repetition) of this desired behaviour in order to maintain it. There are four types of reinforcement schedules that can influence the rate of repetition of the desired behaviour. These are:

- *Fixed ratio* Reinforcement follows a fixed number of repetitions of a particular activity (for example, one pellet of food every 20 lever presses). This tends to produce a consistently steady rate of response in order for the respondent to be able to maximise the reward.
- *Variable ratio* The number of repetitions required to produce the reward is randomly varied. This produces a consistently rapid rate of response as the respondent has no way of predicting which response will produce the desired result. In human terms this is like feeding coins to a 'gaming machine' or buying lottery tickets as the player can never be certain which 'purchase' will result in a win.
- *Fixed interval* This produces reinforcement after the first appropriate behaviour following a set time interval. The behaviour pattern under this regime almost stops after a reward until the next time interval is due, when it starts again. The implication here is that the subject can judge the time interval and adjust their 'work' activity accordingly.
- *Variable interval* The time interval at which food becomes available is randomly varied between upper and lower parameters. Under these

conditions, the subject responds with a consistently rapid rate of behaviour – because it cannot know which display of behaviour will activate the reward.

It is the partial reinforcement schedules described above that produce sustained and rapid response rates and are therefore the most effective in maintaining the desired behaviour. So far the discussion has only involved positive reinforcement (that is, the subject being rewarded for doing something that the designers of the conditioning programme wanted). Other reinforcement options available include:

- *Negative reinforcement*   An unpleasant event that precedes a behaviour and which is removed when the subject produces appropriate behaviour. For example, a torturer may stop abusing a prisoner if they confess to a crime.
- *Omission*   The stopping of reinforcement. This leads to the reduction and eventual extinction of a particular behaviour. For example, employees who do an excellent job may stop doing so if managers do not continue to acknowledge their contribution.
- *Punishment*   An unpleasant reward for particular behaviours. Issuing a written warning to an employee who is frequently late for work would be an example. This form of reinforcement decreases the occurrence of the behaviour in question.

This approach has been adopted for use in controlling the behaviour of humans and is referred to as behavioural modification, the basis of the approach being that managers should seek to encourage appropriate behaviours among employees through the application of the above reinforcement principles. The model begins with an assessment of the behaviour requirements compared with actual behaviour patterns in the specific context. The reinforcement adopted will depend on whether the current behaviour pattern is to be maintained, unwanted behaviours are to be eliminated, or desired behaviours increased. Once selected and operational, the results of the reinforcement approach would then be monitored and any remedial or follow-up action taken in a continual cycle of reinforcement. Among the criticisms of this model is that it is managers who decide what defines appropriate behaviour and it is therefore an attempt at social engineering and management control. In addition it is very difficult to maintain the application of such a model in practice as most managers are not in enough permanent contact with subordinates to be able to ensure consistency in the application across time. Also the range of rewards available within organisations is limited and needs to be controlled in ways which limit fraud, favouritism, discrimination and unfairness. This inevitably restricts the ways in which behaviour modification can be used in practice. The process also encourages instrumental approaches to work based on compliance rather than a commitment on the part of employees – namely, only doing things if a reward is offered.

Discipline is also about the control of human behaviour and will be discussed in more detail below. In seeking to encourage particular behaviour and attitudinal patterns there are many other possible ways to achieve delivery on a consistent basis, including:

- *Resourcing* People recruited with appropriate skills and competencies who fit in with the ethos of the company, work colleagues and the type of work involved are more likely to behave in consistent ways over time.
- *Induction* This eases the individual into the company, job and work group in such a way that they acquire the dominant standards of behaviour and attitudes. Done thoughtfully, this process can help to support management's objectives.
- *Training* Training courses can upgrade and reinforce an individual's competencies. But they also present opportunities to reinforce management preferred behaviours and attitudes. For example, selection for attendance on training courses sends a signal – 'punishment' (remedial training) or 'developmental' (someone worth investing in); during training an opportunity exists to reinforce management messages about preferred behaviours and attitudes.
- *Culture* Some organisational cultures are more supportive of management intentions than others.
- *Rules* Every organisation has rules that should be kept up to date and relevant to the needs of the organisation. Equally knowing that the rules will be enforced also encourages compliance.
- *Management style* The style of management adopted within an organisation can also strongly influence how employees behave.
- *Expectations* The expectations that management have in relation to employee behaviour will shape to a significant extent what actually happens.
- *Delegated responsibility* The degree of delegated responsibility given to employees can significantly influence the way that they respond to their work.

- *Job design* A well designed job can provide a number of benefits, including scope for an individual to develop a commitment to the achievement of management's objectives.
- *Team working* Team members can exert pressure on individuals to conform to the team norms of behaviour. Key to this aspect of behaviour control is that teams need to have developed behaviour norms that will support management intentions – if not they can exert a subversive and malign influence.

See also: absence management; counselling, coaching and mentoring; discipline and grievance; employee relations and conflict; high performance working; organisational culture; performance management

BIBLIOGRAPHY

Martin, J. (2005) *Organisational Behaviour and Management* (3rd edition). London: Thomson.

Benchmarking

> A technique allowing a company to measure its performance against the 'best in class'. It determines how comparators achieve their performance and uses that information to improve its own performance.

There are many definitions of benchmarking and all offer some insight into it as a process. The above definition is generic and contains the general flavour of the process while leaving several key terms vague. For example, what does 'performance' mean – highest profit level, lowest cost, raw material conversion rate, and highest customer satisfaction rating are all possibilities. Also 'best in class' has little direct meaning as an objective term. Who decides what qualifies an organisation to be the best in class and on what criteria? No organisation is perfect in all aspects of its activities and performance, so what should be compared in the benchmarking process – every aspect whether good as well as bad, or just the superior features? Having said all of this, benchmarking is a potentially valuable process involving the comparison of two situations in order to be able to make judgements and take actions intended to improve the functioning of an inferior situation. Given the lack of clarity in the meaning of some of the terms used to define benchmarking, it gains significance as an organisational process from the fact that an organisation's strategic capability is also a 'relative' issue since it is about meeting and beating the performance of competitors. In other words, benchmarking encourages a continuous improvement at many levels of organisational functioning in the search for a competitive advantage.

Benchmarking as a process can involve quantitative and/or qualitative techniques as the basis of comparison. However these are measured the basic process is to compare the inputs and outputs of particular processes in order to be able to draw meaningful conclusions about the relative performance of the activities under investigation. Such comparisons do not have to be restricted to whole-company inter-organisational scenarios; they can be made between parts of organisations or between different sections within the same organisation. It is not a new idea, although it is only over recent years that it has been widely publicised and embraced as a formal part of management practice. In essence there are four different types of benchmarking:

- *Internal* Comparisons between similar activities within the same organisation.
- *Competitive* Comparisons with direct competitors.
- *Functional* Comparison with similar functions or operations but from different industries or sectors of the economy. For example, an aircraft manufacturer could compare their metal cutting and bending practices with those used in shipbuilding.
- *Generic* Comparison of work processes with other organisations with innovative but not directly comparable work practices. For example, a rail infrastructure company could compare its track building and repair practices with the processes used in coal mining to cut and extract coal.

The basic benchmarking process comprises 11 stages grouped under four categories. These are:

- Planning:

  o Identify own organisation benchmark target.
  o Identify benchmark comparator.

- Determine the data required and collection methods.
- Collect appropriate data.

• Analysis:

- Determine the gap between the target and comparator.
- Determine an action plan and performance targets/timescales.

• Integration:

- Communicate the results and garner support.
- Establish the specific goals in collaboration with appropriate stakeholders.

• Action:

- Develop appropriate action plans.
- Implement these plans and monitor their progress.
- Recompile the benchmark comparisons.

It is generally understood that benchmarking is an iterative process and so the conclusion of this first cycle of 11 steps would be followed by beginning the cycle again, the justification being that change is an ever present feature of organisational life and that continuous improvement is necessary because existing comparators will also improve their performance and new and innovative practices are to be found in unexpected places. For example, some years ago an airline studied the maintenance, refuelling and support processes provided in Formula 1 racing car facilities in order to improve the turnaround times of their aircraft at the passenger gates of international and domestic airports.

Common issues and potential problems associated with benchmarking include gaining access to appropriate comparisons within other organisations. Most organisations are wary of releasing information about their activities and processes, particularly if they see them as a source of competitive advantage. These concerns can become even greater if the organisation seeking the information is a direct competitor or there are separate concerns that the information may be made available to such a competitor. There is a danger of deliberate misinformation or only partial information being supplied unless adequate safeguards and reciprocal arrangements are put in place. In order to ensure both fair play and an honest supply of information, it is usual for protocols to be agreed upon regarding how the contributors should behave in the benchmarking process. The American Productivity and Quality Center suggests

benchmarking

that the following points can help with the appropriate exchange of mutually beneficial information:

- Know and abide by the Benchmarking Code of Conduct.
- Have a basic knowledge of benchmarking and follow a benchmarking process.
- Prior to initiating contact with potential benchmarking partners, determine what needs to be benchmarked, identify the key performance variables to study, recognise the superior performing companies, and complete a rigorous self-assessment.
- Develop a questionnaire and interview guide, and share these in advance if requested.
- Possess the authority to share and be willing to share information with benchmarking partners.
- Work through a specified host and agree mutually on scheduling and meeting arrangements.

If the benchmarking process involves face-to-face meetings or site visits, then the same source encourages that the following be adopted:

- Provide a meeting agenda in advance.
- Be professional, honest, courteous and prompt.
- Introduce all the attendees and explain their role and presence.
- Adhere to the agenda.
- Use a universal language, not company-specific jargon.
- Ensure that no party is sharing proprietary information unless prior approval has been obtained by all parties from the proper authority.
- Share information about your own process, and, if asked, consider sharing your study results.
- Offer to facilitate a future reciprocal visit.
- Conclude meetings and visits on schedule.
- Thank the partners for sharing their information and processes.

In human resource management terms there are many possibilities for benchmarking to take place. These include (based on issues indicated by the CIPD (2008), and for which some benchmark data are available based on surveys carried out on behalf of the Institute):

- The level of spending on training.
- Learning and development issues and trends.

- Absence management and levels.
- Recruitment, retention and turnover levels and issues.
- Reward issues.
- Diversity issues and trends.

In addition there are of course many aspects of human resource management operation, strategy and practice that could form part of a benchmarking exercise. For example, resourcing practice, reward practice, salary levels, benefit provision, and so on. Any form of benchmarking is a comparison with what already exists elsewhere. At its most basic it is a comparison with similar organisations or those in the same industry and so it is in danger of becoming an incestuous process, even assuming that competing organisations can be trusted to be honest and open in the benchmarking process. At its best it encourages comparisons with dissimilar organisations in perhaps very different industries but with processes that contain lessons for others to learn from. Carried out on such a basis, benchmarking can be a creative process only limited by the ability of those involved to seek out and find meaningful comparisons. But even in such cases it is still ultimately limited to comparing what exists, however creative (or lacking in it) that may be.

As a methodology, benchmarking does not require or encourage the application of creative development and innovative thought in seeking to develop/change/improve organisational processes in order to achieve an improved performance; it assumes that as long as such processes are comparable (or better than) others that is good enough. It also assumes that somewhere, someone will have found the best way to do something and that 'we can capture it, if only we can find them'. These two assumptions presume that someone will indeed have found the best way to do something, that they can be found, and that they will be willing to pass on their expertise. In short this reflects the 'me-tooism' approach to management based on 'we do what others do, and so we don't have to think too deeply or fundamentally challenge ourselves to be the best we can, or to develop new ways of doing things'.

The terms 'best practice', 'best in class' and 'world class' are often used in relation to the identification of benchmark comparison targets. Indeed the term 'best in class' is used in the definition at the start of this section. But what do these terms mean, particularly in relation to human resource management activities? Usually they are taken to refer to organisations either in whole or part that are commonly accepted as being exemplary by journalists, academics, practising managers, graduates or some other group able to give (and have publicised) an opinion. For example, every year articles appear listing organisations by such criteria as the 100 best companies to work for as rated by graduates and so on. Also most professional magazines will publish articles written by practitioners (or journalists) reflecting on the 'good practices' adopted by particular organisations in relation to a specific topic or theme. However, in relation to HR activity in particular such examples should be viewed using a sceptical eye. For example, for any issue being held up as an example of good practice would everyone actually subjected to that issue within the company agree with that view or how many people would need to agree before it could be accepted as good practice? Say a particular form of flexible benefits package was being described as a means of reducing labour turnover and of maximising employee engagement – how could that be demonstrated? There are many types of data that could be presented in support of the claim (reductions in labour turnover, higher productivity, improved satisfaction levels, etc.), but in each case there are many other possible reasons for such changes. Labour turnover depends on numerous factors including economic conditions, alternative job opportunities, working relationships, job design, etc. Likewise productivity depends on many factors including the pressure to work harder, the use of incentives, effective administrative systems and procedures, etc. Also what proportion of employees and/or managers would have to support the claim before it could be substantiated? Most (if not all) articles appearing in the professional press will appear with permission and so some degree of public relations presentational expertise will be involved in their writing up and the publication process. It is never totally clear just how close to the 'truth' any article is (even if the 'truth' could be known). For example, I know from my own research that in one large organisation a number of senior staff in the HR department were dismissed in ways and for reasons that would have undoubtedly resulted in successful claims for unfair dismissal (had they not been facilitated by generous settlements contained within compromise agreements) at the same time as an article appeared in the professional press claiming that the very same organisation had a superior HR department and extremely good diversity and employee relations policies!

See also: *behaviour management; benefits; discrimination, diversity and equality; employee empowerment and engagement; high performance working; job, job analysis and job design; organisational structure; performance management; reward management; total reward*

American Productivity and Quality Centre. Available at www.apqc.org/portal/apqc/site (last accessed June 2009).

CIPD (2008) 'Benchmarking training activity and spend'. *Factsheet*. Available at www.cipd.co.uk (last accessed July 2009).

Benefits

> *Employee benefits are the rewards that an employee gains over and above their basic wage or salary. Benefits can broadly be categorised as either transactional if they are formally part of the reward system and have a monetary value, or relational if they are not formally quantified but reflect a positive advantage gained by an employee as a result of working for an organisation.*

Benefits are offered by employers for two reasons. Firstly, for commercial reasons based on the need to design cost effective reward systems that are capable of attracting, retaining and engaging employees. Secondly, based on the moral imperative to 'look after' employees. The basis for benefit provision has changed over the years between these two reasons depending on the prevailing social, labour market, political, commercial and economic conditions. During the 1990s it became apparent that a wide range of factors played a part in attracting, retaining and engaging employees and that each individual had a different mix of reasons for their decisions in relation to employment matters. This led to the development of the total reward concept with its emphasis on the combination of transactional and relational rewards in being able to maximise the level of impact on attracting, retaining and engaging employees. Brown and Armstrong (1999) developed a four cell matrix to describe the total reward model with three of the four cells relating to what would be classified as benefits in the broadest sense of the term. These include transactional benefits such as pensions, holidays and health care, as well as relational benefits associated with the

benefits

opportunities for learning and development for the job, organisation and career. They also include relational benefits associated with leadership style, job design, quality of working life and work-life balance.

There are different ways of grouping together under common headings the range of different benefits offered by an organisation, but they are usually based on the type of benefit. For example:

- *Personal security benefits* These include a pension; health care; death in service; personal accident; sick pay; redundancy pay; long-term sick or incapacity pay; and outplacement/career counselling services. Some are required by legislation (sick pay and redundancy pay) but many organisations offer enhanced terms.
- *Financial assistance benefits* These include mortgage assistance; company loans; relocation expenses; season ticket loans; travel allowances (including fuel costs) and fees to professional bodies.
- *Personal needs benefits* These include maternity and paternity leave; leave for personal reasons (paid or unpaid); career counselling; career development and training; the chance to work as part of a team; the existence of well-designed jobs; employee assistance programmes; sports and social facilities; discount on company products/services; the existence of good/effective management practice; flexible working opportunities; and childcare nurseries or vouchers, etc.
- *Affinity benefits* These include providing employees with the opportunity to purchase reduced price medical and insurance cover; retail vouchers/discounts; discounted gym memberships, bicycle and other leasing facilities, etc.
- *Holidays* Although there is now a statutory requirement to allow paid holidays most organisations include this benefit as part of their contractual obligations.
- *Company cars or a car allowance* Many organisations will provide a company car (or car allowance) to employees either because their job entails a considerable amount of travelling, or because of the job status of the individual.

According to the CIPD (2007a), some employers will pay higher wages rather than offer employee benefits. Employees can subsequently buy their preferred range of benefits reflecting their individual circumstances. Referred to as clean pay, such an approach is easily communicated, understood and administered. The consequences of 'clean pay' include:

- That it may cost an employee more to buy benefits than it would their employer.
- For the employer the administration cost is reduced and simplified.
- It allows the employer to advertise apparently high wages
- Employees may spend their work-time looking around for the best deals.
- Employees may make bad decisions that may not become apparent for many years.
- There are tax advantages associated with the provision of some benefits.
- The employer will have to deal with the consequences of misselling benefits to employees, or of poor employee choice, or face a potential public relations problem.
- Although high wages are attractive, it limits the ability to design a reward package containing a mixture of benefits aimed at attracting, retaining and engaging high calibre employees.
- Some benefits are a legal requirement and employees will expect certain benefits to be provided.

Alternatively some employers will offer the opportunity to employees to purchase additional benefits through what are called salary sacrifice schemes. For example, an employee may agree to give up part of their gross pay in return for a matched contribution to their pension scheme, saving tax and National Insurance contributions for both employer and employee. Salary sacrifice can also be used to purchase additional leave days and other benefits.

Another approach to employee benefits that allows individuals to select a personal benefits package, up to a set limit and from the total range available, has emerged over the last few years. Usually called flexible benefits (or sometimes by its older name of cafeteria benefits) it represents an opportunity for employees to select specific benefits and/or a level of particular benefits as appropriate to their circumstances. This reflects a benefit in itself as it provides for the benefit entitlement of the employee to be quantified and each benefit available to be valued. The result is a pick-and-mix approach to matching the benefit package with employee needs and preference which can be achieved to maximise the benefit and impact for an employee and minimise cost to the employer. The advantages of a flexible benefits arrangement are (CIPD, 2007b):

- Employees choose benefits that best match their needs.
- Employees value the chosen benefits more highly.
- Flexible benefit schemes can help to minimise reward arrangement difficulties following mergers, acquisitions, harmonisation, etc.
- Employers know the full cost and value of the benefit package.
- Employees can change their choices as their circumstances change.
- Employees know the full worth of the benefits package they receive.
- Employers can eliminate benefits that are not valued and can negotiate very favourable terms with providers of popular items.
- Employees are given a sense of control and involvement by having a choice.
- Dual career couples can minimise the duplicated benefits offered by their respective employers (and maximise the total range of benefits taken).
- Employers are seen to be more responsive to the needs of individuals.
- A wide ranging competitive benefits package is valuable in attracting and retaining high quality employees.

The disadvantages are:

- They are complex and expensive to set up and maintain (although technology reduces the cost and administrative burden).
- The choices made may over time cause problems to either or both employers and employees.

In providing flexible benefits it is necessary to determine which benefits are to be covered by the scheme and how frequently changes to selections are to be allowed. For example, it may be decided that employees should not be allowed to opt out of the company pension scheme, or that a company car will be provided to sales personnel in order to protect the corporate image. How frequently an employee should be allowed to review and change their benefit package is also an important decision. Usually it is restricted to once each year unless specified circumstances such as promotion, marriage or bereavement occur in between reviews. It may also be difficult for employees to understand the choices that they face and the consequences of the decisions that they will make. Some organisations provide educational support for employees in helping them to make informed choices.

It would be usual for each level within an organisation to have a range of benefits specified as available for that level and for the range and cost of benefits to rise in line with seniority. That and the use of flexible benefit schemes require each benefit to be costed and each level within the organisation to be allocated a value of benefits available to it. In some flexible benefit schemes employees can elect to purchase (or sell) holiday leave days at the expense of (or to gain) other benefits that they might have access to. Equally it is not uncommon to find that employees are allowed to 'purchase' some benefits outside of the formal benefit scheme, for example a manager entitled to a particular size of company car could be allowed to upgrade it to a more expensive model in return for a monthly deduction from their salary.

There are tax implications associated with a number of benefits, the main areas affected being (CIPD, 2007a):

- *Pensions* Employees may obtain income tax relief at their highest marginal rate for their pension contributions and employers can offset their contributions to pension schemes against corporation tax.
- *Childcare vouchers* Employers can pay up to a specified sum of money each week in childcare vouchers and be exempt from paying any National Insurance contributions on them. The employee does not have to pay any National Insurance or income tax on the vouchers provided.
- *Home computing initiative* This government initiative to encourage home working and the adoption of technology was scrapped in April 2006, but employers can still operate any existing arrangements until their scheme ends.
- *Bicycle loans* Employees can save up to half the cost of bicycle and related accessories used for commuting to work. The firm would purchase the bicycle and then lease it to the employee. In addition, employers can also provide tax-free meals and drinks to those who cycle to work.
- *Other tax free benefits include* season ticket loans, worth up to £5,000 to cover the cost of public transport; an annual party, worth up to £150 per head; and independent financial information, worth up to £150 per employee (all these are 2007 rates).

benefits

35

See also: benchmarking; employee assistance programme; employee relations and conflict; expatriation and international management; quality of working life and the psychological contract; resourcing/retention; reward management; total reward

BIBLIOGRAPHY

Armstrong, M. and Stephens, T. (2005) *A Handbook of Employee Reward Management and Practice*. London: Kogan Page.

Brown, D. and Armstrong, M. (1999) *Paying for Contribution*. London: Kogan Page.

CIPD (2007a) *Factsheet – Employee Benefits an Overview* (February). Available at www.cipd.co.uk (last accessed December 2007).

CIPD (2007b) *Factsheet – Flexible Benefits* (April). Available at www.cipd.co.uk (last accessed December 2007).

Bullying and Harassment

> **Bullying can be offensive, intimidating, malicious or insulting behaviour, an abuse or misuse of power intended to undermine, humiliate, denigrate or injure the recipient. Harassment is unwanted conduct towards another and may be related to age, sex, race, disability, religion, nationality or any personal characteristic, and may be persistent or an isolated incident.**

The key to both terms is that they represent 'events' that are demeaning and unacceptable to the recipient. They are actions or behaviours that often serve the intention of intimidating or forcing someone to do something by subjecting them to persecution intended to undermine their confidence and self-esteem. They can also represent an intention to exercise power or control over someone else, or they can reflect interpersonal dislike or conflict. Some commentators use the term 'mobbing' to reflect such actions, being based on the behaviour observed in some birds whereby a group of birds will 'pick on', 'mob' or 'attack' another bird. In that sense it reflects actions based on some supposed difference between the bully and the victim. The terms are often used interchangeably and many definitions would recognise bullying as a form of harassment.

Bullying or harassment is often perpetrated by someone in authority over a subordinate. However sometimes managers can be bullied or intimidated by subordinates. It can also involve groups of people picking on other groups or perhaps individuals. Bullying and harassment may be obvious to all observers in a particular situation who may all be able to see what is going on, or it may be insidious and carried out quietly away from the public gaze. Whatever form it takes, it is unwarranted and unwelcome to the victim. It is for the observers or victims of bullying or harassment to classify it as unacceptable based on their perceptions of what is happening and how it makes them feel. So, for example, a manager might think that their manner is direct and forthright, but to the subordinates it may be experienced as bullying or harassment. Among the consequences of that perspective are that each manager has to take responsibility for how their behaviour and actions appear to others. The CIPD (2006) survey found that 20 per cent of respondents reported being bullied or harassed during the previous two years, a rise of some 7 per cent since the survey was carried out in 2004. The consequences of bullying identified in the survey included poor performance, conflict, stress, negative psychological states, low morale, dysfunctional teams not focussed on their work tasks and high levels of the intention to resign (or actual resignation) among those experiencing it.

A national survey carried out since 2005 by the Andrea Adams Trust and Digital Opinion (2007) found that 75 per cent of respondents had discussed their bullying experiences with family or friends and 58 per cent had talked about it with colleagues. Just 32 per cent of employees experiencing bullying made a formal complaint, while 53 per cent started looking for another job and 22 per cent sought legal advice. Only 5 per cent of individuals being bullied said that the way that they dealt with the issues solved the problem and only 32 per cent said that they were able to achieve some degree of resolution to it. However, more significantly over 38 per cent reported that their actions had no effect, and 25 per cent of victims actually felt that the situation had been made worse as a result of their actions to try and seek a resolution. 44 per cent of respondents said that they did not know how their employer would deal with complaints of bullying, with 25 per cent reporting that their organisation had specific policies and procedures in place. The remaining 31 per cent said that bullying complaints would be dealt with through the normal grievance procedures.

Examples of bullying or harassment include:

- Spreading malicious rumours, or insulting someone by word or behaviour.
- Circulating memos that are critical of someone.

- Ridiculing or demeaning someone.
- Picking on people or setting them up to fail.
- Exclusion or victimisation.
- Unfair/unreasonable treatment.
- Overbearing supervision or misuse of power or position.
- Unwelcome physical contact or sexual advances.
- Jokes, offensive language, gossip, slander, sectarian songs and letters.
- Posters, graffiti, obscene gestures, flags, bunting and emblems.
- Isolation, non-cooperation or exclusion from social activities.
- Intrusion by pestering, spying and stalking.
- Shouting at staff.
- Setting impossible deadlines.
- Making threats or comments about job security without foundation.
- Undermining a competent worker by overloading, and constant criticism.
- Preventing individuals progressing by intentionally blocking promotion or training opportunities.
- The use of text messaging, the internet or other digital device to spread harmful or hurtful images – 'cyber bullying'.

While it is not possible to make a direct complaint to an employment tribunal about bullying, other possibilities include:

- *Sex*   The Sex Discrimination Act gives protection against discrimination and victimisation on the grounds of sex, marriage or because someone intends to undergo, is undergoing, or has undergone, gender reassignment.
- *Race*   The Race Relations Act gives protection against discrimination and victimisation on the grounds of colour or nationality. The Act also gives a right to protection from harassment.
- *Disability*   The Disability Discrimination Act gives protection against discrimination and victimisation.
- *Sexual orientation*   The Employment Equality (Sexual Orientation) Regulations give protection against discrimination and harassment on the grounds of sexual orientation.
- *Religion or belief*   The Employment Equality (Religion or Belief) Regulations give protection against discrimination and harassment on the grounds of religion or belief.
- *Age*   The Employment Equality (Age) Regulations give protection against discrimination and harassment on the grounds of age.

- *Duty of care* Every employer has a legal and moral duty of care for each employee.
- *Health and safety* If bullying or harassment is not prevented or dealt with effectively then employers are potentially failing to ensure the health and safety of the victim.

The Andrea Adams Trust exists to promote awareness of bullying and harassment in the workplace and to offer employers and employees advice and guidance on how to deal with such situations. They and the CIPD offer the following guidance on dealing with bullying:

- Recognise that bullying exists and that it can be damaging in terms of cost, reputation and commercial success. Provide examples of such behaviour.
- Don't assume that no complaints mean that there are no problems. Emphasise that every employee is accountable for their behaviour.
- Ensure that a culture exists within which bullying cannot thrive and that effective measures are in place to deal with it.
- Assess possible contributory factors such as:

    o Signs indicating a lack of mutual respect between groups/individuals.
    o Management style.
    o Consultation, involvement and communication processes.
    o Job design, workplace layout and workflows.
    o Performance expectations and management.
    o Diversity.
    o Inadequate staffing levels and heavy workloads.
    o Behaviour of clients and competitors.
    o Content, level, type, access to and attendance at training events.

- Undertake stress audits particularly in relation to dignity at work and a listening culture.
- Develop and implement a specific policy and procedure for dealing with bullying at work. Reinforce that such behaviour will not be tolerated. Establish alternative confidential complaints channels.
- Ensure appropriate grievance procedures are in place and that they are regularly reviewed. Clarify the legal implications of such behaviour.
- Recognise that whatever the facts of the case, the victim believes that they have a problem and provide practical help and support whilst inquiries are underway.

bullying and harassment

- Ensure that there is positive support from the key stakeholders (HR professional, trade union officers and occupational health staff).
- Provide relevant training on bullying policies and procedures for key stakeholders and awareness training for all employees.

In seeking to deal with bullying and harassment, organisations are widely advised to adopt both informal and formal procedures to ensure that issues can be resolved in the most effective way for all the parties involved. That might involve the use of:

- *Mediation*   Harassment or bullying can be one person's word against another's and mediation can provide an effective way of clarifying and surfacing issues and the identification of future behaviour patterns that will satisfy both parties.
- *Guidance and counselling*   Guidance or counselling in relation to behaviour at work can be an effective way of exploring the impact of particular types of behaviour on the people who experience it.
- *Informal*   Acting quickly and informally can reduce personal embarrassment and suffering; avoid disruption to work and working relationships. The use of an informal process should not preclude the victim from being accompanied if they feel the need for support.
- *Formal*   Formal procedures are needed if the bullying is of a serious nature, where it is the individual's preference or where an informal attempt to deal with the situation has failed.

Whatever route is taken to dealing with a complaint it should be clear to all employees that disciplinary action will be taken against those who bully or harass at work. As such, dealing with suspected instances of it should involve investigative procedures that are robust and able to meet the requirements of both grievance and discipline proceedings. Comprehensive records would also be needed of the complaint, the persons involved, actions taken, etc. Depending on the result of investigations disciplinary action might be taken against the perpetrator. However, in addition it might be necessary to consider moving one or more of the people involved to other departments or duties within the organisation. It should not automatically be the complainant that would be expected to move, but they might be offered the choice to do so where practical. Forcing either the perpetrator or the victim to move might give rise to claims of constructive dismissal if it is not handled within the terms of the existing contracts of employment, or as an alternative to dismissal if the allegations have been proved. Where no job moves result it would be necessary to make periodic checks to ensure that the bullying or harassment has stopped and that no subsequent victimisation has occurred.

See also: *behaviour management; counselling, coaching and mentoring; discipline and grievance; discrimination, diversity and equality; labour turnover; organisational culture; quality of working life and the psychological contract*

BIBLIOGRAPHY

ACAS (2007) *Bullying and Harassment at work: Guidance for Employees.* London: ACAS. Available at www.acas.org.uk/index.aspx?articleid=797 (last accessed December 2007).

Andrea Adams Trust Available at www.andreaadamstrust.org (last accessed January 2008).

CIPD (2006) *Working Life: Employee Attitudes and Engagement* (research report). London: Chartered Institute of Personnel and Development.

CIPD (2007) 'Harassment and bullying at work'. *Factsheet.* London: CIPD. Available at www.cipd.co.uk (last accessed December 2007).

Digital Opinion (2007) Available at www.digitalopinion.co.uk/bullying-natsurvey-results.html (last accessed January 2008).

Career Management

> *A career path refers to the actual or planned sequence of jobs that an individual has enjoyed (if looking backwards) or might be expected to follow during the course of their working life (if looking forwards). Career management refers to the design and implementation of processes that enable individual job moves to be managed in a way that encompasses organisational and individual career perspectives.*

Career management is about balancing the needs of the individual with the needs of the organisation. It inevitably forms part of the HR planning process and has close links to succession planning, employee development and management development. From an individual perspective therefore, career management reflects the developmental practices and processes that the person undertakes when seeking to pursue their particular job and work preferences over time. From an organisational perspective, career management reflects the policies and practices undertaken to ensure that the short-, medium- and long-term need for an appropriate number of suitably trained and capable people required by the organisation at all levels of the hierarchy are available internally. As such career management has a major part to play in the recruitment and retention of high calibre individuals who through the career development and opportunities offered by an organisation find that their personal aspirations coincide with those of the organisation. Of course there can never be a guaranteed or specific match in the long run between the career aspirations of an individual and those of the employing organisation. Individuals may develop interests and seek opportunities that the employer cannot offer; an individual may seek promotion at a time when the employer does not have such an opportunity available; an employee may seek to change their work-life balance. Equally the employer may decide to change their business activity in the future which may adversely impact on future job opportunities for individuals; as part of succession or diversity planning an organisation may decide to appoint people from outside thereby reducing the opportunities available to existing employees; or it may be that during a recession or economic slowdown redundancy impacts on an individual's career. Consequently career management is never a perfect match between the needs of an individual and the ability of the organisation to meet them (or vice-versa). The balance is at best an optimal one in that for unspecified periods of time the needs and expectations of both parties can be met.

King (2004) has identified a number of principles that it is claimed underpin the effective provision of career management within an organisation. These are:

- *Consistent* Messages about career opportunities and intentions are gleaned by an individual from many sources including from their line manager, HR specialists and company practice. Consistent information needs to be ensured so that potential opportunities are known without unrealistic expectations being raised.

- *Proactive*   Career management is a balancing act based on a wide range of assumptions. It is necessary for career management practice to take account of changing business and organisational requirements by being proactive in the way it seeks to align individuals and opportunities.
- *Collaborative*   It requires employers and employees to work together in achieving the needs and expectations of both parties.
- *Dynamic*   The need to flex career management practice and compromise over career choices to meet the changing needs and expectations of individuals and the organisation as circumstances change.
- *Senior management involvement*   It can only be achieved if employees see that senior managers take it seriously and are prepared to provide meaningful support.
- *Integration with other business and HR strategies*   If career management is not effectively linked to other strategies then it will appear to favour a 'chosen few' for reasons that are not connected with talent, potential or business needs.

King (2004) has also suggested that effective career management contains five components:

1 *Career planning and support*   This involves activities including setting objectives through personal development plans, appraisal and development reviews, development programmes and work experience.
2 *Career information and advice*   This involves activities including career counselling and coaching, career workshops and courses.
3 *Developmental assignments*   This involves activities including external or internal secondments, project assignments and work shadowing, and international assignments.
4 *Internal job markets and job allocation processes*   This involves activities including the internal advertising of job opportunities and encouraging internal applications and effective and thorough recruitment processes.
5 *Initiatives aimed at specific populations*   This involves activities including talent spotting, high potential development schemes, succession planning, graduate entry schemes, diversity management, development and assessment centres, and managed career moves.

One interesting issue within career management is to whom (if anyone) does a 'career' belong? Is it the property of each individual employee;

is it the property of the employing organisation; or is it a joint responsibility? This is an important question for many reasons as it has a direct impact on who should take the lead for planning career management and developmental activity, and who should take responsibility for ensuring that the career of an individual unfolds appropriately for both the individual and the employer. It is not an easy question to answer as there are many perspectives associated with career development that will impact on both individuals and organisations. For example, the individual gains a number of benefits from a career such as a financial reward, job satisfaction, status, life-style, and so on. But in order to do so they have to find organisation(s) that will provide appropriate opportunities, development and encouragement. On the other hand, organisations also gain many benefits from having effective career management strategies and policies.

For example, they are more likely to have high numbers of motivated employees, high levels of employee retention, higher levels of productivity, and a positive reputation among actual and potential employees as well as among customers, suppliers and the wider community. Clearly there are mutual benefits accruing from career management but that does not provide an answer to the original question as, for example, the failure of an organisation to provide effective career management support does not mean that individual employees do not have careers or their own career management strategies, just that they will do so to their own advantage which may not provide any benefit to the current employer. Conversely, no organisation can force an employee to undertake career management or development activity against their will. External resourcing can always provide 'people' to fill any job. Some people (an unquantifiable number) will be satisfied with their current jobs and so on and will not be interested, or perhaps may feel that they could not cope with the greater responsibility or commitment that a career advancement implies. In addition, there may be personal, family, organisational or other reasons why an individual may not seek a career development opportunity.

Pringle and Gold (1989) found that only about 25 per cent of respondents had plans for the future and that a combination of luck, being in the right place at the right time and opportunity provided them with promotion and career development 'chances'. However, if the employer does not take some responsibility for career management then those employees willing to manage their own careers will do so and those unable to will stagnate; neither of which helps the organisation to achieve the high performance status so keenly sought these days. The other reasons for organisations taking a keen interest in career development include the strong possibility that those individuals who are willing and able to take responsibility for their own career management are likely to seek opportunities outside of those offered by the current employer (to the detriment of the old employer). A career management survey carried out by the CIPD (2003) found that 95 per cent of respondents felt that individuals would be expected to take responsibility for their own careers in the future and that 90 per cent felt that organisations must offer support for this to happen.

Using a range of sources Torrington et al. (2005) identified a range of strategies that could be adopted by an individual in pursuit of career management goals both within a single organisation and in the wider world of work:

- *Self-nomination/presentation*   Making sure that senior people are aware of an individual's career desires and willingness to take on more responsibility.
- *Search for career guidance and a mentor*   Actively looking for advice, guidance and sponsorship from sources both inside and outside the organisation.
- *Interpersonal attraction*   Building effective working relationships, particularly with the immediate line manager – who has an obvious impact on access to promotion and career development opportunities.
- *Networking*   Making contacts both inside and outside the organisation that can provide information and general support networks.
- *Extended work involvement and work-life balance*   The individual making themselves indispensable by being prepared to do 'whatever needs to be done'. However, that can be at the expense of a balance between work and other interests/commitments and is not sustainable in the long run.
- *Building competencies as well as competence*   Being aware of the need to develop a wider range of competencies, but also being competent in delivering outcomes accurately and on time.
- *Creating opportunity*   Seeking out opportunities to put into practice the other items in this list.

- *Collect intelligence/information and understand market trends*   Understanding what is going on within the organisation, the local area, industry and economy, etc.
- *Be aware of personal strengths and weaknesses*   Knowing personal limitations and strengths helps to avoid mistakes and identify those areas where support might be needed.
- *Look after your health, wellbeing and fitness*   Being physically and mentally able to stand up to the rigours of modern working life requires these issues to be taken seriously.
- *Respond quickly to changes in business need*   Being flexible in adapting to changing priorities and trends in business need and job requirements prevents competency stagnation.
- *Develop the means to improve personal performance and future employability.*
- *Be prepared to move employers when a win/win relationship no longer applies*   Recognising that ultimately career achievement is a personal responsibility that might or might not align with the current employers needs or intentions.

See also: assessment/development centre; counselling, coaching and mentoring; employee development; human resource planning; management development; performance management; resourcing/retention; strategic HRM; succession planning and talent management

BIBLIOGRAPHY

CIPD (2003) 'Managing employee careers – issues, trends and prospects' (Survey Report: June). London: CIPD.

King, Z. (2004) *Career Management: A CIPD Guide*. London: CIPD.

Pringle, J.K. and Gold, U.O'C. (1989) 'How useful is career planning for today's managers?', *Journal of Management Development*, 8(3): 21–26.

Torrington, D., Hall, L. and Taylor, S. (2005) *Human Resource Management* (6th edition). New Jersey: Prentice Hall.

Competency

A competency can be regarded as the characteristics and capabilities of an individual which directly lead to superior job performance. Looked at from a job perspective, competency is usually explained in terms of behavioural dimensions that affect job performance.

The starting point in thinking about competency is to recognise that there is a difference between what someone knows and what they can actually do effectively. For example, there is a world of difference between a child knowing (say) how to drive a car because they have watched someone and played with a toy steering wheel and them actually being able to drive a real car properly, safely, and without accident. There is an inbuilt tension between what someone might know and what in practice they can actually do with that understanding. The competency movement sought to move away from the acquisition of knowledge for its own sake and to focus on what people could actually do after whatever intervention had taken place. In an organisational context the focus on competency rather than knowledge should ensure that there is a detectable impact on operational effectiveness and performance as a result.

There is some debate about the relationship (if any) between the terms 'competency', 'competence' and 'skill' in relation to this topic. Some writers and indeed practitioners tend to regard the terms as interchangeable, others see a difference between them. For example, competency has already been defined above as broadly reflecting the behavioural requirements that impact on job performance. Competence on the other hand can refer to an ability of an individual to actually deliver what is required in terms of output. In driving a car an individual would be deemed competent when they had passed their driving test – they could demonstrate that they could meet the expected standard. But of course every time the individual subsequently drives their car they have an opportunity to demonstrate that they are a competent driver (and acquire additional competency). The distinction between competency and skill is less easy to identify, as in its broadest sense a skill reflects the ability to 'do' something. For example, skill can be defined as, 'Practised ability or expertness'. This definition suggests that someone with a skill is 'competent' to carry out certain specified tasks, which is what the term 'competency' also implies. Boyatzis (1982) overcame this difficulty by suggesting that (based on a definition broadly similar to that above) competency comprised any or all of the following elements:

- *Traits*   This aspect of competency reflects the characteristics or innate qualities that an individual possesses and which impacts on their performance at work.
- *Motives*   Some people are motivated to deliver superior performance and to achieve good results for many reasons.
- *Skills*   This aspect would be a skill as reflected in the traditional sense of the term as outlined above.
- *Self-image*   The self-image that an individual holds about themselves influences how they interpret the world around them and their circumstances and will consequently form the basis of how they decide to interact with those situations.
- *Social role*   This aspect of competency reflects the acceptable and conventional social norms and behaviours that exist in a particular context.

In that sense Boyatzis regards competency as something more than skill in the traditional sense of the term. Some of the factors in the above list are able to be manipulated and/or encouraged as a result of organisational interventions. For example, career management policies can help motivate individuals to deliver a high performance but some items from the above list are difficult to influence or even measure in relation to the achievement of a superior job performance. It is the behaviour of employees that are the subject of measurement and appraisal in terms of competency profiling as contributing to team and/or organisational success. For example, the CIPD have identified ten core competencies that form the professional standards for people working within HR. As such these are the general competencies that all practitioners should aspire to hold, but each level and area of specialism within HR practice will have specific competencies relevant to that role. Each business discipline (marketing, finance, etc.) will have their own competency frameworks similar to these, and of course similar frameworks will exist for many other areas of work within organisations and particular industries. The core competencies within HR are (www.cipd.co.uk):

1 *Personal drive and effectiveness* The existence of a positive, 'can-do' mentality, anxious to find ways round obstacles and willing to exploit all of the available resources in order to accomplish objectives.
2 *People management and leadership* The motivation of others (whether subordinates, colleagues, seniors or project team members) towards the achievement of shared goals not only through the application of formal authority but also by personally role-modelling a collaborative approach, the establishment of professional credibility, and the creation of reciprocal trust.
3 *Business understanding* Adoption of a corporate (not merely functional) perspective, including an awareness of the financial issues and accountabilities of business processes and operations, of 'customer' priorities, and of the necessity for cost/benefit calculations when contemplating continuous improvement or transformational change.
4 *Professional and ethical behaviour* Possession of the professional skills and technical capabilities, specialist subject (especially legal) knowledge, and the integrity in decision-making and operational activity that are required for effective achievement in the personnel and development arena.
5 *Added-value result achievement* A desire not to concentrate solely on tasks, but rather to select meaningful accountabilities – to achieve goals that deliver added-value outcomes for the organisation, but simultaneously to comply with the relevant legal and ethical obligations.
6 *Continuing learning* Commitment to continuing improvement and change by the application of self-managed learning techniques, supplemented where appropriate by a deliberate, planned exposure to external learning sources (mentoring, coaching, etc.).
7 *Analytical and intuitive/creative thinking* Application of a systematic approach to situational analysis, the development of convincing, business-focused action plans, and (where appropriate) the deployment of intuitive/creative thinking in order to generate innovative solutions and proactively seize opportunities.
8 *'Customer' focus* Concern for the perceptions of personnel and development's customers, including (principally) the central directorate of the organisation; a willingness to solicit and act upon 'customer' feedback as one of the foundations for performance improvement.
9 *Strategic thinking* The capacity to create an achievable vision for the future, to foresee longer-term developments, to envisage options

competency

(and their probable consequences), to select sound courses of action, to rise above the day-to-day detail, and to challenge the status quo.

10 *Communication, persuasion and interpersonal skills* The ability to transmit information to others, especially in written (report) form, both persuasively and cogently, and to display listening, comprehension and understanding skills, plus sensitivity to the emotional, attitudinal and political aspects of corporate life.

The national (UK) arrangement for utilising the notion of competency is the National Vocational Qualification (NVQ) framework (in Scotland this is referred to as the Scottish National Vocational Qualification or SNVQ). This sought to bring within a single framework the previously existing (and largely unstructured) wide range of vocational qualifications. NVQs are based on national occupational standards. These standards are statements of performance that describe what competent people in a particular occupation are expected to be able to do. They cover all the main aspects of an occupation, including current best practice, the ability to adapt to future requirements, and the knowledge and understanding that underpin competent performance. There are five levels of NVQ broadly defined (by the Qualifications and Curriculum Authority) as follows. Management level NVQs exist at levels 3, 4 and 5:

- *Level 1* Competence that involves the application of knowledge in the performance of a range of varied work activities, most of which are routine and predictable.
- *Level 2* Competence that involves the application of knowledge in a significant range of varied work activities, performed in a variety of contexts. Some of these activities are complex or non-routine and there is some individual responsibility or autonomy. Collaboration with others, perhaps through membership of a work group or team, is often a requirement.
- *Level 3* Competence that involves the application of knowledge in a broad range of varied work activities performed in a wide variety of contexts, most of which are complex and non-routine. There is considerable responsibility and autonomy and control or guidance of others is often required. It is argued by some that this level is broadly equivalent to A level awards.
- *Level 4* Competence that involves the application of knowledge in a broad range of complex, technical or professional work activities performed in a variety of contexts and with a substantial degree of personal

responsibility and autonomy. Responsibility for the work of others and the allocation of resources is often present. It is argued by some that this level is broadly equivalent to a first degree level of award.

- *Level 5*   Competence that involves the application of a range of fundamental principles across a wide and often unpredictable variety of contexts. Very substantial personal autonomy and often significant responsibility for the work of others and for the allocation of substantial resources feature strongly, as do personal accountabilities for analysis, diagnosis, design, planning, execution and evaluation. It is argued by some that this level is broadly equivalent to a postgraduate degree level of award.

The annual survey of learning and development carried out by the CIPD (2007a) found that some 60 per cent of organisations surveyed already had a competency framework in place within the organisation, and of the remaining 40 per cent almost half intended to introduce one in the near future. The respondents that had no immediate plans to introduce competency frameworks were predominantly small employers with less than 250 employees; perhaps not an unexpected result as they may not have an understanding of such arrangements or the expertise available to develop them. Of those respondents with competency frameworks in place they covered just under 80 per cent of all employees within the organisation and 50 per cent reported that they used a single competency framework for the entire organisation. The most popular terms used to describe competencies identified in that survey were:

- Communication skills.
- Team skills.
- Customer service skills.
- Problem-solving skills.
- People management.
- Results orientation.

According to the CIPD (2007a) survey the following were the main areas of contribution for competency frameworks:

- They contributed to the achievement of effective performance management.
- They contributed to the achievement of greater employee effectiveness.

- They contributed to the achievement of greater organisational effectiveness.
- They contributed to the achievement of effective training needs analysis.
- They contributed to the achievement of effective career management.

Salaman and Taylor (2002) identified that a number of weaknesses were inherent in the application of the competency approach in relation to management jobs, including:

- An emphasis on behaviour marginalising the effect on success through other factors in the social, cultural and organisational context.
- Most will emphasise a small, narrow set of behaviours and attitudes whereas most management jobs will involve a wide range of tasks and requirements.
- There is a tendency to focus on current competency requirements rather than on long-term management development.
- There is an inbuilt assumption that management decision making and action are always rational and aimed at achieving the highest performance.
- There is an assumption that managers are results driven whereas in practice they must balance many competing pressures in deciding which outcomes must take precedence.

Other criticisms of competency frameworks include (CIPD, 2007b):

- They can be over-elaborate and bureaucratic.
- The language used can be off-putting.
- It is difficult to achieve a balance between reviewing competencies often enough to remain relevant but not so frequently that they become confusing.
- If too much emphasis is placed on 'inputs' at the expense of 'outputs', there is a risk that it will favour employees who are good in theory but not in practice.
- Competencies are based on what good performers have done in the past and different skills and attitudes may be required as work changes over time. They also run the risk of failing to encourage teams with mixed skills who balance each other's strengths and weaknesses.
- They can become out of date very quickly due to the fast pace of change.

- Competencies can exclude the attitudes of previously disadvantaged groups so it can become difficult for women, people with disabilities, or ethnic minorities to match their underlying assumptions.
- Some competencies are essentially personality traits which an individual may be unable (or unwilling) to change.

See also: assessment/development centre; employee development; job, job analysis and job design; management development; performance management; succession planning and talent management.

BIBLIOGRAPHY

Boyatzis, R.E. (1982) *The Competent Manager: A Model for Effective Performance.* London: Wiley.

CIPD (2007a) *Learning and Development: Annual Survey Report 2007.* London: CIPD.

CIPD (2007b) 'Competency and competency frameworks'. *Factsheet: April.* London: CIPD. Available at www.cipd.co.uk (last accessed January 2008).

Salaman, G. and Taylor, S. (2002) 'Competency's consequences – changing the character of managerial work'. Paper presented at the ESRC Critical Management Studies Seminar: Managerial Work, The Judge Institute of Management, Cambridge University.

Compliance/ Commitment

> *Compliance – following the rules, requirements and obligations associated with a job whilst paying only 'lip-service' to the underlying aims and objectives sought by management. Commitment – employees identify with management to the extent that they adopt management's values and norms and commit themselves enthusiastically to their work and to the achievement of management's aims and objectives.*

The distinction between compliance and commitment and their relative significance for HRM practice may at first glance seem obvious, especially to the psychological contract and high performance working. In brief, commitment is sought from employees in order to achieve high performance working through progressive, leading edge and effective human resource policies and practices. It is associated with the democratic management style and the stakeholder view of the status of employees relative to the organisation. Achieved successfully, commitment should make the job of management much easier as employees will have internalised the appropriate ethos. They will also work enthusiastically in pursuit of the organisation's objectives and so reduce the level of control and management required. This is a win-win situation in which employees are allowed freedom of action and managers achieve high levels of effectiveness and customer service and a reduced cost of operations. Compliance on the other hand represents a situation in which employees will do what is required of them but only if they are managed and 'driven' appropriately. It is generally associated with autocratic management styles based on the paradigm that managers are responsible for taking decisions and giving instructions whilst employees are simply required to do as directed. It requires close supervision and management along with the existence of comprehensive control procedures and the regular monitoring of work quantity and quality. It all adds up to an expensive way of running an organisation. From that simple explanation it should be apparent why commitment is thought desirable and that compliance is not. That so many organisations now claim to adopt such approaches should make it apparent that commitment is the norm these days and compliance a thing of the past. But is that so? Can compliance be so easily ignored? Are democratic management styles really the norm? Do progressive HR policies really deliver conditions that encourage commitment and are employees actually stakeholders, equal in status and rights with management?

The starting point for this discussion needs to be a consideration of organisations within a capitalist system. The basis of capitalism is the pre-eminence of the achievement of profit as a return for the risk in investing capital. In the basic capitalist model employees are not expected to think or to have any interest in the business beyond selling their labour to be used at management's direction. However, it is being increasingly recognised that in today's social context it is necessary for managers to work closely with (rather than simply directing) employees if they are to be able to harness effectively the human resource available to them. These basic views of capitalism have become distorted over the years as many managers and employees have become shareholders and/or receive profit based payments in one form or another; also share ownership is widespread among the working population through investment, savings and pension schemes. However, such adaptations do not completely negate the underlying argument about the way in which control is exercised and the relative power balance between employer and employee.

As far back as the 1960s writers such as Fox (1966) were suggesting that the employment relationship in Britain (being based on the traditional relationship between master and servant) was responsible for much of the hostile industrial relations climate and conflict at the time. It has since been argued that much of the recent move towards human resource management and away from personnel management, is driven by the desire to 'go beyond the contract' in getting better value for money from the employee resource. In addition the traditional compliance based authority structures have been replaced with an emphasis on a commitment based work organisation. However writers (such as Legge 2005) suggest that simply softening the language used to underpin HRM can hide the contradictions implicit within capitalism and that the rhetoric adopted by organisations adopting an HRM approach to manage people could mask the reality of managerial prerogative in the service of capital. Some would argue that whilst things may have changed it has not produced a commitment based relationship as the working relationship continues to be based upon a fundamental inequality. Capital can take its need for labour elsewhere or dispense with it altogether through the use of technology. Modern HR practice seeks to overcome this difficulty through the inclusion of the encouragement of employees to take significant responsibility for their own career and development planning and management, implying that as employees have the freedom to choose and decide about their own future they become stakeholders in a business and less susceptible to the demands of a particular employer. Of course this entire debate becomes even more complex when the focus of the discussion moves away from the private sector and onto the public and voluntary sectors. In these sectors there is no 'for profit' imperative underpinning the reason for an organisation's existence and equally it can be difficult to identify the 'beneficial owner' – the individual or group who will 'take away' the ultimate benefit resulting from the organisation's activity. It is sometimes argued that the citizen, customer, client or recipient of the service provided is the ultimate beneficial owner (because the service is provided for their benefit) and therefore the dominant stakeholder. This is an argument that frequently does not work in practice – try arguing that you should not pay your income tax this year because you are a bit short of money for example!

The relationship between individual employees and the organisations that employ them is a complex one. At a basic (and perhaps cynical) level, the human employee is simply a cheaper, flexible alternative to a machine or computer, to be replaced as soon as a more reliable and/or cheaper alternative becomes available. However, that view is overly simplistic and there are many forces that will act upon the relationship between employees and employers. The reliance on compliance as the means of managing the human resource within an organisation will inhibit any real connection between employer and employee at a time when the quality of that connection offers real potential for a competitive advantage. Hence the emphasis on commitment as the driving force for the employment relationship. However, there are two major questions about commitment in organisations that need to be considered:

1 Is the employer attempting to seek a committed workforce because it is the right thing to do, or are they simply attempting to manipulate a particular working environment in order to maximise the profit potential? As a supplementary question – does this distinction matter?
2 Is it possible to distinguish between employee behaviour and attitudes when the individual is 'committed' as compared to when the individual feels that they must display (comply with) certain behaviours and attitudes in order to retain a job or career? As a supplementary question – does such a distinction matter?

The answer to both of these questions and the supplementary ones are very difficult to determine and to some extent depend on personal belief and ethical standpoint. Managers are employees with one distinction – they are supposed to act in the interests of the beneficial owner of the business; ordinary employees have no such special status. At best they are one of the stakeholders within the organisation, at worst a necessary resource to be manipulated in pursuit of organisational objectives and replaced whenever practical. The behaviour and attitudes of employees towards work and organisations also cover a wide range of variation. Sometimes employee behaviour might reflect favourable attitudes and the adoption of management's underlying values; sometimes an open hostility and rejection of organisational purpose and management objectives; sometimes a superficial demonstration of commitment to the organisational objectives and management's values as a situational imperative based on job, career and income objectives. Which of these is active for a particular employee depends upon factors including their personality, prior experience of organisations and managers, and the treatment that individuals expect from them. Given that it is not possible to 'see inside the heads' of employees it is never certain what motivates particular behaviours or if particular statements or expressed opinions are a true reflection of what an individual actually thinks or believes.

It is management that determines how an organisation will position itself relative to the various stakeholder groups and therefore how the employment relationship will be arranged. Employees must adapt and reach an accommodation within that reality if they are to survive and prosper within it. This is the basis of the labour process debate, one that is grounded in the use to which human labour is put in the transformation of organisational inputs into outputs for sale within capitalist markets and the part played by managers in the organisation of that work. It is argued that management actions will lead to a reinforcement of the dominant position of managerial control over organisational functioning and the cost of operational activity. The debate also seeks to understand and explain the degree of 'malice aforethought' in management decision making. For example, is it done to control labour and reinforce management's superior position; is it done to further the commercial objectives of the organisation; or is it done for the benefit of employees, customers and society? It is also argued that by allowing some of its power to be dissipated, managers can retain effective control over labour activity and use, leading some writers to talk of the 'manufacture of consent'. This explains how workers are encouraged to support (consent) to the relative imbalance of power in a capitalist society as a consequence of being allowed some degree of influence in decision making over aspects of their work – aspects carefully prescribed by management. One of the difficulties in researching in this area is that of being able to find out the true causes of particular managerial decisions and actions. Managers attempting to manipulate employees, for example, are unlikely to admit to this!

Reliance on compliance as the basis of employee engagement could lead to alienation – a reaction expressed as a 'switching off' from any real engagement with the organisation or the work being done. Thompson provides a definition of alienation as follows:

> Work performed under conditions in which the worker is estranged from his or her own activity in the act of production, through the sale of labour power and the subordination of skills and knowledge to the capitalist, or other external social forces. (1989: xiii)

compliance/commitment

57

Alienation is about separation, ownership and the rights of workers as stakeholders. It is argued that alienation occurs as an inevitable reaction to the control of work by managers. The key features of alienation include:

- *Powerlessness*   A lack of control or influence over the pace and methods of work.
- *Meaninglessness*   Being a very small part of a large process with work of little real significance in terms of the finished product or service.
- *Isolation*   A lack of belonging, or of a feeling of not being part of a team or group.
- *Self-estrangement*   A lowered feeling of self-worth as a consequence of being reduced to a number in the 'system'.

It is easy to see why alienation would not be desirable as state of employee engagement and why commitment would be preferred as the means to effectively connect employees with their work and organisation.

French et al. (1985) suggest that there are nine expectations that organisations have in relation to what they expect from employees. These include:

- The pursuit of organisational goals that are different from and take precedence over personal objectives.
- The delivery of appropriate levels of involvement, commitment and initiative from individuals.
- Acceptance of authority and taking responsibility.
- Compliance with leadership direction and influence.
- Requiring individuals to fulfil expected roles within the organisation.
- Requiring high levels of effectiveness and efficiency from employees.
- Co-operating with others in pursuit of defined organisational objectives.
- Adhering to rules, policies and procedures.
- Displaying loyalty to the entire organisational system.

From the above list of expectations it would seem that both compliance and commitment are expected from employees so perhaps it is unrealistic to consider them as an either/or reflection of what employees understand as the requirements placed on them. One way that such expectations could be transmitted and reinforced throughout the employee group is by what has become known as compulsory sociability. This reflects an approach to building teams with a strong culture by requiring individuals to join in group activities and follow particular patterns of behaviour or face sanctions of some description. It reflects the ways in which management preferred patterns of behaviour and attitude can be inculcated across the workforce through apparently innocent and voluntary group activity, but which in practice contains strong elements of compulsion in compliance with both process and outcomes.

See also: employee communication and consultation; employee development; employee empowerment and engagement; employee relations and conflict; high performance working; management development; organisational culture; performance management; strategic HRM

BIBLIOGRAPHY

Fox, A. (1966) *Industrial Sociology and Industrial Relations*, Royal Commission Research Paper No. 3. London: HMSO.

French, W.L., Kast, F.E. and Rosenzweig, J.E. (1985) *Understanding Human Behaviour in Organisations*. New York: Harper & Row.

Legge, K. (2005) *Human Resource Management: Rhetorics and Realities* (anniversary edition). Basingstoke: Palgrave Macmillan.

Thompson, P. (1989) *The Nature of Work: An Introduction to Debates on the Labour Process* (2nd edition). Basingstoke: Palgrave Macmillan.

Contract of Employment

> *A verbal or written agreement that seeks to establish the basis of the working arrangements between those seeking the services of others and providing services which it is intended by both parties will be enforceable at law. A contract is only formed when an offer is made and accepted and a consideration is exchanged. Consideration in this context means that both parties exchange benefits (or commit themselves to do so) such as the payment of wages or work.*

There exists a legal basis to many aspects associated with the employment of people by an organisation including the contractual relationship between them. Specific statutes relating to employment legislation are enacted by parliament in the UK (including the devolved parliaments in Scotland and Wales) and through provisions originating from the European

Commission. The common law also has a significant impact on HR policy and practice and establishes the basic duties and responsibilities of both employer and employee. Case law continually adapts and clarifies statutory provision in the light of particular circumstances presented to the superior courts which then become binding on the judgements of the lower courts (employment tribunals). Inevitably therefore the discussion of anything related to the contract of employment will be out of date shortly after it is written.

The basic question surrounding the relationship between a worker and an organisation revolves around the issue of whether someone is an employee or not. That can be difficult to ascertain but it is important as employees have more rights in law than non-employees. In contract terms this distinction would be between a 'contract of service' and a contract for services'. A contract of service grants the status of employee to the worker, whereas a contract for services defines an independent/ self-employed contractor without the rights of an employee. Some employers have deliberately used this distinction to seek to minimise their responsibilities towards employees by classifying workers as self-employed in some way or other. Ultimately only the courts can provide a definitive answer to the question if it becomes an issue of legal significance.

Employee and worker rights include:

Some of the rights that only apply to employees include:	Some of the rights that apply to all workers include:
• Right to a statement of terms and conditions of employment. • Right to an itemised pay statement. • Statutory sick pay. • Time off for public duties. • Trade union rights. • Minimum notice periods. • Maternity/paternity leave and pay rights. • Unfair dismissal rights.	• Equal pay for equal work. • Non-discrimination on the grounds of sex, race, religious belief, sexual orientation and disability. • Health and safety rights. • Minimum wage and working time rights. • Data protection rights. • Carer's responsibility rights.

The main obligations of employers and employees under the common law include:

Owed by employer to the employees:	Owed by employees to the employer:
• Duty of care. • Duty to pay agreed wages • Duty to provide work. • Duty not to treat employees in an arbitrary or vindictive way. • Duty to provide support to employees. • Duty to provide safe systems of work. • Maintain a relationship of mutual trust and confidence.	• Duty to cooperate with employer. • Duty to obey reasonable/lawful instructions. • Duty to exercise reasonable care and skill in duties performed. • Duty to act in good faith. • Duty of fidelity (also applies to ex-employees). • Maintain a relationship of mutual trust and confidence.

A contract of employment does not have to be written to exist, which is why the legislation requires employees to be provided with a statement of the main terms and conditions of employment. The legislation specifies what information must be included in such a statement, but it is less than the complete terms contained within the contract proper. In addition to the written contract, the totality of a contract of employment will include things that are 'custom and practice' within the organisation; elements from both the common and statute law; and also (if it is applicable) agreements with trade unions, staff associations or trade associations (which might determine issues such as pay review practices).

A contract comes into existence when an offer is made by one party, is accepted by the other, and a consideration is exchanged. Once formed, the contract cannot be unilaterally changed by either party without the agreement of the other. However, an employer might argue (say) that it is essential for the survival of the organisation to cut wages. Employees are then faced with the option of seeking legal redress for a breach of contract, taking some form of industrial action, or accepting the change. In seeking to impose change, an employer may give notice to terminate the employment of existing employees (under the existing contract) but offer continued employment based on different terms and conditions of

contract of employment

employment in a new contract of employment. If the new terms are not accepted by employees then their employment would be terminated and they would be forced to seek legal redress if they felt that they had a case in law. Clearly, it makes sense to have a specific clause in the contract of employment allowing flexibility and change to influence the terms, although these would still be subject to the general tests of reasonableness by an employment tribunal.

A contract of employment comprises three different types of terms. These are:

1 *Expressed terms*   These reflect the terms that are specifically referred to in writing, including starting salary, hours of work, holiday entitlement, job title and notice period, etc.
2 *Implied terms*   These reflect terms that while not written down can be safely implied to be applicable, including the right to breaks, duty of care, etc. There is an inevitable ambiguity with implied terms (potentially leading to confusion, argument or dispute) and as much as possible should be documented.
3 *Incorporated terms*   These are incorporated into an employment contract as a result of a requirement or obligation: for example, as a result of employment legislation or agreements with trade unions in relation to terms and conditions of employment.

There are two main forms of contract that have already been identified above. They are a contract for services and a contract of service. To decide whether or not a contract of service applies to a particular context (whether the worker is an employee) three main questions need to be addressed (CIPD, 2007):

- *Mutuality of obligation*   This question asks 'Does the employer have to provide work for the worker, and does the worker have to do the work provided by the employer?'
- *Control*   This question asks 'Does the employer control how the worker does the work, and does the employer's disciplinary and grievance procedure apply to the worker?'
- *Substitution*   This question asks 'Can the worker send a substitute to do the work for the employer on their behalf?'

In addition to the formal contract of employment there is currently a heavy emphasis on the psychological contract. This refers to the unspoken and unwritten expectations that both parties have in relation to the role and responsibilities of the other party in the employment relationship. It is about the expectations that both parties have on what they have to give and what they stand to gain in return from the relationship at work: in short, the mutual obligations of one towards the other. As such it does not exist in the sense of being written down nor is it likely even to be referred to specifically, but nevertheless it is a potent force in determining how the working relationship will function on a day-to-day basis within the work dynamic. The psychological contract is easily broken by either party and once damaged is difficult to repair as it involves issues of trust, fairness, equity, and informal obligations.

Current experience suggests that a balance of give and take exists in the employment relationship, albeit in a different form to that which existed previously. Today there is more emphasis on personal careers with individuals taking responsibility for themselves and their own development. The differences between the old and new psychological contracts are highlighted in the following table:

Traditional psychological contract	Evolving psychological contract
• Work hard on behalf of the employer. • Act loyally towards the employer. • Work in best interests of the employer. • Expect long-term employment in return. • Expect development and career advancement should the opportunity arise.	• I will contribute creatively and with appropriate effort. • I don't expect/want long-term employment. • I expect development to be provided to maintain and enhance my market worth. • I will take personal responsibility for my career. • I expect a salary commensurate with my contribution and market worth.

See also: employee relations and conflict; negotiation; quality of working life and the psychological contract; statutory bodies; trade union/employee representation

contract of employment

BIBLIOGRAPHY

Broady, D. (2005) *The Employment Contract: Legal Principles, Drafting and Interpretation.* Oxford: Oxford University Press.

CIPD (2007) 'Contracts of employment'. *Factsheet: September.* Available at www.cipd.co.uk (last accessed February 2009).

> **Counselling** A process involving a confidential meeting to explore some difficulty, distress or dissatisfaction that an employee is experiencing. The purpose being to encourage the employee to identify options to help relieve the identified difficulties.
>
> **Coaching** A process intended to develop a person's skills and knowledge so that their job performance improves, hopefully leading to the achievement of organisational objectives.
>
> **Mentoring** The process intended to provide ongoing support and development to a less experienced individual by passing on advice and guidance with the intention of improving performance.

Counselling helps the client to explore conflicts and difficulties that they are facing with the intention of helping them to find areas to begin to instigate change that might have a positive impact on the difficulties experienced. Counsellors will seek to assist the client to focus on constructive behaviours which will help them reach specific goals. In an organisational context, counselling would be likely to be available as part of an employee assistance programme with open, free access to employees but within the total number of sessions available (restricted to perhaps a maximum of six). Consequently, counsellors will work within a relatively short timeframe and must be conscious of the potential need to refer clients to more long-term support provision through primary care institutions and probably not made available through the employer. Hughes and Kinder (2007) identified several points that were significant in the provision of counselling support in an organisational context. These include:

- Attendance at counselling should not adversely impact on the career development or status at work of any employee.
- Attendance should be voluntary.
- Counsellors should not judge or exploit their clients in any way.
- Counsellors are expected to have an understanding of organisational culture and circumstances that might impact on their work.

- Counsellors should be aware of (and sensitive to) the potentially differing and sometimes conflicting needs and expectations of the various stakeholders to any counselling intervention.
- Counselling is only one of a number of employee support services that could be made available within an employee assistance programme.
- Stress audits can be a useful means of identifying pressure points impacting on all employees and the subsequent development of coping and resilience strategies.
- Self referral to counselling by an employee should be a completely private and confidential process with no information being made available to the employer. Counsellors can be placed in a difficult situation if the sessions identify significant workplace problems that need to be addressed.
- Managerial referrals present particular difficulties in relation to issues such as client attendance requirements, the purpose and consequences of the counselling process, and the type and nature of any feedback provided to the employer.

Hughes and Kinder (2007) incorporated the work of a number of writers to identify the benefits of counselling, including:

- *Cost reduction*   Lower cost of operations as employees are more likely to attend work and be more productive.
- *Reduced risk of legal action*   An improvement in employee wellbeing, working relationships, etc. and less need to claim compensation. It is also less likely to result in prosecutions for breaches of health and safety requirements.
- *Reduction in levels of sickness and other absence*   Employees who have access to counselling are more likely to attend work and to have lower levels of sickness.
- *Improves productivity*   Employees who are not affected by problems at work are more likely to produce higher productivity.
- *Positive impact on work effectiveness*   Attitude improving when counselling was available leading to improved work effectiveness.

Coaching is a recognised 'helping behaviour' along with counselling and mentoring, but has a slightly different approach to both. In comparison to counselling it is more directive in approach with the intention of improving an individual's job, knowledge and skill profile with a specific organisational purpose in mind. It can be thought of as a style of managing in which a commitment to improving the organisation is part of a commitment to improving people. The obvious analogy is that of a sports coach who is tasked with improving a player's capability in relation to the sport and their contribution to the overall team performance. The CIPD (2007) reported that over 60 per cent of the organisations surveyed used coaching as part of their development processes and that over 70 per cent regarded it as a part of the preferred management style within the organisation. The same source identifies a number of coaching characteristics within an organisational context, including:

- A non-directive form of development.
- A focus on improving performance and developing skills.
- Both organisational and individual goals.
- Is not a substitute for counselling or other clinical interventions; neither is it appropriate for individuals suffering psychological, personal or social distress or difficulty.
- It provides an individual with feedback on their strengths and weaknesses.
- It requires the use of appropriately trained and experienced practitioners.
- A recognition that line managers are not necessarily the best people to serve as coaches for their staff.

One of the difficulties with coaching is trying to identify when it represents the most appropriate option in particular circumstances. Factors to take into account include the objectives and outcomes sought; the nature of the issues to be dealt with and their amenability to resolution through coaching; the alternatives available; the relative cost of coaching compared to other options and the likely benefits; employee preferences; employee readiness for the coaching approach; and whether the organisation has access to coaching facilities.

Whereas coaching is often described as having a relatively short-term timeframe; mentoring is generally considered to be based on a long-term relationship. Often it involves a more senior individual passing on advice and guidance, giving the junior partner the benefit of their greater understanding, knowledge and experience. The CIPD (2008) identified the main characteristics of mentoring as:

- A supportive form of development.
- A focus on helping an individual to progress their career and improve their skill base.
- Personal issues and difficulties being integrated into the mentoring relationship process more effectively than in coaching with its focus on performance development.
- Having personal as well as organisational objectives and benefits.

Clutterbuck (2004) suggested that the benefits to the organisation and individual are as follows:

- Organisation:

  o Assists with the provision of effective succession planning. Encouraging people to think about and beyond their current job, and to think about what being more effective means. That should encourage individuals to prepare and have the confidence to move into larger jobs.

  o Positive and significant impact on recruitment and retention rates. Encourages prospective employees to think of the organisation as caring about long-term development. It encourages people to stay with the organisation as they can see opportunities for personal and career development.

  o Improved organisational effectiveness through higher levels of job engagement and job satisfaction. It can raise the level of engagement by introducing a non-judgemental dimension into performance and developmental issues. Higher levels of engagement also positively impact on levels of job satisfaction.

  o Encourages organisations to adapt more easily and effectively to change. Mentoring should provide the catalyst and support for individuals to reduce the perceived risk and stress that can adversely impact on how change is viewed.

- Individual:

  o Improved clarity in the management of career goals and expectations.

  o Improved levels of self-confidence and self-awareness that can also impact positively on contribution and performance.

  o The acquisition of knowledge, skill and experience that they may not have otherwise encountered, or if they had it would have been over many years.

  o Development of a wider network of advisors, contacts and potential supporters.

  o Mentors gain benefits and satisfaction as a result of being able to pass on their experience, skill and knowledge to the benefit of others.

  o Line managers gain from the impact of mentoring on individual employees as a result of the focus, clarity and purpose that they acquire because of the development process.

Alred et al. (1998) identified a simple three-stage model of mentoring as a process. The first stage involves identifying the issues that the individual being mentored wants to explore and establishing a relationship between the parties. The second stage involves seeking to introduce and develop new understandings for the mentored individual through listening and challenging, providing constructive feedback, discussing strengths and weaknesses, identifying developmental opportunities and priorities, and demonstrating new skills. The third stage involves action planning in seeking to encourage new ways of thinking and working, exploring options for actions and possible consequences, developing an action plan and monitoring progress. Mentoring is based on an effective working relationship over a long period of time and it carries the risk of becoming one that is based on dependency or on spilling over into a strong personal relationship. Of course such a relationship can also turn sour after a period of time or simply not work at all if the individuals do not 'hit it off'. The CIPD (2008) identified several things that an HR specialist should consider when setting up and running a mentoring programme, including:

- Determining when mentoring represents an appropriate intervention as compared to the other development options available.
- Appointing, training, and monitoring the activities of a pool of mentors across various levels of the organisation.
- Determining how to match mentors with those who are to be mentored.
- Understanding differing approaches to mentoring and the necessary tools and mechanisms/processes involved.
- Establishing any contractual arrangements and monitoring the effectiveness of the process formally and on a regular basis.

See also: *career management; employee assistance programme; employee development; management development; performance management*

BIBLIOGRAPHY

Alred, G., Garvey, B. and Smith, R. (1998) *Mentoring Pocketbook*. Alresford: Management Pocketbooks.

CIPD (2007) 'Coaching'. *Factsheet*. Available at www.cipd.co.uk (last accessed March 2008).

CIPD (2008) 'Mentoring'. *Factsheet*. Available at www.cipd.co.uk (last accessed March 2008).

Clutterbuck, D. (2004) *Everyone Needs a Mentor: Fostering Talent in Your Organisation* (4th edition). London: CIPD.

Hughes, R. and Kinder, A. (2007) *Guidelines for Counselling in the Workplace*. London: British Association for Counselling and Psychotherapy.

Data Protection

The basic legislation that provides data protection requirements is the Data Protection Act 1998, which came into force in 2000 and implemented the relevant European Union Directive from 1995. In addition, there are many other statutory provisions that provide data protection rights in particular circumstances including the following and a number of other statutory instruments covering particular areas, such as telecommunications, electronic communications, and the holding/use of sensitive personal data:

- The Human Rights Act 1998.
- The Freedom of Information Act 2000.
- The Regulation of Investigatory Powers Act 2000.
- The Public Interest Disclosure Act 1998 (this provides protection for those dismissed or subject to other sanctions for 'whistleblowing' or any similar act in relation to information in the 'public interest').

The basis of data protection legislation is that those who hold and use personal data in an electronic, manual or other form (referred to as data controllers) must comply when doing so with the principles contained within the appropriate legislation. The people about whom information is held and/or processed (referred to as data subjects) are provided with particular rights under the legislation. In addition to the legislation mentioned above, there is a common law requirement that confidential information obtained in an employment context should not be used for the benefit of the holder of that information without the appropriate consent. Eight principles are enshrined within the legislation which stipulate how data should be handled by data controllers. They are that data must be:

- Fairly and lawfully processed.
- In relation to the intended purpose, should be adequate, relevant and not excessive.

- Accurate and up to date.
- Processed for limited purposes.
- Not kept longer than is necessary.
- Processed in line with the rights of data subjects.
- Held securely.
- Not transferred to countries outside of the EU without adequate safeguards for data protection being in place.

The Information Commissioner was established under the Data Protection Act 1998 to oversee issues associated with data protection, offer guidance on how data should be managed, and to investigate complaints about data mismanagement. In 2005 the Commissioner produced a Code of Practice in relation to employment-based data management which covered four major areas of HR work in relation to data. These are:

1 Recruitment and selection.
2 Employment records.
3 Monitoring at work.
4 Information about the health of workers.

The legislation requires that data controllers must register with the Information Commissioner unless they hold and process personal information only for the purposes of the following, in which case an exemption from the requirement to register may be possible (Information Commissioner, 2007).

- Staff administration (including payroll).
- Advertising, marketing and public relations for one's own personal business.
- Accounts and records.
- Some not-for-profit organisations.
- Processing personal information for personal, family or household matters.
- Maintenance of a public register.
- Processing personal information without an automated system such as a computer.

The legislation also requires that organisations abide by the eight principles outlined above and that they be prepared (subject to payment of the stipulated fee) to provide information within 40 days about any of the data held about an individual to that person if they request it.

The website of the Information Commissioner (2008) sets out the basic rights that data subjects have in relation to data about them held by organisations. These include:

- To find out what information is held on computer and some manual records.
- To apply to a court to require a data controller to correct, block, remove or destroy personal details if they are inaccurate or contain expressions of opinion based on inaccurate information.
- To request a data controller to not process information about them that will cause substantial unwarranted damage or distress.
- To prevent unsolicited marketing material being sent to them.
- To object to automated decision making involving actions to be taken in relation to them.
- To claim compensation from a data controller through the courts for damages or distress caused by any breach of the legislation.
- To ask the Information Commissioners Office to investigate and assess whether some aspect of the legislation has been breached by a data controller.

The same website identifies a number of questions that data controllers should ask themselves in relation to actual or potential information issues in order to assess the type, level, form and purpose of the data held, together with the organisational responsibilities in relation to it:

- Do I really need this information about an individual?
- Do I know what it will be used for?
- Do the people whose information I hold know that I have it and are they likely to understand what it will be used for?
- If I am asked to pass on personal information, would the people on whom I hold information expect me to do this?
- Am I satisfied that the information is being held securely, whether it is on paper or computer?
- What about the website, is it secure?
- Is access to personal information limited to those with a strict need to know?
- Am I sure that the personal information held is accurate and up to date?

- Is personal information deleted and destroyed as soon as there is no more need for it to be held?
- Are staff trained in their duties and responsibilities under the data protection requirements and do they practise these?
- Do I need to notify the Information Commissioner that I am a data controller and are the notification details up to date?

In terms of an employer's action plan, the CIPD (2008) suggest that it should contain the following elements:

- Appoint a data controller – an individual to be responsible for all data and information held and used within the organisation in relation to the relevant legislation.
- Audit information and data systems to identify who it is that holds which information and for what reason.
- Consider what information is collected and how it is used.
- Issue guidance to managers and departments on how to gather, store and retrieve information.
- Ensure that all the information collected complies with the relevant legislation and data principles.
- Check the security of information storage.
- Check on the what, how and why aspects that are associated with the transfer of data outside of the European Economic Area and on provisions for its subsequent security.
- Check and monitor the use of automated decision-making systems used within the organisation.
- Review any policy and practice in relation to references.
- Review any policy in relation to the private use of phone, fax, email and the internet.

If an individual makes a request about the information that might be held about them they are entitled to be told:

- Whether the personal data about them are being processed.
- A description of the data being processed.
- The purposes for which these are being processed.
- The recipients or classes of recipients to whom these are being or may be disclosed.
- In an understandable form, the personal data held and any information available to the data controller about the source of these data.

Data controllers need not respond to identical repeated requests (or similar ones) from the same individual unless some time has elapsed. Employers should not make any attempt to alter, amend or disguise any data that might make the data more acceptable (for example, amending, hiding or changing comments in performance appraisal records). In 2005 the Information Commissioner produced a Code of Practice in relation to employment-based data management (outlined above) which covered employment-related data. The code made it clear that health-related information, including sickness, mental health, medical screening, drug and alcohol testing and genetic testing, all fell under the sensitive personal data heading for the purposes of the legislation. Given its sensitive nature such information should only be collected in relation to health and safety matters, to avoid discrimination, to satisfy other legal requirements, or if each worker has given individual and explicit consent to such information being collected and held. These records should be kept separate from general absence records. There is no general guidance on how long employment-related records should be kept as it will depend on a number of factors relevant to each individual and the type of record.

One area of potential difficulty in relation to data protection is in monitoring employee behaviour and use of facilities such as the phone, fax, intranet, internet and email. It is advisable that employers have appropriate policies in place for the business and private use of such facilities including the monitoring of such use. Monitoring like this is a sensitive issue and there is no definitive advice covering all eventualities. It may be possible for employers to monitor such use if the employees have given their specific prior permission through (say) the contract of employment. It might also be possible for an employer to justify particular monitoring when an employee had not given such specific prior permission – for example, if a breach of company policy was suspected – but even then employees should preferably know that there is a possibility of being monitored. The reporting by an employee of another employee downloading pornography or other offensive material from the internet, or of circulating such material by email, is a relatively common issue that can involve data protection and other employment rights-based issues.

See also: absence management; assessment/development centre; career management; counselling, coaching and mentoring; discipline and grievance; interview; psychometric and other tests; statutory bodies; succession planning and talent management

BIBLIOGRAPHY

CIPD (2008) 'Data protection'. *Factsheet: January*. Available at www.cipd.co.uk (last accessed March 2008).

Information Commissioner (2005) *The Employment Practices Code*. Wilmslow: Information Commissioners Office.

Information Commissioner (2007) *Notification Handbook: A Complete Guide to Notification*, Wilmslow: Information Commissioners Office.

Information Commissioner Available at www.ico.gov.uk (last accessed March 2008).

Discipline
and Grievance

There are different interpretations of the terms discipline and grievance which depend upon their intended purpose:

1 *Punishment   Discipline and grievance represent processes for punishing the other party for some wrongdoing.*

2 *Justice   Discipline and grievance represent mechanisms through which some injustice can be brought to the attention of the other party and redress sought.*

3 *Contract breach   Discipline and grievance represent the means through which breaches in the contractual rights, obligations, expectations and implications that exist between the parties can be brought to the attention of the other party and redress sought.*

4 *Behaviour management   Discipline and grievance are the means through which inappropriate behaviour and actions by either party can be brought to the attention of the other and if necessary appropriate measures put in place to 'correct' the inappropriate or unwanted behaviour.*

Irrespective of the underlying view of the purpose of discipline and grievance procedures, people can do the 'wrong thing' at work for many reasons.

It can be the result of a lack of training; a misunderstanding about what is expected; illness; an 'off-day'; wilfulness; interpersonal conflicts; and many other reasons. Equally employees can feel aggrieved at some aspect of their treatment by managers and other employees for many reasons. It may be that a busy manager is rather brusque in their approach one day; that the manager and subordinate do not get along at a personal level; that a manager is underperforming and under considerable pressure from their boss (causing aggressive behaviour towards subordinates); that a manager may be trying to take advantage of a subordinate in some way or another; that an employee may have been passed over for promotion and feels that they are being discriminated against; that an individual may feel that work has been allocated unfairly, etc. However these arise, such situations need procedural arrangements to deal with them in order that such problems can be resolved speedily.

However, as with many aspects of human experience within organisations it is not quite as simple as this might imply. For example, it is not realistic to expect every individual to work and to behave perfectly all day every day and to never make a mistake. Neither is it realistic to expect everyone to be happy about their job, pay, career, colleagues, and superiors all of the time. That variability may have a temporary or longer-lasting impact on the ability of a business to function smoothly and effectively. Consequently, there exists a range of intervention options that seek to allow for this variability in human behaviour and its impact on organisational functioning. Examples include employee assistance programmes, counselling, employee relations procedures, and discipline and grievance procedures.

There are two possible approaches to the use of discipline, including:

- *Informal* Informal approaches to discipline can cover many interventions but they are usually carried out as part of normal interpersonal interaction between managers, employees and between colleagues. They include:

  o Guidance or instruction to perform a particular task in a particular way or at a particular time, etc.
  o A 'telling-off' for doing something wrong, not working as they should be, or making a mistake.

However, that very informality can lead to problems if for whatever reason the employee needs to be 'dealt with' a number of times. As a result, there exists the need to draw a fine line between an informal approach to managing people during the everyday interaction at work and a need to ensure that formal procedures are used when appropriate.

- *Formal* There are usually a number of stages or steps in a formal company discipline procedure. These normally include:

  o A verbal warning: This would be applied to situations involving minor episodes of misconduct. Although classed as a verbal warning it should be recorded in writing, and a copy given to the employee. The document should summarise the problem; set out what the employee is required to do and by when; identify what support will be provided by management during the process; and also what will happen if repeated occurrences of the 'problem' arise. Review meetings should also be included in the outcome to monitor and encourage employee progress in meeting the stated requirements.

  o A written warning: This might be used for repeated occurrences of minor misconduct (where the verbal warning has not changed the employee behaviour) or for events that are more serious than would warrant a verbal warning. The written warning document given to the employee (and kept on file) should be very similar in content to that described under the verbal warning stage. Review meetings would also be similar.

  o A final written warning: This might be used when the behaviour expected as the outcome from a written warning does not materialise, or when a significant event occurs that is almost serious enough to justify dismissal. The final written warning document given to the employee (and kept on file) should be very similar in content to that described under the verbal warning stage. Review meetings would also be similar.

  o Dismissal: This level would arise when the requirements of the final written warning stage have not been met or when a serious event occurs that could result in dismissal. The most serious events would be referred to as potentially leading to dismissal on the grounds of gross misconduct. Dismissal for gross misconduct means that the individual's employment is terminated without the contractual right to notice. It represents a category of misconduct which is so serious that it allows the employer to dismiss the employee without giving them the opportunity to redeem themselves. As an alternative to dismissal some procedures allow for disciplinary transfer, demotion or suspension without pay, but these should only be used if the appropriate contractual provision exists.

In addition to the procedural steps there exists a need to take into account other aspects of this process:

- A reasonable investigation process to identify the 'facts' associated with the case.
- Reasonable hearings so that the case can be fully explored and the individual is given the chance to put their side of the story and challenge the evidence.
- Allowing representation from a trade union representative, another representative or a colleague.
- Hearings should be held as quickly as is practical and within a stated timescale. The right of appeal should also be exercised within a specified and reasonable time, as should the period during which the disciplinary action stays 'live' on an employee's file.
- Allowing the right of appeal against a decision to a higher authority not previously involved in the disciplinary case.
- Some managers may not have the right to dismiss an employee and so the procedure should indicate the appropriate level of management to deal with each stage.

In disciplinary situations the main legal aspect is the right to raise a claim of unfair dismissal if the employee considers that their employment has been terminated unfairly. The law requires that any dismissal should be based on a reasonable belief (of guilt) following a reasonable investigation and that a fair hearing is carried out within the provision of an appropriate procedure (or in the absence of a company procedure the application of the statutory procedure). The law makes provision for a dismissal to be fair if it falls into one or more of the following categories:

- Redundancy.
- Legal bar.
- Capability.
- Conduct.
- Some other substantial reason (SOSR).

Where an individual feels that they have been unfairly dismissed they would make an application to an Employment Tribunal to hear their case. This would be done by completing an application form (within three months of the effective date of termination) outlining the basis of the claim. A copy of the form would then be sent to the former employer who would be asked to respond within a specified timescale. The response would be sent to the applicant and a date would then be set for a tribunal hearing. Copies of all of the paperwork would also be sent to the Advisory, Conciliation and Arbitration Service (ACAS), who would seek to offer conciliation to the parties in an attempt to resolve the matter without the need for a tribunal hearing. Should that not prove possible then the tribunal would meet and hear the case and make its award either in favour of the applicant or the employer. If the dismissal was found to have been unfair then the tribunal will make an award, which can be:

- *Reinstatement* The employer is ordered to take the employee back into the same job and on the same terms of employment and with no loss of service. If the employer refuses then the tribunal can award additional compensation.
- *Re-engagement* This is similar to reinstatement, but there is no continuity of employment.
- *Compensation* This represents a financial award to compensate the employee for the loss of their job. There are rules covering how the award is calculated, based on service, job prospects and the employee's contribution to their dismissal.

Either or both parties can opt to be represented by a legal representative, trade union officer or another person during the tribunal hearings. In certain circumstances it is possible for the losing side to appeal against the findings of a tribunal to the Employment Appeal Tribunal (EAT), and potentially beyond that to the other superior courts within the judicial system.

Grievance procedures tend to mirror disciplinary procedures in terms of the steps provided, for example:

- *Informal hearing* The employee would present this informally (in writing) to their immediate supervisor. A meeting would follow at which the issues would be explored; subsequently the decision would be communicated to the employee within specified timescales.
- *Formal hearing* If the matter is not satisfactorily resolved by the immediate supervisor then the individual should have the opportunity to raise the grievance (in writing) with a more senior manager. A meeting to discuss the 'problem' would be arranged within a reasonable timescale and the issues would then be explored. An outcome should then be made known to the employee within a specified timescale.

- *Appeal* If the matter is not satisfactorily resolved by the manager holding the formal hearing then the individual should have the right of appeal to a more senior manager for one last review. In some cases, rather than an appeal to a senior company manager there might exist an appeal panel – perhaps involving both management and union members, or perhaps reference to an external arbitration stage.

It would be possible in some circumstances for an individual having a grievance rejected by the employer to resign and claim that they had been constructively dismissed. By doing so they would have the opportunity to seek redress before an Employment Tribunal. There are areas such as discrimination or victimisation that allow claims to an Employment Tribunal without the need to have been dismissed first. Part of the case may involve the way in which an employer dealt with the issue when it was brought to their attention by an employee.

See also: behaviour management; contract of employment; employee relations and conflict; organisational culture; performance management; statutory bodies; trade union/employee representation

BIBLIOGRAPHY

Torrington, D., Hall, L. and Taylor, S. (2005) *Human Resource Management* (6th edition). Harlow: Prentice Hall.

Discrimination, Diversity and Equality

Discrimination is about favouring one group of people (or an individual) to the detriment of others. Equality seeks to prevent discrimination. Diversity is about seeking to go beyond equality and ensuring that organisations are able to capture the benefits of 'difference' between human beings as a means of achieving a competitive advantage.

Discrimination, diversity and equality are areas associated with the practice of HRM that are about ensuring that, as a minimum, the law in relation to equality of opportunity is complied with, but also that the maximum potential and contribution to the organisation from each individual can be realised. The law seeks to ensure that employers do not discriminate against particular categories of people and that management decisions and actions are applied fairly and constantly to all employees. Legislation applies to all aspects of the employment relationship including resourcing, reward, career development, pension and termination rights. The main themes covered by the requirement for equality are:

- Gender, marital status or sexual orientation.
- Disability.
- Race, national origin or ethnicity.
- Religion or belief.
- Ex-offenders with spent convictions.
- Membership (or non-membership) of a trade union.
- Part-time or fixed-term contract workers.

There are four types of discrimination that have been recognised within the legislation:

- *Direct discrimination* This arises when an employer uses (say) sex or race in a particular situation or decision. For example, a job advert for a male computer operator would directly discriminate against females – unless the employer could show that a 'genuine occupational qualification' existed. For example, the need for a female actor to play a female part in a play.
- *Indirect discrimination* This arises when a 'requirement or condition' for a job will disadvantage a particular category of people. For example, including a job requirement for people to be over six feet tall would indirectly discriminate against women as they tend to be smaller than men.
- *Positive discrimination* This arises when an employer seeks to overcome previous discrimination by giving preference to a group previously discriminated against (for example, seeking only women applicants for senior jobs). Such actions would be unlawful, however 'positive action' is permissible (e.g. seeking to prepare and encourage more women to apply).

- *Victimisation* This arises when an employer seeks to take action against an employee (or group) because they sought to (or assisted others to) claim their legal rights. For example, an employer might victimise an employee (by failing to promote them) because they had previously raised a grievance over equal pay.

In most situations it does not matter if an employee is male, black, Asian, white, female, or married, and so the legislation seeks to prevent such factors from being taken into account. In addition, such factors would not be expected to have an impact on the level of reward, promotion, access to development or other aspect of employment. Unfortunately, management decision making in relation to employees usually involves a need to 'discriminate' or to differentiate between people in some way or another. For example, if ten people apply for one vacancy then nine people will be 'discriminated' against as they will not be selected. Equal opportunity legislation and management practice seeks to ensure that such decisions are not based on inappropriate factors whilst recognising that some basis for selection is unavoidable.

Diversity is often taken to mean the same as equal opportunities, the argument being that by providing an equality of opportunity a diverse workforce matching the composition of society will be achieved – along with fairness. However, equal opportunities is grounded in legislative provision and the specific categories covered by it do not match the breadth of diversity within society. There are other forms of 'difference' between people which form no part of the legislative provision but which may have an impact on organisational performance. For example, people will differ in terms of their personality, work role preferences, level of enthusiasm, and so on – all of which might be expected to have an impact on organisational effectiveness. Consequently, the management of diversity involves recognising that every individual differs from every other individual in some way or another, and that if that potential can be harnessed, high performance organisational activity could result along with improved working relationships, culture and atmosphere. As such diversity in its broadest sense represents a business results-based approach to managing the differences between people, whereas the equal opportunities approach represents a moral approach to fairness in employment as reflected in the legislative provision.

The equal opportunities approach is not specifically concerned with individuals, but with company policy and practice in the provision of the opportunity for disadvantaged groups to make progress in areas that have previously been denied to them. Legislation is used as the primary means of defining the rights of disadvantaged groups and of seeking to ensure a compliance with the law by employers. Current legislation does not require that disadvantaged groups should have preference (positive discrimination) in the allocation of jobs, etc. However, the use of positive action is encouraged in supporting and encouraging previously disadvantaged people to be able to compete more effectively for jobs and promotion, etc. A more extreme approach to equality of opportunity argues that the legislation does not go far enough and that quotas and positive discrimination need to be used to forcibly change previous discriminatory practice, the intention here being to ensure that disadvantaged groups spread quickly into previously inaccessible areas of the workforce. However, such approaches can be argued to restrict the ability of organisations to select and promote the best individuals in an attempt to socially engineer the workforce profile. Some of the organisational implications of the term 'diversity' include:

- A means of being able to meet the requirements of equality legislation.
- A means of being able to match employee and customer profiles in an attempt to align business capability with customer needs and expectations.
- A means of providing planned difference among the workforce in order to avoid the potential commercial dangers that can arise from high levels of conformity.
- A means of being able to embrace the different and unique qualities each individual can bring to the workplace, contributing to the achievement of high performance working and a greater level of commercial success.

The foregoing discussion does not answer questions about what difference means in an individual context, nor how much is appropriate to a specific job or context. To consider the first question, people 'differ' in many ways – height, weight, gender, ethnic grouping, intelligence, personality, skill range, to identify just a few. Some of the ways in which people differ might have a work-related or commercial benefit to an organisation and some will not. It is very difficult to answer the question about what differences are of relevance to an organisational context. In general terms it is about seeking to identify the 'things or characteristics' that can provide a potential contribution to an organisation, remembering also that any such differences have to be capable of surviving a legal challenge. In relation to the issue of 'how much' difference is appropriate, that is also a very difficult question to answer. For example, Belbin (1993) argues that a number of team roles exist and that a balanced team composition is necessary if teams are to have a pronounced and positive impact on company performance. So does that imply that because most work in organisations is undertaken by teams, the recruitment, promotion, and training of people with specific team roles required at level of management should be the norm?

There are three organisational approaches that can be taken to tackle the issues of equality and diversity, according to LaFasto (1992):

- Compliance as the result of pressure and legal requirement.
- Managing diversity because it provides a potentially useful business opportunity, based on an instrumental approach in which management commit to diversity in return for a commercial advantage.
- Valuing employees because they represent the most important asset and resource for the business. A recognition by managers that valuing employees builds self-esteem and is significant in creating a high performance organisation.

Jackson et al. (1992) suggest a slightly different way in which organisations respond to diversity, emphasising the cultural basis of the six stages identified which are conveniently grouped into three levels:

- *Level 1*:
  - o Stage 1: The exclusionary organisation. The dominant groups seek to exclude others and maintain the status quo.
  - o Stage 2: The club. The dominant group is prepared to moderate its explicit power by allowing 'outsiders' to join – providing they conform to the norms of the dominant group.

- *Level 2*:
  - o Stage 3: The compliance organisation. A minimalist approach complying with the essential legislative requirements. Such organisations may encourage equality of opportunity at the lower levels but the dominant groups at the top remain largely unaffected.
  - o Stage 4: The affirmative action organisation. One that actively seeks to adapt to changing circumstances. Will encourage staff to change attitudes and also encourage the development of people from minority groups.

- *Level 3*:
  - Stage 5: The redefining organisation. Such organisations seek to ensure that the culture supports a multicultural workforce and that power is redistributed across all groups.
  - Stage 6: The multicultural organisation. This is based on a culture that values individual contributions and recognises everyone as a full member of the organisation. They also recognise the existence of a broader social responsibility to encourage the development of other organisations, individuals and society.

Ross and Schneider (1992) suggest that organisational approaches to diversity are based on the following criteria:

- They originate from internal intentions rather than external requirements.
- They are focussed on individual rather than group levels of activity.
- They are focussed on the cultural aspects of organisational activity rather than the procedures, processes and systems adopted.
- They are the responsibility of every function and person in the organisation and not just a reflection of HR policy.

They suggest a six step process for achieving a diversity culture within an organisation:

1 *Diagnosis* Identify what exists in relation to culture, policy and levels of diversity – the outcome will identify the baseline from which to move forward.
2 *Set the aims* Identify the business case (to justify changes) as well as senior level sponsorship (to champion and support the changes). Determine the aims, objectives and outcomes from the proposed change.
3 *Spread of ownership* Raise awareness of the benefits of diversity among everyone within the organisation. Encourage individuals at all levels to question their attitudes and pre-conceptions about diversity. Move ownership towards everyone being actively involved.
4 *Policy development* Everyone can be involved in policy development to some degree, which is why it is appropriate to begin this stage after widespread ownership is achieved.
5 *Managing the transition process* Includes activities such as training, positive action programmes, policy implementation and cultural awareness/change initiatives.

6 *Maintain momentum* Measure and celebrate achievements, introduce initiatives to keep progress flowing. Monitor the impact on customer relations, productivity and cost/profitability.

See also: *employee development; employee relations and conflict; high performance working; human capital; interview; job evaluation; quality of working life and the psychological contract; resourcing/retention; statutory bodies; strategic HRM*

BIBLIOGRAPHY

Belbin, M. (1993) *Team Roles at Work*. Oxford: Butterworth-Heinemann.

Jackson, B.W., LaFasto, F., Schultz, H.G. and Kelly, D. (1992) 'Diversity' in B.N. Jackson, F. LaFasto, H.G. Schultz and D. Kelly (eds), *Human Resource Management*, 31(1–2), Spring/Summer.

LaFasto, F. (1992) 'Baxter healthcare organisation' in B.N. Jackson, F. LaFasto, H.G. Schultz and D. Kelly (eds), *Human Resource Management*, 31(1–2), Spring/Summer.

Ross, R. and Schneider, R. (1992) *From Equality to Diversity – A Business Case for Equal Opportunities*. London: Pitman.

Downsizing, Reorganisation, Outsourcing and Redundancy

> *Downsizing means to reduce the number of employees in an organisation, usually in order to improve productivity. Reorganisation means rearranging the activities in the organisation usually in order to improve productivity. Outsourcing means sub-contracting an area of work to an outside specialist provider. Redundancy means the employer no longer needs the work done by particular employees.*

The alternatives to downsizing are generally identified as including:

- Resourcing linked to future needs for flexibility and adaptability among employees.
- Training and development linked to the need to develop flexibility and rapidly changing skill/knowledge requirements.
- Effective succession planning.
- The effective use of redeployment within the organisation.
- Encouraging intrepreneurship – motivating and encouraging existing employees (and managers) to develop new business ideas.
- Undertaking a range of cost-saving initiatives across all aspects of the business.
- Introducing policies that will reduce working hours, reduce labour costs, allow for sabbaticals and study leave.
- Not replacing people as they leave or retire and actively seeking work opportunities by developing links with other companies.
- Introducing phased retirement in which individuals nearing retirement work progressively fewer days each week until finally retiring permanently.
- Engaging in various forms of participation including allowing employees to buy parts of the business being closed, or 'swapping' part of their pay for share ownership.

In essence, there are alternatives to simply cutting the number of employees; the process of identifying alternatives is a creative one; it needs to be thought about before the organisation is facing a crisis; and the HR department has a major role to play in identifying and providing many of the alternatives. The HR department also has a significant role to play in helping line managers to identify how the same amount of work can be done by fewer people and also in the development of appropriate severance, redeployment, retraining, employee relations, and transitional arrangements.

Reorganising is an umbrella term for the many different approaches to the use of change management techniques in an attempt to 'do things differently' – usually in the search for higher productivity and/or reduced costs. It can involve any or all of the following: a redesign of the organisation; a redesign of parts of the organisation; the combining of departments or teams; the elimination of teams, departments or divisions (as the result of closure, outsourcing or sale); the redesign of work or administrative systems; the relocation of business activity; a reduction in the numbers employed; and the streamlining of a product/service range or features. It can also be another term for downsizing or delayering. However, downsizing (usually) implies that the number of employees will be reduced relative to the output of the organisation in order to improve productivity, whereas reorganising does not automatically imply a reduction in the numbers employed. Delayering refers to the elimination of layers within the hierarchy – usually involving the reduction of middle management jobs, levels and numbers. Reorganising has as its focus the rearrangement of the ways in which the organisation functions and operates in order to meet customer needs more effectively which may or may not mean that fewer people will be employed as a result. In that sense it is a broader term than downsizing. There are many approaches to reorganising the work of an organisation, including use of the following techniques and models:

- *Work study*   At its simplest level, this is about the identification and introduction of the 'best' and most efficient ways of working and the development of incentive arrangements to encourage employees to work at a motivated rate. It has a long history and is most frequently associated with the scientific management approach to the design and organisation of work.
- *Business process re-engineering (BPR)*   This is based on the premise that organisations tend to elaborate themselves over time (in relation to administrative and operational processes, management information systems and the numbers employed) and so become slow at responding and lose their focus on the key purpose of meeting customer needs. BPR as a process is about the fundamental rethinking and radical redesign of business processes to achieve dynamic improvements in performance, costs, quality, service, and speed. The approach proposed by BPR is that a rapid and radical approach is needed to remove any surplus activity that is not relevant to the essential business processes of an organisation. It begins with an identification of the essential business processes – the things that are vital for getting the product or service into the hands of the customer – as they are the only true 'givens' necessary for an organisation to continue in business. Only once the bare essentials are identified can the minimum level of additional administrative requirement and other support activity be identified and built into the organisational system.
- *Organisational development (OD)*   This involves the systematic application of behavioural science to organisational processes in order to

improve effectiveness. The strands of practice within OD include the use of encounter groups, process consultation, survey feedback, action research, and a planned approach to interventions.

- *Systems thinking* There are a number of systems approaches to the reorganisation of organisational activity, for example the viable systems model, total systems intervention, etc.
- *Business restructuring* This approach simply refers to a redesign process involving the reorganisation of business activity in terms of functioning and hierarchical purpose.

Outsourcing means the delegation of a defined area of business activity to an external provider who is required to deliver the delegated activity to a defined performance standard. In many ways it is a modern form of sub-contracting. It is not uncommon to find outsourcing being used for specific areas of a business such as all or part of the HR function. The CIPD (2008) have identified a number of benefits and potential problems associated with the outsourcing of HR activity and the following list has been adapted from that source to be applicable to any area of work to be outsourced:

- *Potential benefits:*
  - Reduced costs.
  - Increased efficiency.
  - Access to high quality IT systems and technology.
  - Improved availability of management/control information.
  - Access to expertise not available internally.
  - Increased flexibility and speed of response.
  - Part of an overall business strategy to outsource a number of functions.
  - Reduced risk of problems in one area of the business 'spilling over' to the areas outsourced.
  - To free up internal resources to operate more strategically.

- *Potential problem areas:*
  - Don't outsource what you don't understand. The outsource provider will have to solve the problem subsequently (at a cost) and the provider's solution might not be most appropriate to your organisation.
  - Outsourcing does not absolve the organisation of its responsibility for the aspect of work outsourced.
  - Because outsourcing arrangements can be long term (five to ten year contracts are not unusual), an understanding by both parties

of the current and future business strategy of each is important.
- o A loss of internal knowledge and understanding of processes which become the 'property' of the outsource provider.
- o Standardisation of processes in line with the outsource provider and not organisational preferences.
- o Fragmentation of organisational activity between internal and outsourced areas of responsibility means that divided loyalties can arise among employees and that day-to-day operations are split from strategy and policy development.
- o The need to constantly review the success of the outsourcing arrangement against specified metrics.

Redundancy reflects the termination of an employment contract under specific circumstances. That involves one of the following three circumstances:

- A total cessation of the organisation's activities.
- A cessation of business activity at the site where the employee works.
- A reduction or cessation of the work for which the employee was employed.

Many situations can arise in which the reorganisation of work in one form or another will lead to redundancy (for example, the relocation of business activity, the restructuring of work activity, or the introduction of a different technology which reduces the need for human intervention). It would be usual for an organisation to have an established redundancy policy that would specify how such situations would be dealt with. Policies should incorporate the guidelines, rules and procedures to be followed for dealing with redundancy situations effectively, such as:

- Planning the scale of the redundancy and how to implement it.
- An identification of the population potentially being made redundant.
- The notification of large-scale redundancies to the Department for Business, Enterprise and Regulatory Reform.
- Considering the possibility of allowing volunteers to apply for redundancy and the rules for selecting the basis on which people will qualify.
- Engaging in meaningful consultation at both a collective and individual level.
- Identifying the objective selection criteria.
- Complying with all three stages of the statutory dismissal procedures, including advance notice of an individual consultation meeting and permitting a colleague to be present at consultation meetings.

- Allowing and notifying individuals of the opportunity to appeal.
- Encouraging the search for suitable alternative employment.
- Calculating the statutory or other redundancy payment.
- Considering other financial support such as assistance with relocation expenses.
- Considering helping redundant employees to obtain training or alternative work through internal support or the services of outplacement consultants.

Organisations should be aware of the possibility of redundancy and plan to avoid the necessity. Many of the possibilities have already been identified above in the alternatives to downsizing. Once it becomes necessary to make people redundant then a mechanism for doing so is important. There are a number of factors that can be used, but in each case it must be shown that these were fair and reasonable and that they were applied in a non-discriminatory and reasonable way. Appropriate factors might include any combination from the following: length of service; attendance records; discipline records; skill; competency; work experience; and performance achievements. It would be possible to develop a scoring approach using a number of such factors as appropriate to the circumstances. Naturally a redundant employee has the right to claim unfair dismissal through an Employment Tribunal – unless this was arranged through a compromise agreement which specifically precluded such an eventuality. Also it is necessary to consider those employees not being made redundant and the effect on them of seeing colleagues (and perhaps friends) being made redundant. This has been referred to as the survivor syndrome – in which those remaining in work feel that they perhaps should have been made redundant and so retain a strong link to those that have left the organisation rather than to the company and its future. This can lower morale, productivity, trust in management, and loyalty to the business, as well as create feelings of guilt and increase absence and labour turnover.

See also: benchmarking; career management; contract of employment; discrimination, diversity and equality; employee communication and consultation; employee relations and conflict; high performance working; human resource planning; statutory bodies; strategic HRM; trade union/employee representation

BIBLIOGRAPHY

CIPD (2008) 'HR outsourcing'. *Factsheet: January*. Available at www.cipd.co.uk (last accessed April 2008).

Employee Assistance Programme

A scheme provided by an employer to offer assistance to employees who experience a problem and who might find it beneficial to have an opportunity to talk to a support worker, the intention being to assist the employee to find a way of dealing positively with the difficulty.

Employee assistance programmes (EAP) are generally made available to employees as part of an organisation's benefit arrangements. They are an attempt to encourage employees to seek help in dealing with issues that might otherwise create difficulties at work in relation to performance and/or attendance. The issues that can be covered by an EAP can be very wide and are not usually restricted to things directly related to work. They could typically (but not exclusively) include:

- Work relationship issues.
- Family/personal/relationship issues.
- Eldercare, parenting and childcare issues.
- Separation, loss and bereavement issues.
- Bullying, harassment or violence at work or home.
- Financial difficulties.
- Legal problems.
- Health concerns.
- Stress-related concerns.
- Drug and/or alcohol abuse.
- Work problems.
- Work pressures or difficulty in coping with work requirements.
- Emotional problems.
- Concerns about housing.
- Work-life balance issues.

EAPs are usually provided free and confidentially to employees within the predetermined limits of contact allowed by the scheme rules. Initial contact between the employee and the provider is usually by telephone at the employee's initiative. But in some cases an employee might be referred (formally or informally) to such provision by their manager as a result of a performance review, or behavioural, attendance or other problems becoming apparent at work. The process involved in conducting the support offered by the EAP is very much based on the counselling model outlined earlier and so will not be discussed in detail here.

Although employers will fund the EAP, they are not generally made aware of which employees (or indeed managers) are making use of the services offered unless there are specific reasons for this confidentiality to be breached and the employee agrees. Such instances might involve bullying, safety issues or other situations in which management action is needed to prevent a continuance or future occurrences of the problem. There are of course underlying concerns about the management referral of an employee to EAP support and about the transmission to management of any information about EAP contacts. Management referral will place pressure on an employee to 'deal' with whatever the issue is (as identified and defined by management) in a management preferred way. That could imply very strongly that the employee has been 'marked out and categorised' and that their continued employment is likely to be at risk unless they co-operate fully in dealing with and resolving their issues in the prescribed way. There is also the issue of what information should be passed back to the employer from the EAP provider. The employer is funding the provision of the service and so at one level needs to be aware of how the money is being used and indeed whether or not the service is being used at all by any of its employees. The employer also needs to be aware of anything that is systemically wrong with the ways in which the organisation functions or of particular issues or people that need to be dealt with (as causes of employee distress) so that employee wellbeing and effectiveness can be maximised. However, in doing so it could be that the rights to confidentiality and privacy of an individual might need to be compromised and such situations need to be carefully handled. It should be obvious from the discussion so far that the provision of EAP is about the employer seeking ways to maximise the potential contribution from employees. Admittedly, an employer offering such provision is seeking to provide employees with the opportunity to improve their wellbeing by having access to support services that can help an individual to find ways to resolve difficulties and cope with the problems that life throws at them. But this is done not for altruistic reasons but for commercial reasons in order to be able to show that every effort was made to take the duty of care seriously and to maximise the employee contribution by removing or minimising any hindrances to it. It is quite clear that the 'client' of the EAP provider is the employer, not the employee. Services are provided to the employees of a client under very specific rules and guidelines, but it is the client to whom an ultimate allegiance is paid.

The usual pattern of EAP provision is that all employees would be made aware of the availability of the service and what it might cover together with any limits on the actual level, frequency and duration of the support offered. Whatever form the general notification to employees takes would also specify confidentiality and other related aspects (including what information would be provided to management) in an attempt to give the scheme credibility and make its boundaries clear. The key role of contact with the EAP provider is to help the employee to find ways of dealing with or coming to terms with whatever the issue was that caused them to contact the provider. The EAP provider is not there to solve the problem for the employee but to guide them in finding their own solutions. It would be usual for the contract between the EAP provider and the employer to specify the number of contacts and/or duration/type of contact between employees and the provider. Should it be necessary to go beyond that agreed limit or to involve specialist support or face-to-face meetings, then the contract would make provision for how this might be arranged without breaching confidentially or privacy rules. Any ultimate limit on cost or time grounds would also need to be specified so that open-ended or very specialised or more appropriate care could be arranged through other agencies and not necessarily provided by the employer (for example rehabilitation, medical or psychiatric care).

There have been a number of studies that have sought to demonstrate that EAP does deliver positive benefits for both employees and employers. For example, Attridge (2001) suggested that in 60 per cent of EAP interventions no absence from work was necessary and that in 72 per cent of cases productivity had increased as a result of the intervention. The average gain in productivity was recorded as 43 per cent. These are very dramatic results but of course it is difficult to be sure if the outcomes were solely attributable to the EAP interventions. It is possible that similar outcomes might have been noticed as a consequence of adopting a more caring management style or as a result of some attention being paid to an employee. But at the very least the EAP appears to have provided a structured process for dealing with employee issues in a positive manner with positive outcomes – at least for the employer.

The criteria for what makes a successful EAP include the existence of the following:

- Open to employees and immediate family members.
- Recognition by management, employees and employee representatives that such a scheme is necessary and demands commitment for its effective functioning
- Appropriate policies and procedures supported by managers, employees and employee representatives.
- Establishment of both formal and informal referral processes to access the EAP.
- Promotion of the EAP and encouragement to use the service.
- Training for managers and employees in the EAP and its functioning/ purpose.
- Strict rules on confidentiality and privacy being applied in practice.
- Regular review of the EAP to ensure that it meets the needs of managers and employees.
- Regular evaluation of the effectiveness of the EAP.

The Canadian Centre for Occupational Health and Safety (2006) suggests the following guidelines for employers seeking an EAP provider:

- What experience does the EAP provider have in providing such services?
- Where is the EAP provider based? The closer to the client organisation the more likely the provider is to understand local concerns and issues.
- What range of services does the EAP provider offer?
- How would employees access the EAP (phone, email, on-site represen tation) and what are the timescales for the provider returning calls, etc.?
- How does the EAP provider decide which staff will have access to its staff and how often is the contact list updated or changed?
- What provision does the EAP provider make for contact out of normal office hours?
- How many specialist staff are available for employees to contact and what are their qualifications, training and experience in EAP counselling?
- What would the EAP provider deliver in terms of on-site training (orientation and on-going) for managers and employees?
- What provision will be made for return-to-work, follow-on or longer-term support?
- What provision will be made for a subsequent evaluation of the effects of individual EAP interventions?
- What type of publicity and promotion of EAP provision will be provided?

- What fee structure is being proposed?
- What employer reports will be available on issues such as use, issues raised and outcomes achieved?

See also: bullying and harassment; compliance/commitment; counselling, coaching and mentoring; data protection; employee empowerment and engagement; employee relations and conflict; organisational culture; performance management; quality of working life and the psychological contract

BIBLIOGRAPHY

Attridge, M. (2001) *Personal and Work Outcomes of Employee Assistance Services.* Presented at the American Psychological Association Annual Meeting (August), San Francisco, CA.

Canadian Centre for Occupational Health and Safety (2006) 'Employee assistance programmes'. Available at www.ccohs.ca/oshanswers/hsprograms/eap.html (last accessed April 2008).

Employee Communication and Consultation

> **Communication: a process of sharing information and creating relationships in environments designed for manageable, goal-oriented behaviour.**
>
> **Consultation: a process in which the views and opinions of employees and trade unions are sought before a decision is made by management.**

Communication is more than the simple passing of information from one person to another in that it implies a two-way process. A manager or team leader giving work priorities to subordinates reflects information transmission because there is no interaction involved. Team members may think about, or discuss with other people the information given, but the two-way interaction with the manager or team leader does not exist. In addition to the vast number of communication links that potentially exist between individuals within an organisation, there are also the large number of teams that need to communicate with other individuals and teams. Consequently, the communication frameworks that exist within any organisation are many and complex. Communication within an organisation serves a number of formal purposes, including:

- *Between superiors and subordinates*   To report or give instruction; to seek approval and clarify; to organise, direct and influence.
- *Between internal peer groups*   To persuade, integrate and influence.
- *Between external peer groups*   To establish boundaries and parameters; to identify options for mutual enterprise and to influence.

In addition to the formal purposes for communication just outlined, there exists a wide range of informal communication networks inside and around any organisation. For example, the 'grapevine', 'rumour mill' or 'water-cooler moments' are all informal aspects of communication that function within any organisation and can often be more powerful than the formal channels of communication as they do not appear to contain the 'spin', hidden agendas or manipulative purposes that are often assumed to exist with formal management communications.

The communication process in large organisations needs to be managed carefully if total chaos is to be avoided and the ways in which this can be achieved include:

- *Limitation*   Not every employee or team would be expected to communicate with every other employee or team within a company. Managing this is achieved through a hierarchical and departmental structure.
- *Procedure*   Appropriate procedures can ensure that information is available only to those individuals and teams requiring it.
- *Teamwork*   The use of teams and committees allows a degree of informality to facilitate communication between members; also the use of team representatives ensures that not every individual is involved in communicating with every other individual or team.
- *Automation*   The use of electronic media should simplify communication as individuals can access parts of the total information available as necessary to their jobs and at a time appropriate to them.
- *Separation*   The identification of 'content' that requires communication and that which can be designated as information flow.

For example, employee communications are often separated into categories such as newsletters or team briefings (one-way) and formal meetings between employee representatives and human resource managers to discuss future staffing plans (two-way).

It has been suggested that good employee communication helps to build and maintain a positive psychological contract through the two way interaction and sharing of ideas involved. Bingham and Suff (2002) identified four key objectives for organisations in implementing employee communication processes. These are:

1 Engaging employees in seeking to achieve business objectives.
2 Encouraging employees to understand the goals and strategy of the organisation.
3 Encouraging employee support for a culture change.
4 Encouraging a climate of open dialogue across the organisation.

The CIPD (2007) suggest that there are 13 points that need to be taken into account when devising an employee communication strategy and process. These are:

1 Convince top management of the importance of communication.
2 Build alliances across the organisation to support initiatives.
3 Recognise that no single method will be effective.
4 Use a mix of approaches and use all available channels where relevant (written, face-to-face, web-based, moving images).
5 Target the forms of communication to the audience; for example, it may be appropriate to use different methods for shopfloor employees and senior managers.
6 Respect cultural diversity and vary approaches accordingly. This is just as important in the UK as it is in a multi-national context.
7 Make sure that messages are consistent, over time and between audiences.
8 Ensure a clarity of message and keep things as simple as possible.
9 Train managers to understand the importance of communication and in the necessary skills.
10 Seek wherever possible to develop and sustain two-way communication, dialogue and feedback.
11 Determine whether employees feel that the culture of the organisation is such that they can say what they think without discomfort; and if they can't, consider how that might be changed.

12   Consider whether communication is built into the planning stages of all major changes and initiatives.
13   Review and evaluate every communication event to check what worked, what didn't, and why.

European employment legislation requires managers to communicate certain information to trade unions in specific industrial relations circumstances including collective bargaining and potential redundancy situations. The legislation expects employers to disclose relevant information in a timely manner so that they can carry out their responsibilities more effectively. Also, organisations with more than 250 employees have to include a statement in their annual reports identifying any actions taken over the year to introduce, maintain or develop communication with employees.

Consultation in its widest sense refers to any attempt by management to seek out employee views before intentions become specific proposals. It also refers to the formal contact between employers and employees in joint decision making as required by European employment legislation. The intention of consultation is that neither party would be tied to a particular decision but proposals could be explored within the process with the views expressed helping to inform the eventual decision. As a result the element of surprise and a large measure of confrontation should be removed from subsequent negotiations and/or change initiatives.

The current legislative framework is governed by the Information and Consultation of Employees Regulations (2004) which came into force in April 2005. These applied to all undertakings of more than 100 people (more than 50 people from April 2008) and were based on a European Directive from 2002. Employers with relevant pre-existing agreements would only be required to consider making changes if more than 40 per cent of employees requested it. Where no formal pre-existing arrangements apply a request by more than 10 per cent of the workforce to have information and consultation arrangements will require an employer to negotiate such facilities. A failure to agree acceptable arrangements will result in the imposition of the standard provisions. Employers can take the initiative and suggest information and consultation arrangements to employees, but a failure to reach agreement would result in the standard provisions being applied. The regulations allow for either direct manager/worker consultation or an indirect process whereby employee representatives meet and consult with managers (or a combination of the two) to continue for pre-existing arrangements. However, the standard provision requires the election of employee representatives and indirect consultation methods through such elected representatives.

The standard provisions require employers to inform and consult with employees over the following issues:

- Information on recent and/or probable developments of the undertaking or in relation to its activities and/or economic situation.
- Information and consultation on the situation, structure and probable development of employment levels together with any measures that might pose a threat to employment.
- Information and consultation on issues likely to lead to substantial changes in work organisation and/or contractual matters.

Although the scope of issues to be included in any information and consultation arrangements should be specified to avoid ambiguity or argument, the following are likely to be the main issues that would be appropriate:

- Levels and trends for profit and loss.
- Sales performance.
- Current productivity and future intentions.
- Reorganisations, restructure, employment plans and redundancies.
- Mergers, acquisitions, divestments and the transfer of undertakings.
- Market developments and strategic plans.
- Working patterns and practices.
- Training and development.
- Equal opportunity.
- Health, safety and environment.
- Pension and welfare issues.
- Data protection issues.
- Outsourcing.
- Pay.

Consultation should be undertaken within an adequate timescale to allow representatives to study the information presented and formulate a response to management, in return being allowed to consider the management reply to any proposals. Management can legitimately withhold information or refuse a consultation where it could be argued that to do so would be prejudicial to the interests of the organisation, but this can be challenged through the courts. A confidentiality clause can be imposed on representatives in relation to the information provided and such a restriction can go beyond the term of office of the representative.

See also: *counselling, coaching and mentoring; discipline and grievance; employee assistance programme; employee relations and conflict; interview; negotiation; performance appraisal; performance management; trade union/employee representation*

BIBLIOGRAPHY

Bingham, C. and Suff, P. (2002) *Internal Communication* (Managing best practice no. 100). London: Work Foundation.
CIPD (2007) 'Employee communication'. *Factsheet*. Available at www.cipd.co.uk (last accessed May 2008).

Employee Development

> *The full range of training and development activities aimed at maximising the actual and potential contribution of an employee to the business over both the short and longer term.*

Development is a generic term covering all educational, training and development activity with both informal and formal intentions. Informal intentions are not directly related to the actual outcomes of the intervention, but they nevertheless represent important reasons for undertaking the activity. For example, by funding employee self-selected development activity the culture of an organisation could change, making organisationally relevant development more acceptable and also making it easier to manage and achieve change. Over recent years the nature of both employment and the psychological contract has changed with a lower expectation of long-term employment and a greater expectation that development would be provided to the individual which would enhance their market worth being more prevalent. This introduces an informal focus (from the organisation's perspective) for development in that employees are likely to have a broader interest in their development needs than employers (who are more likely to focus on current job/organisation needs). The formal intentions of development are what might be regarded as the traditional perspectives on it in relation to meeting an organisation's needs for employee capability development, etc.

Traditionally any training or development activity has been viewed as a cost rather than an investment. Often employers will have taken the view that the better trained employees were the easier it would be for them to find better paid employment elsewhere. In practice, employers resented providing a well trained labour force for their competitors and there were indeed organisations that were only too willing to pay high rates of pay to attract well qualified and trained employees but who provided little or no training or development themselves. Over the years various government initiatives have sought to encourage (or force) employers to change their attitudes to the provision of training and development, but with a limited lasting effect. The current national approach is that the government seeks to encourage rather than directly intervene which might distort development purpose in ways that might not have organisational relevance. It is the commercial imperative that has changed the traditional situation to a significant degree over recent years. Organisations, products, services, markets and labour markets have been changing so fast and frequently (hyper-competition some have termed it) that it has become a prerequisite for staying in business that the potential strategic and commercial benefits available through development are taken seriously.

McCracken and Wallace (2000) have proposed that there are nine elements involved in seeking to link development activity within an organisation to its strategic direction and plans. These are:

- That development should help to shape and achieve the mission and goals of the organisation.
- That development strategies, policies and plans should relate to the present and future direction and intention of the organisation.
- That development should be integrated with other HR activity.
- That senior management should lead rather than just support development activity.
- That senior management (as well as HR specialists) should propose development opportunities based on their scanning of the business environment.
- That line managers have a role as partners in the selection, design and delivery of development activity.

- That trainers should have an expanded role as change agents.
- That trainers have a role to play in influencing the organisational culture.
- That the evaluation of development should be based on future cost-effectiveness, not just current cost.

The starting point for any development activity is to identify the need that it is intended to fulfil. There can be many such triggers for development but they can be generally categorised under one of three headings:

1 *Gap* This category suggests that there has been a gap or deficiency identified in relation to what the organisation, department, team or individual can do relative to what is currently (or anticipated to be) required.
2 *Problem* This category suggests that a problem has arisen and that a possible training intervention could resolve it.
3 *Need* This category is more aligned with the longer-term direction and intentions of the organisation than the previous two. It is about the linking of business and people strategies so that a synergy is achieved between human capability and business needs over the long term.

The above are examples of approaches to the identification of training needs which in general represent any systematic process intended to identify the development needs relevant to a particular individual and/or group in a particular context. The basic model of development is based around the circular and iterative stages of:

- Identifying the need.
- Designing an appropriate development activity to meet the need.
- Carrying out the development.
- Evaluating the outcomes and achievements from the development activity.

That basic four-stage model would be applied as part of the development strategy which in turn links to the business strategy. The outcome of the evaluation process would invariably contribute to the identification of further development opportunities as there exists a never-ending range of possibilities for human beings to contribute to the evolution and future success of organisations. The CIPD (2007) has identified a number of choices that need to be taken in relation to the degree of planning and its effect on development activity. These are:

- *Choice one: Planned or not?*   Much learning takes place informally – for example, when asking a more experienced colleague how to do something. But such approaches cannot be relied upon to meet all the needs of a business. The question is therefore how much planning should be applied to the development activities carried out within the organisation? The answer will depend on many factors including the business and HR strategies involved and the degree of change being faced, anticipated, etc.
- *Choice two: Learning or training led?*   Historically, much training was carried out through the provision of standardised courses with employees being directed to (or choosing) ones that they thought would be appropriate. These days learning has more to do with matching the needs of individuals and business through the creative application of a range of development activities, not just classroom-based courses.
- *Choice three: Who does it?*   Development will be more effective if the individual receiving it 'buys into' the process. This implies that individuals should be heavily involved in the identification of their own development needs and the choice/type of interventions intended to meet those needs. However, such an approach might not capture the business-based needs for development and consequently there exists a need to incorporate this into the planning process.
- *Choice four: Vertical versus horizontal?*   Development planning is usually envisaged as a vertical process predominantly involving individuals and their line managers. However, it is also possible that the work team or peer group might have the potential to influence the type of development that an individual engages with as well as their willingness to do so – e.g. horizontal influences.
- *Choice five: Use diagnostics or not?*   In development planning, diagnostic instruments (including assessment/development centres, performance appraisals and psychometric tests) all have the potential to identify needs that could be met through development.
- *Choice six: Demand or supply based?*   Demand-based planning is about making provision for development based on the identified needs of individuals and the business. Supply-based planning is about individuals selecting or being directed towards pre-determined (often standardised) offerings.

- *Choice seven: Competence-based or not?* The use of competence-based frameworks is widespread in organisations these days and not just in relation to development activity. However, not all development needs can be fitted neatly into company-based competence lists – for example, the need to pursue and acquire professional qualifications or an MBA.

- *Choice eight: Strategic versus tactical?* This choice is about the long-term versus the short-term perspectives taken in relation to the planning of development. Line managers have a short-term imperative to deal with immediate pressures and can easily lose sight of the longer term. Effective planning is about finding ways of meeting immediate and longer-term objectives for individuals and organisations.

- *Choice nine: Individual versus team?* This choice is about the potential benefits to be gained (by individuals and organisations) through developing learning communities and cohorts rather than a sole reliance on individual development needs. It is possible that groups of peers, like-minded or job-related groups can plan much of their development in a type of collegiate approach to meeting the needs of individuals and the group as a whole.

- *Choice ten: Choosing learning approaches?* There is a wide range of approaches to learning that can be used and deciding on the most effective or appropriate in any context can be very difficult.

- *Choice eleven: Within a performance review or separate?* Although performance issues can identify development needs, the annual performance appraisal is not automatically the best or most effective means of doing so.

- *Choice twelve: Planning versus contracting?* Some organisations have developed a contract-based approach to the implementation of development plans as an alternative means of trying to ensure that 'plans' are acted upon and results delivered to the benefit of the individual and the organisation, the idea being that a development contract would be drawn up between the individual, line manager and development specialists that would form the basis of what was to be delivered when, how, and with what outcomes.

No organisation has an unlimited supply of money for development activity. As a result it is necessary to ration development in some way or another in order to deliver that which could be justified or accommodated within budgetary constraints from the full range of developments that could be undertaken (assuming unlimited resources). The obvious aim should therefore be to seek out those development interventions which offer the best value for money or return on investment as the most important to carry out. However, it is not that simple in practice. Estimates of value for money or return on investment are invariably estimates based on a wide range of assumptions and 'guestimates' of the costs or savings available. For example, a fall in the level of absence might follow a training programme on 'How to manage absence', but how much of the reduction was the result of the training and how much as a result of absence being given a higher emphasis within the organisation is difficult to determine. Hamblin (1974) suggested that training could be evaluated against a range of criteria in order to evaluate its effectiveness, cost and access to it. He used five factors to reflect a range of aspects associated with the training event. These included:

1   *Reaction*   This would be based on the immediate responses of trainees on issues such as any perceived benefits, feelings about the experience and content. It is also based on the assumption that if trainees enjoyed the learning event (or felt it was 'good') they would be more likely to gain from it.
2   *Learning*   This reflected the benefit taken away from the training event in the form of new competencies, etc. This might be reflected through an end of course test and would be intended to reflect the exit capability of the people trained. This would not guarantee, however, that they actually utilised the new competencies in their work.
3   *Job behaviour*   This seeks to determine if the effect of development through individuals' work-related behaviour changes and is one way of attempting to judge both the transfer of knowledge to the workplace and the impact of such changes. This could be done through the observation of trainees; data collection on such issues as productivity, customer complaints, etc.; or through interviews of trainees and their managers some time after the event.
4   *Organisation*   At an organisational level development is intended to improve effectiveness in terms of issues such as productivity, quality, output and customer relations. It might be possible to quantify some aspects of this level of evaluation, but it would probably include a significant degree of qualitative evaluation or judgement and it would be difficult to separate other influences on the measures adopted. In some situations this aspect of evaluation could not be attempted for about one year after a particular development intervention.

5   *Ultimate value*   This refers to the intangible benefits that the organisation gains from any development activity. This could be its ability to survive in a hostile market, its profitability, or even its contribution to society as a whole. This aspect is also very difficult to measure and links specifically with a particular development activity.

In more recent times, Thomson (2008) has suggested that there are two major areas that should be addressed in seeking to evaluate training activity. They are:

- *What was done and was it of value?*   Under this heading there is a range of hard and soft metrics that can be introduced to measure issues such as the reduced cost of quality and increased output; to looking for evidence that people search for ways of combining development opportunities to gain increased added-value through different routes.
- *How was it done and was it of value?*   This category seeks data from questionnaires and interviews with individuals and managers in relation to how the development was done and the effects on them and their work.

See also: *assessment/development centre; career management; competency; high performance working; human resource planning; management development; performance management; succession planning and talent management; teamworking*

BIBLIOGRAPHY

CIPD (2007) 'Development planning', *Factsheet: September*. Available at www.cipd. co.uk (last accessed May 2008).

Hamblin, A. (1974) *Evaluation and Control of Training*. Maidenhead: McGraw-Hill.

McCracken, M. and Wallace, M. (2000) 'Towards a redefinition of strategic HRD', *Journal of European Industrial Training*, 24(5): 281–290.

Thomson, I. (2008) 'Evaluation of training', *Factsheet*, CIPD. Available at www.cipd. co.uk (last accessed May 2008).

key concepts in human resource management

Employee Empowerment and Engagement

> **Empowerment:** *The process of enabling an individual to control their work, take actions and decisions beyond the requirements of their normal job function without reference to a more senior authority.*
>
> **Engagement:** *The opportunity for employees to become involved in decision making and/or the running of the business beyond the normal scope of their job.*

Empowerment allows the individual to take action beyond that normally allowed by their job and status, and engagement seeks to increase motivation, commitment and general support for the business by allowing employees to have a contribution beyond that which would be expected at their job level. The purpose of both empowerment and engagement is to capture a more effective contribution from the employees than would usually be expected. The benefits for the employee are more interesting work, a feeling of value to the organisation, and perhaps the possibility of personal or career development. The value to the organisation is improved productivity, improved decision making, a more willing acceptance of management decisions, reduced costs through fewer levels in the hierarchy being needed to deal with queries and problems being passed upwards for resolution, improved customer service, faster decision making, and improved recruitment and the retention of high calibre employees.

There are also a number of other related terms in this area of human resource management. Delegation refers to the passing on of some area of responsibility to a subordinate. It is often said that authority can be delegated but accountability cannot. So for example, a sales manager may delegate the authority to set discount levels to the sales force, but they cannot delegate (or abdicate) their personal accountability for ensuring that appropriate sales volumes are achieved and that they are profitable for the organisation. Employee involvement and participation are terms that have a broadly similar meaning to engagement. Involvement and participation represent the ways in which employees are allowed to engage with the business and management beyond carrying out their job responsibilities. That could be through quality circles, joint consultation, or the many other forms of interaction and contribution that are offered by many organisations. Financial participation represents a particular form of involvement by allowing and encouraging employees to build a financial stake in the business. Profit sharing and various forms of share option are the most common forms of this type of participation. Employee voice is also a related term used to reflect the nature of the ability of employees to find ways of expressing their ideas, opinions, desires, complaints and general viewpoints as part of a broader contribution, involvement and employee relations process (see for example, Marchington and Wilkinson (2005) Chapter 10, and index entries for 'employee voice'). All of these themes have relevance in the search to achieve the high performance working much valued today.

So far the discussion has not made reference to how employees can take part in empowerment and engagement activity. Empowerment tends to be a personal experience in which employees will be empowered to take actions (within specified limits) beyond their normal job requirements. It has been widely suggested that it produces personal changes in the individuals experiencing it, namely displaying higher levels of motivation and greater levels of problem solving. It also alters expectations in that empowered people become more confident and they also seek greater levels of involvement and participation. Engagement and its various forms such as participation and involvement can either be mechanisms that include everyone up to the level that personal time, interest and inclination takes them, or it can be carried out through representatives who would be selected either by the direct vote of the workers or through the trade union representatives depending upon the various agreements and procedures within the organisation.

Empowerment and engagement seek to encourage employees to willingly give more of themselves in return for the benefit of more interesting and meaningful work. It was the early Marxist view of capitalist organisations that identified the notion of alienation. This was regarded as the normal detachment of worker and work that was created under the capitalist mode of production. Alienation emerges as a result of the lack of engagement and ownership and the severe limitation of the rights of workers as stakeholders. It is argued that alienation occurs as an inevitable reaction to the control of work by managers and results in the following employee feelings towards their work:

- *Powerlessness* A lack of influence over the pace of work, work methods and working conditions.
- *Meaninglessness* A feeling that employees' contribution has little significance.
- *Isolation* A feeling of not belonging, of not being part of a team.
- *Self-estrangement* A lack of self-worth as a consequence of being a faceless number within a large organisation and the failure of work to offer a significant focus in life.

It is in trying to minimise the level of alienation that various approaches to employee involvement and engagement have developed over the years. It seeks to encourage the employee to deliver discretionary behaviour – those behaviours that cannot be required under the contract of employment; neither can employees be forced or bullied into delivering them. The CIPD (2008) provide the following view of employee engagement: 'a combination of commitment to the organisation and its values plus a willingness to help out colleagues (organisational citizenship). It goes beyond job satisfaction and is not simply motivation. Engagement is something the employee has to offer: it cannot be "required" as part of the employment contract'.

Engagement can be said to have three dimensions (CIPD, 2008):

- Emotional engagement – being very involved emotionally with one's work.
- Cognitive engagement – focusing very hard whilst at work.
- Physical engagement – being willing to 'go the extra mile' for your employer.

Employers can develop an engaged workforce by:

- Measuring employee attitudes through surveys and similar mechanisms.
- From such data identifying areas such as pay and benefits, communications, training and development, career progression, line management style and approach, and work-life balance, etc. that are in need of attention and improvement.

- Developing appropriate policies, procedures and practices across all three dimensions of engagement including:
  - Involvement in decision making.
  - Freedom to voice ideas, to which managers listen.
  - Feeling enabled to perform well.
  - Having opportunities to develop the job.
  - Effective leadership and management.
  - Feeling the organisation is concerned for employees' health and wellbeing.

Bloisi et al. (2007) describe three different ways in which empowerment can be brought about. These are:

- *Self-initiated empowerment*   This involves the individual taking the initiative in expanding their job by simply doing more than would be usually expected of them. This might involve voluntarily taking on additional responsibilities or by changing the way that they work. This represents the actions of people who are intrinsically motivated or who are looking to become so by making their work more interesting and rewarding. Of course it can also be used politically in seeking to increase the level of power, authority and significance held by the job-holder.
- *Empowerment by others*   Similar to the foregoing approach, this originates from the work group and colleagues seeking to empower themselves and the group as a whole rather than the individual.
- *Empowerment by managers*   The most usual form of empowerment discussed in the human resource literature is this allowed formally by managers. In this case the manager delegates some of this to subordinates and so empowers them in specific areas of work.

It has already been suggested that empowerment has the potential to deliver benefits to both the organisation and individual. However, there is the suggestion that it does not automatically or even generally deliver the expected benefits. For example, difficulties can arise because of a lack of clarity and certainty about where responsibility lies and the general weakening of hierarchical control. Equally some employees do not welcome empowerment as they may not want the additional responsibility or authority that it requires them to take. For empowerment to be successful it is necessary for other employment policies and practices including performance management, mistake toleration and information availability to be supportive. It takes time to develop effective empowerment processes that can be supported and sustained through the beliefs and attitudes of both employees and managers.

Collinson (1994) identified two forms of resistance to management control which suggest that involvement, empowerment and engagement strategies might not be easily achieved or deliver the positive benefits envisaged. The first he terms 'resistance through distance' in which employees refuse to accept any involvement in or responsibility for the running of the organisation. It is an approach which refuses to accept any weakening of the capital/labour split in relation to management and worker responsibilities and role. As a resistance strategy it rejects attempts by managers to achieve control through any form of participation. Collinson points out however that this resistance strategy can create conflict between colleagues if some are willing to become involved with management and some are not. Resistance through persistence, by way of contrast, challenges the managerial prerogative at every opportunity. As the title suggests it persists in pushing for more information and explanation as a way of challenging managers to engage in more significant engagement activity. However, this approach could also create conflict between colleagues if not all of them agree with the strategy, and also with managers because they will be constantly challenged.

See also: behaviour management; competency; compliance/commitment; employee relations and conflict; high performance working; organisational culture; performance management; quality of working life and the psychological contract; teamworking

BIBLIOGRAPHY

Bloisi, W., Cook, C.W. and Hunsaker, P.L. (2007) *Management & Organisational Behaviour* (2nd European edition). Maidenhead: McGraw-Hill.

CIPD (2008) 'Factsheet: employee engagement'. Available at www.cipd.co.uk (last accessed May 2008).

Collinson, D. (1994) 'Strategies of resistance: power, knowledge and subjectivity in the workplace', in J.M. Jermier, D. Knights and W.R. Nord (eds), *Resistance and Power in Organisations*. London: Routledge.

Marchington, M. and Wilkinson, A. (2005) *Human Resource Management at Work: People Management and Development*. London: CIPD.

employee empowerment and engagement

Employee Relations and Conflict

> *Refers to the management of activities related to developing, maintaining, and improving relationships between employer and employee through processes including communication, consultation, dealing with grievances and disputes effectively and quickly, involvement, and negotiation with employee representatives.*

Employee relations represents that aspect of HR practice which seeks to offer proactive management of the employee relationship with the intention of minimising the risk of conflict whilst maximising the level of engagement and commitment of employees. In essence it seeks to create and maintain a 'partnership' approach to the relationship between employer and employee. Should a conflict arise then the aim of employee relations would be to overcome the issues quickly and appropriately in order to minimise the damage and risk to the organisation and its business functioning. Employee relations is often closely associated with collective bargaining. Collective bargaining is traditionally associated with negotiations between management and trade unions. However, with the relative decline in trade union membership over recent years and the economic, social, organisational, managerial and cultural changes surrounding the working relationship this has become less significant in many organisations. Purcell and Sisson (1983) identified five styles of employee relations from their research. These are:

- *Traditional* An approach grounded in dealing with issues only when they become problems. Management are broadly hostile to the trade unions, seek to minimise pay and adopt an authoritarian style.
- *Paternalist* Management consider themselves 'enlightened' and so think that trade unions are irrelevant. They focus on encouraging employee identification with management's objectives.
- *Consultative* Recognition of trade unions along with an informal approach to problem solving in dealing with issues, supported by regular two-way communications.

- *Constitutional* Reflects an emphasis on formal procedures to regulate all aspects of the relationship between trade unions and management. Use of procedures to equalise the power balance between management and the trade unions.
- *Opportunistic* Usually found in large organisations with no overarching employee relations strategy with each sub-unit allowed to adopt its own approach. Emphasis is on achieving unit profitability.

These days there is a different approach to seeking to understand employee relations as a reflection of the dominant (at a particular point in time) internal and external pressures on an organisation. Such pressures can include the level and trend in trade union membership, market conditions and trends, employment patterns and trends, legislative obligations and technology. To that could be added the major forces based on economic and globalisation trends and patterns. Employee voice and social partnership are also important features within employee relations, with the term 'voice' being preferred over traditional terms such as 'consultation' or 'communication' as it reflects the bringing together of individual and collective techniques into a cohesive framework of dialogue and encouraged employee influence on events at work. Marchington and Wilkinson (2005: 286) identified three main barriers to the effective embrace of employee voice:

- Lack of employee willingness or enthusiasm to participate in voice dialogue programmes.
- Lack of necessary skills among managers to facilitate, implement and manage 'voice' programmes.
- Issues associated with the blockage of initiatives by middle managers, or their unwillingness/ignorance of how to participate. Electronic forms of employee voice can circumvent problems arising from middle management, but this could raise different problems if they thought that they were being deliberately bypassed.

Employee involvement within Europe is being directed by initiatives from the European Union based on a belief in a partnership between employers and employees as part of the citizenship rights of employees. These are in addition to the general belief in the business and performance benefits available through involvement. The Department of Trade and Industry (2002) identified outcomes and benefits to individuals and organisations arising from the creation of a good working environment

employee relations and conflict

based on high levels of involvement and high performance working practices. Examples include:

- Examples of the benefits to individuals arising from a good working environment include:

  o Better job satisfaction.
  o Better climate for avoiding and resolving potential conflict.
  o Better awareness of an organisation's prospects and future employment opportunities.

- Examples of the consequence on employee behaviour and attitudes:

  o Greater commitment, dedication and support for the organisation.
  o Greater receptivity and better prepared for change.
  o Greater levels of productivity.
  o Greater support for the organisation's strategy and delivery of energy in support of it.

- Examples of the consequences for the organisation:

  o Lower levels of absenteeism.
  o Lower staff turnover and improved retention.
  o Higher rate of innovation.
  o Quicker and easier reaction and adaptation to changing circumstances and opportunities as they present themselves.

The role of trade unions in employee relations still has a significant influence on how this functions in many organisations. There are different forms of trade union recognition, including the recognition of different unions for different categories of employee in which each union would act independent of the others in representing the interests of its members. Single table bargaining arrangements exist where there are a number of different trade unions recognised within a single organisation, but they negotiate as a single entity with management. Single union bargaining exists where only one union is recognised within an organisation and it would represent all categories of employee. The partnership concept has already been mentioned and there is some movement towards the adoption of partnership agreements between management and trade unions. Such trends have been encouraged by the British government, the European Union and the Trade Union Congress (TUC). Partnership agreements focus on the creation and support of high trust working arrangements, including a willingness to engage in joint problem solving rather than the traditional adversarial negotiation approach to conflict resolution.

There are many areas of employment that fall under the umbrella of employee relations including the right to consultation in various situations associated with issues such as redundancy; the transfer of undertakings; health and safety; pensions; European Works Councils; and workplace agreements in relation to maternity/parental leave, working time regulation, and based on the Information and Consultation Directive. In addition collective bargaining arrangements, dispute resolution, and discipline and grievance procedures are also frequently regarded as an important aspect of employee relations practice.

Issues will occasionally arise that cannot be easily resolved and therefore pressure and power enter the employee relations process. Although there are many possible areas that might give rise to such events, pay and changes to working arrangements are the most common causes. In simple terms, employees may seek a higher pay rise than their employer is willing to afford. In such circumstances the existence of a dispute procedure will offer guidance on the stages involved in seeking a resolution to the problem and may include reference to conciliation, mediation or arbitration as external stages in the search for a solution to the 'problem'. Usually in the UK this would involve reference to the services of ACAS (the Advisory, Conciliation and Arbitration Service). ACAS is an independent body funded by government that is charged with the improvement of employee relations and the resolution of disputes. The three opportunities for their assistance in finding a resolution are:

- *Conciliation* This involves a conciliation officer meeting in private with the two parties to the dispute in seeking to identify any possibilities and options to overcome the problem. Whilst the conversations with each party are private, encouragement to change their position or adopt a more flexible stance may be explored. If and when the conciliation officer feels that there is some prospect of common ground being identified preliminary joint meetings may be held, perhaps chaired by the conciliator, the purpose being to encourage a common understanding and for solutions to be identified. However, this may not be possible and a cycle of several side and joint meetings may be necessary perhaps over several days or weeks before a resolution is agreed. It may be that no resolution emerges, in which case other action by either party may result.

- *Arbitration*   In some instances either after or instead of conciliation the parties may ask ACAS to appoint an arbitrator to help resolve the problem. In such cases the parties will have to agree to abide by the arbitrator's decision (although this is not usually legally binding). The parties will then present their case to the arbitrator who will make a decision as to what the resolution should be. There are different types of arbitration available. Traditionally the arbitrator was free to decide on a solution that they thought appropriate – often part way between the two cases. So, for example, if the union case was for a 10 per cent pay rise and the employer offered 2 per cent the arbitrator might award something in the region of 6 per cent. Pendulum arbitration requires the arbitrator to accept one case or the other and not to impose their own solution. So in the example just outlined they would have to award either 2 per cent or 10 per cent based on whoever had presented the strongest case, the logic of this approach being that it would remove any tendency to present extreme cases as they would be more likely to fail. Consequently, a resolution before any reference to arbitration would be more likely.
- *Mediation*   This option falls in between conciliation and arbitration. It involves reference of the problem to a mediator who would make recommendations to the parties that they could then use as the basis for further negotiations.

If no resolution can be found then one party may take industrial action in an attempt to force the other party to concede more of what that party wants. Industrial action can involve employees going on strike; employers refusing to allow employees to work – called a lock-out; employees going slow – not working at a normal pace or level of productivity; either the employer or employees refusing to offer or work overtime or enforcing a work flexibility restriction of some type; employees possibly withdrawing their goodwill and only following precise instructions, etc.; or employees may work to rule in which case procedures, policies and rules will be followed to the letter. Given the current practice of employers seeking to go beyond the contract and engage in flexible high performance working it could be argued that there is a higher risk of these types of industrial action having a significant and immediate impact on organisations. Hence there is a focus in current HR practice on employee involvement, engagement and voice in order to minimise such a risk. This has been described by some as a modern form of the traditional 'manufacture of consent'. This term was originally intended to describe attempts by management to achieve employee consent to control by managers through the adoption of such practices as collective bargaining.

See also: benchmarking; benefits; compliance/commitment; discipline and grievance; employee communication and consultation; employee empowerment and engagement; flexibility; human resource planning; negotiation; organisational culture; reward management; statutory bodies; strategic HRM; trade union/employee representation

BIBLIOGRAPHY

Department of Trade and Industry (2002) *High Performance Workplaces: A Discussion Paper.* London: DTI.

Marchington, M. and Wilkinson, A. (2005) *Human Resource Management at Work: People Management and Development* (3rd edition). London: Chartered Institute of Personnel and Development.

Purcell, J. and Sisson, K. (1983) 'Strategies and practice in the management of industrial relations', in G.S. Bain (ed.), *Industrial Relations in Britain*. London: Blackwell.

Expatriation and International Management

117

Expatriation refers to labour used by an organisation in a location that would not count as the home location of the employee. There are different forms of expatriate labour including home country nationals who transfer to another country; third country nationals; an international cadre; and secondments in the medium or long term. These are also examples of international management.

Sparrow (2006) identified a wide range of different types of expatriation, including:

- International commuters.
- Contract expatriates.
- Employees used on long-term business trips.
- Assignees on short-term or medium term business trips.
- Cadres of global managers
- International transferees (from one subsidiary to another).
- 'Self-initiated movers' who live and work away from their home country.
- Virtual international employees active in cross-border project teams.
- Domestically-based employees dealing with international suppliers and/or clients.
- Immigrants attracted to a domestic labour market.

The most usual justifications for using expatriate labour include:

- Where no local staff are qualified.
- To train local nationals to take over roles previously occupied by expatriates.
- To transfer technical expertise.
- To give employees international experience in preparation for more senior roles.
- As part of talent management and succession planning.
- To facilitate knowledge sharing between employees in different parts of the organisation.
- To create an international corporate culture.
- To encourage employees to develop an international mindset.

Among the competencies usually identified as necessary for a successful expatriate assignment are: cross cultural sensitivity; conflict resolution; emotional maturity; self-motivation; adaptability, flexibility and resilience; communication listening and influencing abilities. According to the CIPD (2008), before even discussing an overseas appointment with an employee it would be necessary to check the following aspects of entitlement, status and arrangements:

- Entitlement? Is the ability to be sent abroad written into the contract of employment, and if not will the employee agree to this?
- Is the organisation giving adequate notice of the assignment given the personal arrangements that the employee will need to make?

- Will the employee retain the right to return to their 'old' job on repatriation?
- What will happen to any replacement upon the employee's return?
- What will happen in the event of a redundancy in relation to the employee's 'old' job during their absence?
- What provision is there for a termination of employment whilst overseas and what repatriation arrangements would apply?
- Is it necessary to review the disciplinary/misconduct policy in line with particular requirements at the new location?
- Has the organisation examined the legal implications for the employee's employment rights, and the organisation's rights and obligations, both in the home and host country?
- How will local legislation affect the contract?
- Have the taxation and National Insurance issues been carefully considered in both the home and 'new' locations?

In relation to the terms and conditions of employment to be applied during the period of overseas employment, the Employment Rights Act (1996) provides that all employees working outside the UK for more than one month must (before leaving the UK) be given a written statement which contains the following information:

- The period of work outside the UK.
- The currency of payment whilst working outside the UK.
- Any additional remuneration and benefits to be provided as a result of working overseas.
- Any terms and conditions in relation to their return to the UK.

Sending someone to work overseas represents a significant commercial, cost and commitment investment and hence risk to the business. For the employee it can also have significant personal and career implications. It is therefore important for the organisation, the employee, and their family to be as well informed as they can be before the actual decision and arrangements to relocate are made. Consequently, in addition to the above requirements, organisations will usually provide information about the following issues:

- Salary, bonus and other incentive payment entitlements.
- Hardship or separation allowances.
- Clothing allowances.

- Benefits such as pensions, life insurance, medical and dental cover for the individual and any family members.
- The payment of local tax and social security contributions.
- Provision and financial support for children's education and other domestic/support staff and arrangements.
- Details of how salary and allowances will be paid.
- Rights, compensation or support in relation to an employed spouse or partner.
- Leave entitlement and arrangements/frequency of travel back to home country.
- Sale and/or storage of personal effects in home country.
- Home country housing arrangements during the overseas posting.
- Shipping of goods to new location.
- Definition of dependants e.g. parents-in-law, step-children, in relation to travel and accommodation, along with other financial obligations and commitments.
- Pets and quarantine arrangements.
- Social or business obligations and expectations required of the employee as a consequence of their role in an overseas location.
- Any special arrangements for employee assistance provision (including their dependant family) during and subsequent to the relocation.
- Repatriation or subsequent postings arrangements.
- Rights on the termination of the assignment (by either party) either at the completion of the posting or at an interim stage.

The determination of pay for expatriates can be a complex process, subject to dynamic economic and exchange rate pressures. It is not uncommon to find many organisations using the expertise of specialist consultancies in this area to ensure that they get the best advice available in establishing effective policies and practice. Armstrong and Stephens (2005: 302) suggested that there were four general approaches that could be used as the basis of pay determination:

- *Home country basis* Sometimes this is referred to as the balance sheet approach. It builds up the salary to be paid using the following steps:
  - o Determine the salary for the expatriate's job in the home country (net of tax and social security payments).
  - o Calculate the level of home country net disposable income.
  - o Apply a cost of living index to that figure to provide a host country equivalent net disposable income.
  - o Add extra allowances for working abroad.

- *Host country basis* This approach is based on paying the market rate for the job according to the local market conditions and norms. It may also have additional allowances for working abroad added on to it.
- *Selected country basis* This uses a nominated country (not automatically home or host countries) as the basis of pay determination – for example, the location of the company headquarters. The build up of pay thereafter would be as for the home country.
- *Hybrid basis* This involves splitting the expatriate's salary into two components. The first (a local component) would be the same for all expatriates working at the same level in the same location irrespective of their country of origin. The second would be based on the level of income necessary in the host country to achieve an equivalent standard of living in the home country.

One of the key areas of any expatriation assignment is the way that family members not directly associated with the job relocation are able to adjust to the move and its consequences for them. A high proportion of expatriate assignment failures or early repatriation are the result of a partner's inability to deal effectively with the stress of relocation and a complete change in lifestyle and culture. Among the most frequent areas of difficulty are:

- A wish by the partner to maintain their career trajectory and path whilst accommodating the expatriation move.
- Family issues associated with children's education, friendships and family/social networks and support in an unfamiliar cultural setting.
- Other family responsibilities in relation to the care, support and contact with elderly relatives.
- A failure by family members to adjust to changes in their cultural and social circumstances or to form any meaningful social networks.
- Reduced time available for family interaction and support by the expatriate employee as they come to terms with the new job requirements and expectations.
- The partner of the expatriate employee not being able to work at all, or perhaps not being able to obtain a job of an equivalent type or status to their home-based career.
- An unwillingness, unfamiliarity, lack of preparation or expectation of the partner in relation to the social obligations, business networking and general support required to facilitate the expatriate employee's role.

- A loss of involvement and contact in the home job market for the partner leading to a degradation of their market and career viability and worth.

Given the potential risk to the success of the expatriate assignment as a result of partner and/or family difficulties (in business, cost and personal terms), it is vital that the entire family unit is involved in decisions relating to a posting. That would involve an involvement in the appointment application and decision; the pre-appointment briefing and training; and any post-appointment acclimatisation and support.

The CIPD (2008) have identified the following as mechanisms through which many organisations try to prepare employees and their families for expatriate assignments:

- Arranging pre-assignment visits to the host country.
- Briefings by host country managers.
- Cross-cultural training for managers.
- Cross-cultural training for families.
- Language training for the employee and their dependents.
- Advice on assistance with the education needs of accompanying children.
- Introductions to other expatriates in the host country.
- Other assistance, advice and information which can help the expatriate family to settle in to the new country quickly.

Repatriation at the end of an assignment represents another potential area of difficulty for the expatriate, their family, and the organisation. The individual will have probably developed whilst they were working overseas and would naturally wish to capitalise on the additional competency gained – perhaps by moving into a more senior role. However, there may not be a suitable role available at the time of this repatriation; employees who have remained 'at home' will have expectations of career development and may resent the 'sudden' promotion of a returnee; the returnee may have difficulty settling back into their 'old' location; the returnee may have lost both touch and their place within previous social, business, professional and support networks; company focus, policies, practices and procedures are likely to have changed during the absence of the expatriate and so they may not be as effective or able to deliver a previously high performance until they become re-established again. Problems of readjustment are also likely for the partner and children when they return to what to them should be familiar surroundings, friends and activities, only to find that things and people have changed during their absence.

There is also inpatriation, described as a situation where someone from a subsidiary is transferred to an organisation's headquarters. This represents a means of immersing the 'inpatriate' in the central company business activities and culture. Such individuals should be subsequently equipped to take that level of understanding back into their local organisation, thus ensuring a more effective blend of local and home perspectives in the globalised management of the organisation. The CIPD (2008) have identified the main advantages here as:

- Inpatriates bringing a depth of insight/knowledge about doing business in other countries.
- Inpatriates providing a central communication link between HQ and the subsidiary to ensure a greater clarity of understanding.
- Inpatriates providing a new and different perspective within the HQ when policies, plans and strategies are being developed in relation to other countries.
- There being a good business case for the use of local nationals: customers, suppliers, the local community will all tend to react more favourably to an organisation seen to value and encourage people of their own nationality.
- Having inpatriates and third country nationals (an American working in China for a British-headquartered organisation, for example) as an essential part of being a truly international enterprise, as opposed to being a national organisation with some overseas subsidiaries.

See also: *career management; employee development; human resource planning; management development; organisational culture; performance management; quality of working life and the psychological contract; resourcing/retention; reward management; succession planning and talent management*

expatriation and international management

BIBLIOGRAPHY

Armstrong, M. and Stephens, T. (2005) *A Handbook of Employee Reward Management and Practice*. London: Kogan Page.
CIPD (2008) 'Managing international assignments'. *Factsheet: May*. Available at www.cipd.co.uk (last accessed July 2008).
Sparrow, P.R. (2006) *International Recruitment, Selection and Assessment*. London: CIPD.

Flexibility

> There are five different types of labour flexibility including: numerical (vary
> the numbers employed); functional (vary the jobs done by employees);
> temporal (change the time of day/week/month/year that people work);
> financial (vary wage levels to match business activity); and locational
> (move locations). Flexibility also refers to a framework based on the
> integration of a core workforce with various categories of peripheral (and
> temporary) employee.

Flexibility emerged as an academic issue in the 1980s with Atkinson's
(1984 and 1987) model of flexibility involving core and peripheral workers.
The model envisages that a core group of workers will deliver normal
operational activity by providing functional flexibility in coping with the
usual demand variations. Such workers would be drawn from the primary
labour market and would enjoy a relatively permanent employment status
in return for the flexibility they provide. They would hold the key skills
valued by the employer as vital to organisational success. Functional
flexibility in this context also implies that employees are capable of
both vertical and horizontal movement. Horizontal movement
implies performing a range of tasks requiring broadly similar skill
levels. Vertical movement implies jobs requiring greater or lesser levels
of skill. Surrounding that group of core workers would be peripheral
groups of workers, who while important to the organisation do not hold
the status of 'core'. Peripheral workers can be part-time, job-sharers,
short-term contracts, or public subsidy trainees with little prospect of
achieving a transfer into the core group of workers, agency workers,
sub-contractors or those self-employed. They are likely to be important to
the functioning of the organisation, but not critical to it, doing jobs which
can be easily changed, replaced by technology, dropped, or amalgamated.
Organisations can become heavily dependent on key contractors, outsourced
functions and the self-employed – all of whom are likely to have other and
different priorities to the host organisation. That is not to suggest that such
employees would not meet their contractual obligations, simply that they
are not integrated into the host organisation to the same extent or in the
same way as the core group. Consequently, they would be more likely to
put their own interests above those of the host organisation.

key concepts in human
resource management

124

Despite the widespread use of elements from the flexible firm model and particularly in the public sector, Marchington and Wilkinson (2005) suggest that there are four areas which can give some cause for concern regarding use of the flexible firm model as a reflection of strategic thinking:

- *The concept*   The literature varies on a definition of the flexible firm. There also exists a lack of clarity in the model. For example, in relation to part-time as a peripheral category this is misleading as many part-time workers are key members of staff.
- *Extensiveness*   Research evidence does not indicate an extensive use of the model in the workplace. Whilst there has been a dramatic growth in different or non-standard work patterns (such as homeworking, contract, outsourced, self-employed labour, etc.) that does not automatically mean that the flexible firm model is driving such changes.
- *Costs and benefits*   There is debate about the relative costs and benefits of flexible working as implied by the model. It is often assumed that application of the model would automatically lead to a more efficient organisation, the justification being that the costs would be lower because the provision and cost of labour would more closely match the need and so would result in a lower cost of operations and higher returns (in productivity and profit) for the business.
- *Single employer*   The model is based on a single organisation and ignores inter-organisational relationships and trading practices, including spin-offs, joint ventures, and strategic alliances.

There are five types of flexibility:

- *Numerical flexibility*   This allows the number of people employed to grow and shrink rapidly in line with business need. A range of staffing practices might be found in an organisation following this approach. For example, there might be high numbers of people employed on short-term, casual, part-time or sub-contract arrangements, perhaps including the so-called zero-hours contracts. It is also likely that such organisations will have organised their supervision, control procedures and reward practices to match the variability of labour levels and also the presumed lack of commitment and experience in relation to the organisations' activities. It might also be expected that a high labour turnover might be accepted and not regarded as a problem in the attempt to minimise service and hence termination benefits to be paid.

- *Functional flexibility*   This reflects the ability of the organisation to achieve multiskilling and non-demarcated working practices, thus ensuring that employees can be used across a range of jobs. Such flexibility could involve moving to similar jobs in other departments as the workload varied. It could also involve doing different jobs requiring different skills in the same department that an individual worked in. In addition it may also involve accepting work of a lower skill or higher level than required by the usual job.
- *Financial flexibility*   This approach to flexibility provides for pay systems alignment with company activity and performance – to vary the pay costs with activity levels. The aim is to reduce the amount of fixed cost in the form of wages.
- *Temporal flexibility*   This approach involves being able to change the time of day/week/month/year in which people are working to match seasonal patterns. For example, banks and fast food restaurants might be expected to have their peak activity hours over lunchtime and so to avoid long queues they might seek to arrange working patterns that mean more staff being available at that time. Other variations might be found in food factories, where seasonal harvesting might involve staff working very long hours for a few weeks at a time and then a large gap with little work to do until the next crop arrives. Such requirements have led to the development of various forms of annual hours contracts (employees must work (say) a total of 1600 hours per year within the range of zero to 70 hours in any Monday to Sunday period).
- *Locational flexibility*   This approach involves moving work between locations to meet the variable demand for labour. At one level this could simply involve a multi-site company allocating work between operating units. Another option would be for organisations to reduce the size and number of physical units used through the adoption of homeworking practices. It could also involve organisations seeking to locate business units in areas offering the lowest cost of operations, with little or no loyalty to a particular location. Individual units would be opened, closed, mothballed and have their work range changed, etc. in line with the changing business priorities and so on.

Flexibility can also apply to employees in their desire to meet the range of commitments they have and achieve an appropriate work-life balance. For example, the Part-time Workers (Prevention of Less Favourable Treatment) Regulations 2000 (amended in 2002) seek to protect staff on part-time contracts from unfair treatment compared to colleagues on full-time contracts. This protection covers issues such as pay, leave, bonuses, career progression, access to training and development, etc. Legislation also requires organisations to consider requests from staff to work part-time. An organisation is not obliged to agree to such requests if it would be detrimental to the business. For example, any employee who has 26 weeks or more continuous employment and has children who are less than six years of age (or over that age but with a disability) has the right to request flexible working.

From an individual perspective, flexible working options can cover a wide range of arrangements, including:

- The number of hours worked in a given period (for example, part-time working).
- The starting and finishing times each day (for example, flexitime or part-time work).
- Where the work is carried out (perhaps homeworking or at a satellite location either on a pre-arranged schedule or according to a business or other need). There are five main types of teleworking (working at a distance, using various telecommunication devices to maintain contact and work activity):

  o Multi-site – including homeworking, telecottage or telecentre locations.
  o Tele-homeworking – based at home involving low-skilled work for one employer.
  o Freelancing – working for a number of clients perhaps at a variety of locations.
  o Mobile – the use of a range of mobile technology and communications equipment by employees who work 'on-the-road'.
  o Relocated back-office functions – specialist centres undertaking a bulk administrative activity.

- The pattern of work including compressed working weeks (four days at ten hours rather than five days at eight hours, or working a nine-day fortnight: term-time working to allow for child care during school holidays).
- Special leave and career breaks to allow for arrangements to care for dependants, study for exams, etc.

CIPD (2005) research looked at the flexible working arrangements in approximately 600 organisations. The results indicated that 26 per cent of organisations had flexible working arrangements, but these were most common in the public sector organisations (42 per cent of respondents). Some 36 per cent of respondents also made special arrangements for employees with dependants. The survey found that 75 per cent of respondents suggested that flexible working improved retention rates and almost as many reported an improvement in morale. Approximately 50 per cent thought that resourcing had been made easier as a result of being able to offer flexible working. The research also reported that the majority of the requests for flexible working (78 per cent) came from women: 97 per cent of organisations offered flexibility to clerical and administrative staff: 86 per cent of organisations had made the provision available to senior managers. Thirty per cent of respondents reported a high take-up of flexible work arrangements by clerical and administrative staff, but only 8 per cent reported a high take-up within senior management levels. The research also reported that operational limitations and concerns over the ability to manage staff working flexibly were the biggest reason for not offering or agreeing to flexible working. Research undertaken for BT (*Happy People*, 2008) also found that flexible working improved productivity by 54 per cent and reduced costs by about 11 per cent.

See also: benchmarking; competency; contract of employment; employee empowerment and engagement; employee relations and conflict; high performance working; job, job analysis and job design; organisational culture; organisational structure; strategic HRM

BIBLIOGRAPHY

Atkinson, J. (1984) 'Manpower strategies for flexible organisations', *Personnel Management*, August: 28–31.

Atkinson, J. (1987) 'Flexibility or fragmentation? The United Kingdom labour market in the eighties', *Labour and Society*, 12(1): 87–105.

CIPD (2005) 'Flexible working: impact and implementation – an employer survey'. Available at www.cipd.co.uk/surveys (last accessed August 2008).

Happy People (2008) Issue 3 (July) page 6 (supplement in *Management Today*). Available at www.hp.com/uk/inspireme

Marchington, M. and Wilkinson, A. (2005) *Human Resource Management at Work: People Management and Development* (3rd edition). London: CIPD.

Human Resource Management (HRM) and Personnel Management (PM)

> **Human resource management (HRM):** *The management discipline that specialises in the management of people in organisations.*
>
> **Personnel management (PM):** *The management function which coordinates the activities associated with the people needs of an organisation, including employee selection, training and development, rewards, and union-management relations.*

Over the course of human history society has changed as knowledge, resources, human development, technology, science, law and culture have evolved. Organisations have also changed over the years as they have adapted to emerging technologies, labour capabilities, markets for products and services, and the prevailing view of work and its role in human life, etc. The approach to managing people has also changed in response to all of the other changes in society and organisations. Personnel management has its origins in the nineteenth century as a consequence of a recognition by managers, business owners and politicians (under pressure from social reformers) of the need to offset the worst aspects of worker exploitation that had emerged during the Industrial Revolution. The trade unions were also emerging as a potent force representing workers rights at about the same time. This could be described as the social justice period in personnel management. Subsequently the emphasis changed and more focus was placed on staffing, training and the work organisation, particularly during the First and Second World Wars when women began to be drafted into jobs traditionally done by men. Since then many other changes – including rising education levels, higher standards of living, attitudes to work, legislation, globalisation and technology – have forced organisations to become more sophisticated in their use of people at work and so personnel management has transformed itself into HRM in order to meet more effectively the needs of modern organisations. (See Torrington et al. (2005: 11–13), for example, for a brief summary of this view of the evolution of managing people.)

There are four main approaches that have emerged over the past couple of decades that seek to explain how the human resource is to be understood in relation to the organisations that employ them. They are:

1   Fombrum et al. (1984) suggested that human beings should be considered as a resource, no different in essence to any other resource within an organisation. This approach to HRM began with an identification of the business strategy which was then converted into an HRM strategy. That then became the basis of the HRM policies and practices adopted in order to deliver the results sought.

2   Beer et al. (1984, 1985) adopted the stakeholder view of people within organisations. Although 'top down' in adopting a business need and strategic focus to the role of people (as with the previous model), it implies that people are more than a static resource to be considered only as machine substitutes. This model holds that people are thinking, dynamic and interactive beings within organisations that can add value. This model proposes four main areas of policy requirement in order to achieve the maximum benefit from people (employee influence on management and the business; human resource flow into, out of, and within the business; reward systems; and work systems).

3   Schuler and Jackson (1987, 1996) suggested a link between strategy of an organisation and the employee behaviours necessary to achieve it. They identified two strategy options representing alternative ways to compete in a particular market. These are cost minimisation and innovation. The model suggests appropriate employee strategies associated with each. For example, cost reduction strategies require repetitive, predictable behaviours; employees with a narrow skill range; and low levels of employee job involvement. By contrast, an innovative strategy requires a long-term focus; flexibility and change from employees; a tolerance of ambiguity and uncertainty; and high levels of job involvement from employees. Relevant HR policies appropriate to the chosen strategy would then need to be developed and implemented. According to this model, what matters is not which strategy is adopted, but that HR policy and practices are consistent with the chosen strategy.

key concepts in human resource management

4   Developed in the UK by Hendry et al. (1989), this model proposes five main interlinked elements that can influence how people will be managed in any particular organisational context. These are:

- *Outer context*   This represents the external social, economic and cultural forces impacting on an organisation. It also includes influences impacting on the organisation that arise from industry and market conditions.
- *Inner context*   This represents the organisational factors that impact on how people are used. Such internal factors can include culture, structure, profitability, technology, products or services, management style, and politics.
- *Business strategy context*   This represents the effect on people management of the business strategy followed by the organisation.
- *Human resource management context*   This reflects the underlying philosophy of the business about how people should be allowed to contribute to its functioning and operate within it.
- *Human resource management content*   This represents the approach to people management practised by the organisation in terms of its reward systems, employee relations, and work arrangements, etc.

This Hendry et al. model demonstrates the complexity of the people management environment for organisations. The five interacting elements reflect the forces acting upon organisations which create a dynamic and fluid situation that is difficult to manage. One aspect that does not come across strongly in any of the four models outlined is the effect of the individual and groups on the way that HRM is practised within organisations. Individuals and groups of employees do not always perceive things in the same way that managers do, and even if this is the case they may choose not to comply with management intentions. The Hendry et al. model reflects the view that HRM does not 'belong' to specialists because it is line managers who are responsible for the management of their subordinates. Consequently, they argue that everyone within an organisation is actively involved in people management as a fundamental part of their daily responsibilities.

Storey (2001) developed a model of HRM based on four main elements. These are:

- *Beliefs and assumptions*   This element includes an underlying belief that the human resource can provide a competitive advantage for organisations. The employee commitment (buy-in) is more important than compliance with instructions and procedures. An appropriate selection of people (with the 'right' qualities) and development (to inculcate the 'right' behaviours) are central processes within HRM.

- *Strategic qualities* This element holds that HR decisions are strategically important for organisations, that senior managers must be involved in HRM decision making, and that HR decisions need to be integrated into the business strategy.

- *Critical role for line managers* This holds that HR activity is too important for business success to be left up to HR specialists alone. Line managers are the ones who must manage people on a day-to-day basis and so it is they who must be closely involved in HR activity as the delivers and drivers of it in practice. Managing line managers is of critical importance in achieving an effective HR policy implementation.

- *Key levers* This holds that managing the organisational culture is more important than managing HR procedures and systems, that integration of the various HRM sub-functions (reward, resourcing, ER, T&D, etc.) is vital to effective overall management of the people resource, that jobs need to be (re)designed to allow and encourage delegation, the taking of responsibility, and empowerment.

A key theme from Storey's model of HR is that it is a shared activity. However, the form such sharing takes appears to have changed somewhat over recent years. HR services within organisations were traditionally regarded as the provision of a service to line managers, usually in the form of a staff function working with (and supporting) a line function. More recent research suggests that it is increasingly adopting a different role – that of mediating and facilitating the line managers' control over their HR responsibilities. Storey (1992) suggested that two variables seemed to be at work that determined how the HR function related to its line 'customers'. These variables were:

- An axis running from the strategic to the tactical in relation to how the HR function approached its responsibilities.
- An axis running from the interventionary to the non-interventionary based on the degree to which an HR department became involved in HR activities along with their line management customers.

From these two variables is produced a four cell matrix, each describing a different role for HR functions. These are:

- *Regulators* This role lies in the quadrant formed by the tactical and interventionary ends of the two axes. HR functions adopting this role formulate employment rules, procedures and trade union agreements. Subsequently their role would be to monitor the adoption, use and functioning of the rules, procedures, etc.

- *Change makers*   This role lies in the quadrant formed by the strategic and interventionary ends of the two axes. HR functions adopting this role would be proactive in seeking to create a different basis for employee relations – one which emphasises the needs of the business. This might be done as a distinctly HR-based initiative, or as a result of being a fully integrated part of the senior management team.
- *Handmaidens*   This role lies in the quadrant formed by the tactical and non-interventionary ends of the two axes. HR functions adopting this role tend to be reactive to the demands of their client or customer, based on a high degree of submissiveness and seeking to meet their short-term needs.
- *Advisers*   This role lies in the quadrant formed by the strategic and non-interventionary ends of the two axes. HR functions adopting this role tend to act as internal consultants and as such can offer advice and guidance based on being aware of recent developments. They would allow line and general managers to decide what HR initiatives to pursue (based on advice and guidance) and would then act as internal consultants on the development and implementation.

See also: *Note there are no specific references as all headings in this text are relevant to these two terms.*

BIBLIOGRAPHY

Beer, M., Spector, B., Lawrence, P.R., Quinn Mills, D. and Walton, R.E. (1984) *Managing Human Assets*. New York: Free.

Beer, M., Lawrence, P.R., Quinn Mills, D. and Walton, R.E. (1985) *Human Resource Management: A General Manager's Perspective*. Glencoe, IL: Free.

Fombrum, C.J., Tichy, N.M. and Devanna, M.A. (eds) (1984) *Strategic Human Resource Management*. New York: Wiley.

Hendry, C., Pettigrew, A.M. and Sparrow, P.R. (1989) 'Linking strategic change, competitive performance and human resource management: results of a UK empirical study', in R. Mansfield (ed.), *Frontiers of Management Research*. London: Routledge.

Schuler, R.S. and Jackson, S.E. (1987) 'Linking competitive strategies with human resource management practices', *Academy of Management Executive*, 9(3): 207–219.

Schuler, R.S. and Jackson, S.E. (1996) *Human Resource Management: Positioning for the 21st century*. Minneapolis: West.

Storey, J. (1992) *Developments in the Management of Human Resources*. Oxford: Blackwell.

Storey, J. (2001) *Human Resource Management: A Critical Text* (2nd edition). London: Thomson.

Torrington, D., Hall, L. and Taylor, S. (2005) *Human Resource Management* (6th edition). London: Prentice Hall.

High Performance Working

There have been many attempts to explain what high performance working means. One definition is that it represents a combination of people, technology, management and productivity which are integrated effectively to provide a competitive advantage on a sustainable basis.

High performance working is associated with the outcomes of particular HR practices designed and implemented in such a way that they can positively impact on the long-term commercial success of the business. There are different ways in which business performance and success can be measured and interpreted. The CIPD in association with the International Labour Organisation suggested that high performance working could be understood as having the following characteristics (Stevens and Ashton, 1999):

- Sustained market success (or the achievement of organisational objectives).
- Innovation in quality and customer satisfaction (or product or service differentiation).
- Customer and continuous improvement focus.
- Use of self-managed work teams.
- Viewing the workplace as a source of added value.

- Clear links between training and development and organisational objectives.
- Support for organisational and individual learning.

In effect the above list reflects the characteristics of high performance working and not those aspects of HR policy and practice that can lead to it. The EEF (2003) produced a report together with the CIPD that considered a wide range of issues surrounding the creation, implementation and results of high performance working and they identified the following range of HR practices that they considered the most important for a successful implementation of this, including:

- Appropriate selection and recruitment processes.
- Comprehensive induction programmes.
- A sophisticated and wide coverage of training.
- Coherent performance management systems with wide coverage.
- Flexibility of workforce skills.
- Job variety and responsibility.
- Teamworking.
- Frequent and comprehensive communication to employees.
- Use of quality improvement teams.
- Harmonised terms and conditions.
- Market competitive pay.
- The use of rewards related to individual and/or group performance.
- Policies to achieve an appropriate work-life balance.

The research also pointed out that where high performance working was sought as a specific objective the HR policies and practice that were introduced for that purpose should display the following characteristics:

- That employee autonomy and involvement should be integrated into decision-making processes.
- That there should be support for employees as they sought to maximise performance.
- That appropriate rewards should be earned by those employees who delivered a high performance.
- That the sharing of information and knowledge was a critical requirement for employees to 'know' enough about 'what' was going on, 'why', 'where', and 'when', so that they could direct their behaviour, energies and attitudes towards achieving high performance working.

high performance working

135

Snell and Bohlander (2007) began their discussion of high performance working by identifying four fundamental principles that underpinned all of the other features associated with it. These are:

- *Shared information*   This reflects the dissemination of information around the organisation as a prerequisite for empowerment and involvement. Traditionally employees were not provided with much information about strategy, performance, plans, etc. The logic of high performance working is that before someone can contribute to it they must have an understanding of what is being sought and where their efforts fit into the overall picture, etc.
- *Knowledge development*   Development of employees follows naturally from the first fundamental. If people are going to be informed and involved then they need to have the capability to be able to process and respond to the greater knowledge that they will have available to them. Equally through development they can have the opportunity to understand how to interact with the knowledge that already exists, thereby creating new knowledge and understanding in relation to the business, its offerings, customers and processes.
- *Performance-reward linkage*   Measuring activity (or performance) is only one part of a complex relationship between behaviour and performance. Measurement implies scrutiny and the 'boss' providing clear signals to those being measured about preferred behaviour as the basis of encouraging a high performance. The link to rewards takes that one step further and seeks to encourage employee behaviour by offering such rewards. The most obvious example of a reward in this context is money, but there are many other possible rewards available: promotion, career development, training and development, praise, greater levels of autonomy and delegation, and working for a successful organisation are just some of the more obvious. The point here is that a reward must be valued (and sought) by the potential recipient for it to have any chance of impacting on behaviour.
- *Egalitarianism*   This is an interesting concept, being based around the notion of membership of an organisation rather than simply being an employee. It is about a lack of status and the recognition that everyone in an organisation has a different role to play but all are equally important to the achievement of success. It is about getting rid of the traditional hierarchical, conflictual, 'us and them' differences between management and workers and encouraging genuine co-operation, collaboration, and working together.

The CIPD (2008) explained these same issues slightly differently and suggested that the component parts of a successful high performance working programme should be based on the following features:

- A vision based on increasing customer value by differentiating an organisation's products or services and moving towards a customisation of its offering to meet the needs of individual customers.
- Given this vision, leadership from the top (and over time throughout the organisation) is necessary to create a momentum, realise the vision, and measure progress.

As a consequence of the previous two points the main characteristics of high performance working were suggested to be:

- Decentralised, devolved decision making. Decisions are to be made by those closest to the customer – so as constantly to renew and improve the organisation's offering to its customers.
- Development of people capabilities and capacities through learning at all levels, with a particular emphasis on self-management, teamwork, and project-based activities.
- To enable and support a performance improvement and employee contribution to realising the organisational potential.

To gain the requirements of the vision to achieve high performance working the following support systems and cultural aspects of work need to be addressed:

- The performance, operational, and people management processes must be aligned to organisational objectives – to build trust, enthusiasm, and a commitment to the direction taken by the organisation.
- Fair treatment for those who leave the organisation as it changes, and an engagement with the needs of the community outside the organisation – this is an important component of trust and commitment-based relationships, both within and outside an organisation.

Sung and Ashton (2005) carried out research into high performance working and proposed that there were 32 HR practices associated with it which fell under three broad areas of HR activity:

- *High employee involvement practices*   These encourage greater levels of trust and communication between employers and employees and generally accompany empowerment and the exercise of discretion by the latter. Common involvement practices include:

o   Circulating information to all employees on the business/strategy plan, targets and subsequent organisational performance.
o   A staff association – a recognition and effective involvement in business decision making.
o   The frequent use of staff surveys along with publication of the results and any actions arising from them.
o   The use of suggestion schemes incorporating recognition of, and reward for, contributions.
o   The creation of self-managed or self-directed teams.
o   Adoption of the principles of Kaizen – the search for continuous improvement in work systems.

•   *Human resource practices*   Many of these practices are intended to directly add value to the human capital within organisations. Common human resource practices under this category include:

o   The adoption of annual performance appraisal processes involving feedback from superiors and customers.
o   Resourcing linked to business strategy and using formal assessment methods and structured induction.
o   The adoption of systems to review training needs.
o   Employee training to facilitate the ability to perform multiple jobs.
o   The use of job design to facilitate improved performance.
o   The adoption of workforce diversity policies in the widest sense.
o   The adoption of mentoring for managers and other employees as part of their career, professional and personal development.
o   The adoption of the Business Excellence Model or its equivalent.

•   *Reward and commitment practices*   These can facilitate a greater sense of belonging and commitment to the organisation. Common reward practices under this category include:

o   The adoption of performance-based pay for most employees.
o   The adoption of profit-sharing and/or share options for most employees.
o   The use of flexible job descriptions to encourage job movement and rotation, etc.
o   The adoption of flexible working (e.g. hours, locations, job-share, etc.).

o   The adoption of family-friendly policies.
o   The adoption of non-pay benefits as a way of being able to target benefit packages towards the needs of employees and dependents.

Huselid (1995) suggested that high performance working was financially viable as the market value of the organisation increased by between $15000 and $60000 per employee as a consequence (but only if the HRM bundle of high performance practices was effectively integrated and fashioned on the business strategy). It was not enough to simply benchmark good practice, it had to be integrated overall to realise the synergies that delivered employee behaviours, attitudes and competencies focussed on sustaining a competitive advantage. In the UK, Patterson et al. (1997) calculated that 17 per cent of the variation in company profitability could be explained by HRM practice, whereas just 8 per cent was by R&D, 2 per cent from company strategy, and 1 per cent as a result of both quality and technology practices.

See also: *balanced business scorecard; benchmarking; competency; compliance/commitment; employee communication and consultation; employee empowerment and engagement; flexibility; human capital; knowledge management; organisational culture; performance management; strategic HRM; succession planning and talent management*

BIBLIOGRAPHY

CIPD (2008) 'High performance working'. *Factsheet.* Available at www.cipd. co.uk (last accessed September 2008).

EEF (2003) *Maximising Employee Potential and Business Performance: The Role of High Performance Working.* London: EEF/CIPD.

Huselid, M.A. (1995) 'The impact of human resource management on turnover, productivity and corporate financial performance', *Academy of Management Journal,* 38: 635–672.

Patterson, M.G., West, M.A., Lawthom, R. and Nickell, S. (1997) *The Impact of People Management Practices on Business Performance.* London: Institute of Personnel and Development.

Snell, S. and Bohlander, G. (2007) *Human Resource Management – International Student Edition.* Mason, OH: Thomson South Western.

Stevens, J. and Ashton, D. (1999) 'Underperformance appraisal', *People Management,* Institute of Personnel Management, London, 15 July: 31–32.

Sung, J. and Ashton, D. (2005) *High Performance Work Practices: Linking Strategy and Skills to Performance Outcomes* (DTI/CIPD report: February). London: Department of Trade and Industry.

high performance working

Most definitions of human capital are based around the view that it represents the total 'value' of competencies, capabilities, experience and motivation of an organisation's employees. Value in that context is to be taken in the economic sense of the term. Human capital is a term closely related to that of social capital which reflects the value of 'trusted' interaction (informal co-ordination, co-operation and innovation) between individuals. Therefore human capital (and social capital) should be assessed in terms of cost and benefit, just as for any other resource.

It was Mayo (2001) who proposed what he termed the 'human capital monitor'. This was conceived as a formula-based expression of the contribution (added value) of people in financial and non-financial terms. It consists of two elements, the results of which would be added together:

- *People as assets*   This comprised the cost of employment, the contributions, capability, potential and values alignment with those preferred by management.
- *People's motivation and commitment*   This comprised elements from the work environment including leadership, reward, recognition, learning and development.
- The outcomes of these two categories would result in a third category, which he termed the 'people contribution to added value'. This would consist of qualitative and quantitative measures of data and should focus on wealth creation rather than just profit.

The problem here of course is a determination of how to 'measure' and compare the information collected under each of these factors. Equally, the notion that human capital is 'measurable' forces it to be subservient to the financial imperative – thereby ignoring the creative and adaptable way that people can respond to or deal with situations (if motivated to do so) which defies the application of such a logic.

According to the CIPD (2007), there are different types of data that can be used in measuring human capital, including:

- *Demographic*   Data under this category would seek to reflect measures of the composition of the workforce such as age, gender and ethnic origin.
- *Recruitment and retention*   Data under this category would seek to reflect measures about resourcing activity including the number of applications received for vacancies, the number of people leaving (and for what reason), length of service and length of time to fill vacancies, etc.
- *Training and development*   Data under this category would include the number of training days provided, the cost of training, the types of training provided, the length of time needed for trainees to reach high competence levels, data on training gaps, etc.
- *Performance*   Data under this category would include performance management practices, processes and procedures, the performance levels achieved, the productivity and profitability trends, targets and achievements, levels of customer satisfaction, customer loyalty indices, etc.
- *Opinion*   Data under this category would be obtained from employee attitude, customer and supplier surveys as well as from focus groups, etc.

The use of the balanced business scorecard has a role to play in measuring the contribution of human capital. It might be recalled that the balanced scorecard requires measures of strategic performance to be developed under four categories:

- Financial.
- Internal business processes.
- Customer.
- Learning and growth.

The intention here is to provide a means of assessing the degree to which an organisation is progressing in the achievement of its strategic objectives. Similarly, benchmarking is another key concept in this book that has a very direct relevance to the determination of human capital metrics.

As well as understanding human capital and its ramifications within organisations, it is necessary to consider how to communicate this to the various stakeholders that will have a legitimate need and use for that information. The CIPD (2007) suggest that there are a number of

human capital

stakeholder groups that will have an interest in aspects of the human capital range of information. For example:

- *Shareholders* These are the legal owners of a business who have an interest in information in relation to factors likely to influence the long-term financial performance in relation to their investment.
- *Customers* This category of stakeholder needs to be assured about such issues as the quality of the products and services offered by an organisation in the long term. Also they will want to know if they will receive good service in relation to order processing and delivery as well as after sales support.
- *Employees* These stakeholders will want to know about the plans, intentions and performance of an organisation. They will want to be sure that their investment in the organisation in terms of effort and commitment is valued and likely to be rewarded in the long term. They will also want to know that their jobs and long-term income are secure and how they can develop both themselves and their skills.
- *Managers* This category has many of the same needs for human capital information as employees, but because of their job function within the organisation they will have additional requirements. For example, they need to be able to take appropriate actions to manage and improve the performance of the business which has an obvious connection with the people who work in it.

Whilst the internal reporting on human capital issues is generally widespread – based around the ideas and frameworks outlined above – the external reporting on human capital is generally rather limited and usually based on an obligation to comply with the need to make available a statement of issues which are likely to affect company performance. The CIPD (2003) have suggested a framework for the external reporting of human capital information incorporating both primary and secondary indicators. The main reporting headings are:

- The human capital strategy.
- The acquisition and retention of human resources.
- The development of human resources.
- Management and leadership issues.
- The human capital performance.

The CIPD (2007) proposed that the internal reporting of human capital should be based on the following principles:

- It should be reliable and open to scrutiny.
- It should be accompanied by an adequate explanation.
- It should be presented in a manner which is easily understandable for the audience.
- It should be related to business needs.
- It should enable managers to identify appropriate actions which will improve the business performance.

The CIPD (2006) identified the following four steps as a basis for the production of good quality human capital information:

1 Start with the basic data and analysis which is restricted to the identification of trends and patterns and what these mean.
2 Demonstrate the integrity of the data by ensuring their accuracy, reliability, and value to the intended audience.
3 Progress to higher levels of data collection that seek to demonstrate the value of particular people management processes, thereby enabling managers to see how their action can impact on performance.
4 Identify the drivers of business performance and their human resource implications for use in human capital data collection and reporting.

See also: balanced business scorecard; benchmarking; competency; employee development; employee empowerment and engagement; flexibility; high performance working; knowledge management; performance management; strategic HRM

BIBLIOGRAPHY

CIPD (2003) *Human Capital: External Reporting Framework* (Change agenda). London: CIPD. Available at http://www.cipd.co.uk/researchinsights

CIPD (2006) 'The four steps to human capital management'. *Impact – Quarterly Update on CIPD Policy and Research*, 17 (October): 11.

CIPD (2007) 'Human capital'. *Factsheet: November.* Available at http://www.cipd.co.uk (last accessed September 2008).

Mayo, A. (2001) *The Human Value of the Enterprise: Valuing People as Assets – Monitoring, Measuring and Managing.* London: Nicholas Brealey.

human capital

Human Resource Planning

HR planning represents the process of analysing and identifying the need for, and availability of, human resources so that an organisation can meet its objectives. HR planning is about making sure that that organisation has available the appropriate number of people with the appropriate skills in the appropriate places at the appropriate time, ensuring that this is done in a way that encourages the organisation to regard people as a source of competitive advantage.

The basic set of HR planning questions for any organisation are:

- How many people do we require?
- When do we need them?
- What range of competencies do we require now and in the future?
- How do we keep the people that we need?
- What do we do when we have more people than we need?

There is also the role of planning and the people who do it (planners) in the organisational desire and intention to achieve its objectives. Mintzberg (1994) suggested that the purpose of planning was to:

- *Act as strategic programming*   Taking a strategy and identifying ways of operationalising through a process of clarification, identifying implementation actions and subsequent consequences.
- *Act as tools for communication and control*   The implementation of strategies can be achieved more easily if co-ordination, communication and control are used to facilitate it.
- *Allow planners to function as analysts*   Before planning can take place a range of both qualitative and quantitative data must be extracted from internal and external sources that can be applied meaningfully to the organisation's current and prospective situation.
- *Allow planners to function as catalysts*   To extract full value from a planning process there needs to be an engagement with the old, the new, and the possible. That requires planners to challenge the mundane,

key concepts in human resource management

routine and received wisdom in relation to their research and existing company activities and plans.

HR planning takes place within an organisation in which it represents continuous processes intended to provide a match between staffing levels and HR policy with organisational 'need' in an uncertain environmental context. Only in the case of the creation of a new business unit would the processes discussed here be used without any precedent or adaptation of past practice being an influencing factor. The traditional approach to HR planning (sometimes described as the hard approach) sought to identify the gap between labour requirements and labour availability and then to develop strategies to deal with any discrepancy identified. It sought to do this in a semi-mechanical way by:

- *Converting future business plans into a projected requirement for labour*
  That stage would involve the conversion of future activity into a total volume of labour broken down into such categories as number of people by location, function, grade, job function and skill requirements.
- *An evaluation or profile of the current stock of labour (internal labour market) available to the organisation.*
- *An evaluation or profile of the current availability of labour in the various external labour markets* There are many labour markets appropriate to every organisation and these often work in different ways and are subject to different pressures.
- *Having assessed the need and the data available through the internal and external labour markets the HR planning process could begin* The first stage involved the reconciliation of the outcomes from the first two steps above – what was required and what was currently available in terms of labour. Traditionally, the HR plans that emerged from that process would suggest either the need to recruit additional people from the external labour market, or to declare existing employees redundant if too many in a particular category were already employed.

Using this model or approach to HR planning there was little by way of retraining, job design or flexibility envisaged as outcomes. Reasons for that included the social, legal, and managerial perspectives on what running a business involved; the comparative cost (compared to labour replacement) would be excessive; seniority-based promotion and career development; job demarcation issues (tight restrictions on who could undertake which tasks); and restricted (often age-based) entry to craft jobs. In more recent times the approach to HR planning has become more sophisticated and complex, partly in response to the changing social, legal and cultural trends surrounding business activity. Currently, HR planning tends to be based on a cyclical and interactive process involving the answers to questions such as:

- What business are we currently in?
- Where are we now in relation to that business strategy?
- Where do we as a business want to be in the future?
- How do we get there?
- How do we reshape what we have now into what we want in the future?
- How do we handle the transition?

The results of asking these open-ended questions about the business and how it seeks to position itself relative to the world in which it operates are essential to an understanding of the current and future need for people. It is not just an understanding of how many people are needed, or when, or of the skills that they will need that results from such an approach to HR planning. The approach also encourages a more creative and holistic approach to the determination of how people can contribute to the long-term success of an organisation. The earlier approach encouraged a mechanistic matching of numbers required and numbers available across time. The HRM approach seeks to encourage the adoption of a dynamic interaction between people and organisational objectives in light of the ever-changing reality of operational and environmental forces. Of course the same basic data and understanding of labour markets and demographics are required for both approaches – the difference comes in how that basic information is used and integrated with other relevant information into the management of the human resource.

Torrington et al. (2005: 53) identified a number of trend areas in relation to planning and also suggested sources of information relevant to them. But of course there are other frameworks that could be used such as the PESTLE, SWOT and similar models. The actual sources used are a matter for personal judgement and represent a creative and dynamic searching for information (and how to interpret it) that has relevance to the organisation and its context. The Torrington framework includes:

- *Social* Sources could include census information, professional magazines and journals, general magazines and news media, government publications such as *Social Trends*, *The General Household Survey* and *Employment Gazette*.

- *Demographic*   Sources could include census information, *Employment Gazette*, *Labour Market Quarterly*, Learning and Skills Council publications.
- *Political and legislative*   Sources could include news media, reports of the proceedings in the UK and European parliaments, *Industrial Law* journal.
- *Industrial and technological*   Sources could include Employment Digest, news media, trade association publications.
- *Competitors*   Sources could include annual reports, trade magazines, sales intelligence.

In the most sophisticated organisational contexts the outcomes of HR planning activity would be allowed a degree of influence back in the business planning process and hence an ability to influence corporate strategy. The general approach so far discussed is essentially top-down. In other words, it is based on the view that broadly speaking the people aspects of an organisation can and should be fitted around the business objectives. But of course that begs the question – could it not be the other way around? Could the availability and competencies of the human resource not determine the business activities of the organisation? To put it another way – make the organisation fit the people. Now clearly there are many issues surrounding that perspective that would need to be considered carefully (marketing, brand issues, equipment, facilities, and so on). But the basic question about how much human resource capability and availability should influence business direction and strategy still exists and is an interesting question to contemplate. The answer is that there is probably a balance to be struck in deciding the relationship between these two important areas of business activity, but that it is impossible to prescribe what it should be as it would likely differ for each organisation. The need to understand the broader picture within which HR planning is to take place is a creative process in seeking to identify trends in society and the business world that might have an influence on how the business goes about achieving its objectives.

The outcomes from the HR planning process include the determination of the impact on a range of more specific HR plans covering topics that are addressed elsewhere in this book. These include such topics as:

- Resourcing plans.
- Organisation design plans.
- People utilisation plans.

- Training and development plans.
- Outsourcing and redundancy plans.
- Organisational culture planning and development.
- Performance management and motivation plans.
- Employee communication, consultation and voice plans.
- Reward plans.
- Employee relations plans.
- Knowledge and talent management planning.
- Provision of HR services planning.

There is considerable discussion elsewhere in this book about many of the human resource planning areas and their implications for HR policy and practice. However, one of the more difficult and sensitive areas of human resource planning is how to deal with a surplus of people. The section above on downsizing, reorganisation, outsourcing, and redundancy has much relevance to this discussion, but it is worth giving some consideration to the general implications of planning in this area of HR work.

See also: career management; competency; contract of employment; discrimination, diversity and equality; downsizing, reorganisation, outsourcing and redundancy; high performance working; human capital; job, job analysis and job design; labour turnover; resourcing/retention; succession planning and talent management

BIBLIOGRAPHY

Mintzberg, H. (1994) 'The fall and rise of strategic planning', *Harvard Business Review*, Jan/Feb.
Torrington, D., Hall, L. and Taylor, S. (2005) *Human Resource Management* (6th edition). London: Prentice Hall.

Incentive Schemes

> *The broadest definition of incentive schemes is that they represent mechanisms that seek to influence the behaviour of the intended recipient in ways determined by the designer of the scheme. There are many different types of incentive schemes and they all seek to achieve the desired influence on behaviour but through different levers depending on a range of factors, including the type of job, type of behaviour desired, employment conditions and traditions, time-scales involved, organisational culture and management beliefs.*

Incentive schemes have strong links with motivation theory. Motivation theory seeks to explain why people do what they do and incentive schemes seek to utilise that understanding to deliver what the scheme designer wants. There are essentially two different types of motivation active in relation to work – intrinsic and extrinsic.

- *Intrinsic motivation*   These are sources of motivation that originate inside the individual as a response to the job itself and the circumstances surrounding it. For example, a sales assistant in an electrical retail outlet may be motivated in their work because they enjoy the satisfaction gained as a result of interacting with customers and helping them to choose the right electrical appliance for them based on their needs, cost, and quality factors, etc. This is an aspect of motivation that management cannot easily control or influence directly as it is based on the individual and their relationship with their work through such factors as job design; management style; control systems; closeness of supervision; level of empowerment; feeling of being encouraged to contribute, etc.
- *Extrinsic motivation*   These are sources of motivation that originate outside the individual and which influence their behaviour. For example, a sales assistant is likely to earn commission as a result of the sales that they make. That results from an externally designated process of encouraging staff to sell more. This is an aspect of motivation that is much easier for an organisation to control and is the most common basis for incentive scheme design.

Both intrinsic and extrinsic concepts have an important part to play in informing the design of motivational practice within organisations. The self-direction and regulation of behaviour implied by intrinsic motivation could provide cost effective motivation practices, as people would give their efforts willingly and without any form of coercion. However, it is in the gift of the individual to offer or withhold this form of motivation based on a wide range of factors which it is difficult to provide and maintain consistently within an organisational context. There are also power, political and control dimensions to organisational activity that will invariably limit the degree to which everyone can be considered an equal partner in the process.

In psychological terms, incentive schemes seek to reinforce certain behaviours – that is, to encourage them. As a psychological process it is based on the early work of theorists including Skinner (1953) in relation to conditioning behaviour through reinforcement. In practice there are four different types of reinforcement that all seek to influence behaviour in different ways. These are:

- *Positive reinforcement* This refers to a situation in which the subject (to use the psychological term, but employee in the organisational context) is offered a reward that they need or desire for doing something that the designer of the conditioning programme (to use the psychological term, but an incentive scheme in the organisational context) seeks.
- *Negative reinforcement* This refers to an unpleasant event that usually precedes particular behaviour but which is removed when the subject (employee) produces the desired behaviour. For example, a manager might stop shouting at an employee when they do what the manager wants. Clearly this is not a recommended form of motivation!
- *Omission* This refers to the cessation of reinforcement. One of the features of incentive schemes (and reinforcement) is that if the reward is stopped or not received then it leads to a reduction and eventually the extinction of the particular behaviour. For example, if the commission paid to sales staff begins to grow to very high levels it is not unusual for senior management to decide that the scheme needs to be redesigned in order to lower the total earnings of staff. However, by so doing it would not be surprising for the level of sales to fall in response to the cut in salary that staff receive.
- *Punishment* This refers to an unpleasant reward being 'earned' for particular behaviours. This form of reinforcement decreases the occurrence

of the behaviour in question. For example, taking disciplinary action against an employee with a very poor attendance record should lead to the employee being present more frequently in the future.

There are many different types of incentive schemes that have emerged over the years including:

- *Productivity bonus payments* These are based on earning additional money if additional productivity and output are achieved. Productivity can be measured in many different ways and such schemes can operate at every level of an organisation. For example, when applied to factory employees productivity might be measured by indices such as machine utilisation or output per hour worked. For a CEO, it might involve a share price increase over a defined period. For middle managers, it might be based on added value improvements.
- *Performance related pay* This can be based on a performance appraisal or similar processes and can be paid either in the form of a bonus in addition to the base pay or as one of the factors in an annual pay review. With this type of scheme, productivity is usually assumed to be reflected in the achievement of objectives or the degree to which the individual performed their role to a high standard.
- *Attendance bonus payments* These schemes seek to reward attendance and typically pay a bonus if full (or near full) attendance over a defined period is achieved.
- *Additional skill payments* These reward individuals with extra money if they acquire additional skills (or competencies) to those necessary for the performance of their current job.
- *Additional responsibility payments* These might be payments for being prepared to accept responsibilities over and above the current job requirements.
- *Profit share/share option schemes* This category can be applied at all levels of the organisation. The intention of such schemes is to encourage long-term commitment and focus behaviour on the 'bottom-line' of the business. The difficulty with such schemes is that the share price and profit are not particularly amenable to the efforts of individuals or small groups of employees. For example, the share price is determined by the market and is as much based on 'sentiment' as it is on actual company performance. Profit levels are susceptible to external forces as much as they are determined by the effectiveness of company operations. For example, if a competitor suddenly decides

on massive price-cuts to acquire greater market share then somewhere along the line the profit for all organisations involved will be hit. Also such schemes will have a long lead-time, paying out only after the end of the financial year and after all the company figures have been computed and audited. So it can be as much as 15–18 months for the performance delivered on the first day of the financial year to result in the payment of the 'reward' once everything is calculated and approved. That stretches the effort-reward link beyond that which would be held as credible.

• *Team/group bonus payments* Incentive schemes can be based on the individual or group achievement depending upon the objectives of the scheme.

The underlying intention of any incentive scheme is to encourage more (or less depending on the scheme) of something than could reasonably be expected under normal circumstances from a worker. The starting point is therefore what should be expected under normal conditions – an important question if additional cost is to be avoided. It is also a very difficult question to answer. That 'something' could be a greater volume of output; fewer defects; greater sales levels; higher profits; improvements in the share price; or working more flexibly – to name but a few possibilities. In an incentive scheme design and implementation there are a number of decisions to be taken, including:

• *Is a scheme appropriate at all?* Incentive schemes are intended to encourage more of something, but what does 'more' mean? It implies that there is a known base level (which can be reasonably expected) and that more could be achieved if people were rewarded for delivering it. There are a number of assumptions in that proposition. For example, what is it reasonable to expect individuals to do in return for their base wage or salary – a very difficult question to answer? How is it known that employees would not willingly deliver the extra if they were simply asked to do so? How is it known that more could not be achieved by other means that would not involve incentive rewards? Also within the public sector there are particular sensitivities in relation to the introduction of incentive schemes as well as difficulty in measuring what should be targeted by such arrangements.

• *Is a scheme being proposed for the right reasons?* Is it that managers seek to introduce incentives because they are not capable of achieving the extra something through the application of 'good management' practice? Is it being introduced to disguise total wage/salary levels for various reasons?

- *How should the scheme operate?* Deciding the rules of a scheme can become a complex process, leading to possible confusion and lack of impact. Issues that need to be addressed include:

  o What type of scheme – what exactly does 'more' of something mean and how can it be measured?
  o Focus of attention – is there a danger that by focussing employee attention on the specifics of the incentive scheme other (possibly equally important) aspects of company activity will be ignored?
  o Who should be included – sales people might be paid commission on sales but what about the support staff who deal with queries and order processing?
  o Can the people subject to the scheme actually have an impact on the result – everyone in an organisation contributes to the profit levels achieved to some degree, but actual profit levels are also subject to economic and competitive forces outside of the organisation so which has the greatest impact in any year?
  o What should the frequency of payment be – weekly, monthly, quarterly, or annual?
  o What should the effect of over or under achievement be on adjacent bonus periods?
  o What will happen if an employee decides not to respond to an incentive scheme and only produces at the minimum level all the time? Can employees be required to participate in a scheme by 'delivering' more as expected? If so how?
  o How much will it cost and how complex will the scheme be to administer?
  o How easy is it to 'fiddle' the result by those subject to the bonus scheme (the so-called sharp pencil problem) and how can that be prevented?

- *Group or individual incentive?* Individual incentive schemes often have the most pronounced impact on the result. But individual schemes encourage individualism and tend not to encourage team working. Team incentives can have the opposite tendency – the convoy effect – where eventually everyone works at the speed of the slowest person as in a group scheme individual efforts are effectively averaged.

incentive schemes

- *How much and how variable should the incentive be?* The greater the reward possible the greater the effort to achieve it (assuming the individuals want the incentive on offer). But also the greater the feeling of disappointment if it is not achieved, or if it is achieved inconsistently.

See also: absence management; contract of employment; employee empowerment and engagement; employee relations and conflict; high performance working; organisational culture; performance management; reward management; strategic HRM; total reward; trade union/employee representation; wage structure

BIBLIOGRAPHY

Armstrong, M. and Stephens, T. (2005) *A Handbook of Employee Reward Management and Practice.* London: Kogan Page.

Skinner, B.F. (1953) *Science and Human Behaviour.* New York: Macmillan.

Interview

> The most basic definition of an interview is that of a purposeful conversation between two or more people intended to allow both parties to the process to obtain information in relation to a pre-identified intention. For example, job interviews, disciplinary or grievance interviews would be clear examples.

Interviews in resourcing are a significant event for both parties and traditionally regarded as a fundamental part of the 'choosing' decision and there can be few employers or applicants who would feel happy with one not being part of the process. Based on the CIPD (2008) the interview provides an opportunity for a candidate to:

- Ask questions about the job and the organisation.
- Decide if they would like to take the job.

For the organisation, the interview is an opportunity to:

- Describe the job and the responsibilities the job holder would need to take on in more detail.

- Assess a candidate's ability to perform in the role.
- Discuss with the candidate details such as start dates, training provision, and terms and conditions such as employee benefits.
- Give a positive impression to the candidate of the company as a 'good employer' (who they would like to work for should they be offered the position).

The same source also points out that a poorly conducted interview may leave a candidate with an unfavourable impression of the organisation that they are likely to share with other potential applicants and customers. In the selection context there are many different types of interviews, including:

- *Biographical* This approach seeks to talk though the candidate's biographical outline provided in the CV or application form.
- *Behavioural* In this type of interview, candidates would be asked to describe and explain how they had dealt with a specific problem or task in the past.
- *Competency* This approach seeks to systematically assess the candidate against the competency profile that would have been developed for the particular role for which they were being considered.
- *Situational* This approach seeks to illicit from candidates information on how they would handle typical situations based on the normal job for which they are applying.
- *Stress* This approach to interviewing is intended to put the interviewee under pressure – usually justified by the argument that the job in question is a pressured or stressful one and that the candidate's ability to cope with such situations is a necessary part of the selection process.
- *Non-directive* The non-directive approach adopts a broadly reactive approach to interviews in that the interviewer would begin with a general question – perhaps about a previous job or experience – and then supplementary questions based on that reply would be asked. In practice the flow of the interview and the questions asked are determined by the answers to questions given by a candidate.

There are also differences in interviewing approaches. There is the single interview carried out by a single interviewer, where the outcome of the interview would be decided after the 'single' episode. There is a panel interview, with the size of the panel varying from two to more than a dozen people in some instances. The decision would usually be made by the panel immediately following the interviews of all the candidates attending. There is the team interview, in which the work team collectively interview the candidate and then decide who they consider most closely meets the selection criteria. In addition to the single interview there are sequential interviews involving the candidates being interviewed a second or even third time by different interviewers. For example, the sequence might be a first interview with the HR department, a second interview with the department manager, and a third interview with the work team. Each of these is designed to assess each candidate against different criteria in relation to the job and how they would fit with colleagues.

Snell and Bohlander (2007: 263–5) identified a number of what they termed 'ground rules' for employment interviews which should form the basis for training those people who will need to conduct interviews as part of their jobs, including:

- *Establish an interview plan* Base the interview plan on a review of the job requirements, candidate data from the CV and test scores, etc.
- *Establish and maintain rapport* By welcoming the candidate pleasantly and explaining the purpose and plan of the interview at the start. Subsequently maintain this rapport by showing a genuine interest in the candidate and listening carefully to what they say.
- *Be an active listener* Listen out for what is not said as well as what is said in response to questions. Respond to what the candidate says and ask further questions for clarification.
- *Pay attention to non-verbal clues* Facial expressions, body language, posture, hand gestures, tone of voice and so on all carry information that contributes to the insights gained about a candidate.
- *Provide information as freely and honestly as possible* Don't seek to hide things or 'dress-up' a job, prospects, or the company to unrealistic levels – the successful candidate will find out about the problems soon enough and if they feel that they have been misled they will become de-motivated or disenchanted or may even leave.
- *Use questions effectively* Don't ask leading or closed questions – all that will happen is that the answers will be those expected or thought by the candidate to be the required ones. Ask open questions that will allow the candidate to respond as best they can in their own way, thereby providing 'their' response to the question.
- *Separate facts from inferences* During the interview collect factual responses. Save the interpretation of those facts and the drawing of

any inferences from them until later – perhaps in conjunction with other interviewers.

- *Recognise biases and stereotypes*   There are many types of bias and stereotyping that can creep into an interview.
- *Control the course of the interview*   Allow the candidate ample opportunity to talk, but control the pace and direction of the interview (based on the original plan) so that its coverage is appropriate to its objectives.
- *Standardise the questions asked*   Recognise that after all the interviews for a particular job are completed it will be necessary to compare the results for all candidates and so the information from the interviews must facilitate that process.
- *To that list can be added the need to be aware of legislative requirements, codes of practice and company policy*   This is in relation to issues such as fairness, diversity, equality and discrimination.

There are many possible problems with an interview that can arise from a lack of practice, training and preparation and Mathis and Jackson (2008: 245–6) identified the main ones as:

- *Snap judgements*   Avoid rushing to judge an applicant in the first few minutes of an interview.
- *Negative emphasis*   Unfavourable information can sometimes gain more prominence or emphasis in an interview and effectively block out any favourable information that becomes available.
- *Halo or horns effect*   The halo effect occurs when one good characteristic exists and is taken to mean that the candidate is 'perfect, good or appropriate' in every other regard. The horns effect is the opposite – when one negative characteristic overrides the recognition of any positive characteristics that the individual may have.
- *Biases and stereotyping*   There are many forms of bias and stereotyping that can arise – these can act the basis of discrimination in all its manifestations. Careful training for all interviewers and monitoring the selection processes can help to minimise their occurrence.
- *Cultural noise*   Candidates and interviewers operate in a cultural context, but may not have the same cultural frame of reference. For example, young people inhabit a different cultural world to their parents, even though they inhabit the same physical space.

Disciplinary and grievance-based interviews are different in that by their very nature they have to be more structured and will contain more

interview

157

pressure on the management members of the process than would be common in a selection interview. Depending on the circumstances and context, the employee participant is also likely to feel greater pressure in such situations as it is usually their behaviour, actions, and intentions that will form the focus of the discussions. Torrington et al. (2005: 584–5) summarised the steps in both grievance and disciplinary interviewing in the following way:

- The steps in conducting a grievance interview are first to understand the nature of the grievance, to explain the management position, to focus on the problem, to discuss possibilities and then decide what to do.
- The disciplinary interview starts the other way around, first explaining the management position, then understanding the employee's position and focussing on the problem. If that does not produce a satisfactory result, the manager may have to move through three more steps, persuasion, showing disproval or invoking penalties.

Another area of management practice that involves interviews is that of the appraisal review. Although the purpose and intention of such approaches are generally simple – to identify the strengths and weaknesses in an employee's performance and to then find ways of building on the strengths (namely, develop potential) and overcoming the weaknesses to the benefit of the employee and employer – it is very rarely that simple in practice. It is natural for individuals to feel apprehensive about being judged and evaluated by their boss, the reason being that the outcome could include the award (or withholding) of a pay rise, promotion, training, development, career opportunities, or perhaps even termination in extreme cases. Among the possible implications of such interviews are:

- Conflict levels increasing as individuals seek to justify the best performance rankings possible.
- Managers resenting the time and administrative effort involved and so making the process as short and simple as possible.
- Reduced levels of trust arising between managers and employees.
- Inaccurate evaluations being given to avoid conflict and other possible difficulties.

See also: absence management; assessment/development centre; career management; counselling, coaching and mentoring; discipline and grievance; employee assistance programme; performance appraisal; resourcing/retention

BIBLIOGRAPHY

CIPD (2008) 'Selection interviewing'. *Factsheet*. Available at www.cipd.co.uk (last accessed October 2008).

Mathis, R.L. and Jackson, J.H. (2008) *Human Resource Management* (12th edition). Mason, OH: Thomson South-Western.

Snell, S. and Bohlander, G. (2007) *Human Resource Management* (International student edition). Mason, OH: Thomson South-Western.

Torrington, D., Hall, L. and Taylor, S. (2005) *Human Resource Management* (6th edition). London: Prentice Hall.

Job, Job Analysis and Job Design

> *Job – A collection of individual and related tasks brought together in a practical way for a particular purpose within an organisation.*
> *Job analysis – A process beginning with the identification of the content and responsibilities of a job; followed by the systematic analysis and evaluation of the findings. Job design – A process of deliberately seeking to change the content and responsibilities of a job in order to achieve a number of objectives including reduced costs, and improved levels of productivity, customer service and job satisfaction.*

At its simplest level, a job is what people do all day every day that they are at work. It represents the way that all of the many thousands of individual tasks that need to be done are actually achieved in a sensible and structured way that allows an efficient use of the human resource within an organisation to be achieved. There is nothing absolute or given about a job; it is a social construction – created and adapted by people, for people. Therefore the design of jobs can serve particular interests. The question is if management do not take an active interest in the design of jobs who will? The answer here is the job holders, and they may have a different basis for deciding what tasks and responsibilities a job should have compared to the interests of management. Martin (2005: 525–6) suggests that:

> the design of jobs reflects a series of compromises that create benefits and problems for both managers and employees. If a manager decides to create a new type of job within their organisation (by grouping together the tasks to be done in a novel way) then it is unlikely that they will find an employee already having the necessary skills and the company will be forced to undertake extensive training. This will inevitably increase the cost of operations and will also make it more difficult to recruit new people quickly. It also means that the employer becomes vulnerable to problems if they do not ensure that they 'keep their employees happy' because employees would not be easy to replace if they left. Alternatively, when using standard jobs that exist across society labour is more likely to be readily available, training (and labour) costs would be reduced and an increased clarity in work activity would exist.

Faced with such a choice, most organisations will opt for the use of 'standard' jobs within their organisations. Employees also gain here through the acquisition of readily transferable skills. From an employee's perspective having skills that are widely used means that it is easier to find alternative work, but it is more likely that the jobs will be repetitive and attract lower wages. A higher level of uniqueness in job skill, by way of contrast, attracts higher wages and provides more interesting work. However, such employees would be more vulnerable to competition from those prepared to accept lower pay for a greater transferability of skill and hence a greater chance of work.

Job analysis is a process for the identification of the content of a job. It can be used to support a wide range of HR activities, including:

- Resourcing.
- Training.
- Career development.
- Reward systems.
- Performance management.
- Equality.

There are five approaches to job analysis according to Snell and Bohlander (2007), including:

1 *Functional job analysis* This approach requires a consideration of employee activity relevant to data, people, and things. Each of these is then sub-divided into a range of 'difficulty' categories (for

example, 'people' has eight levels from 'taking instruction-helping' to 'mentoring').

2   *Position analysis questionnaire*   This approach requires a consideration of 194 different worker oriented tasks. The degree to which a particular task is present in a specific job is 'measured' on a five point scale.

3   *Critical incident method*   The purpose of this approach is to identify the critical job tasks that will lead to job success.

4   *Task inventory analysis*   This approach develops a personalised set of tasks peculiar to the organisation adopting the method. It would be applied to all the jobs within the host organisation using a five point scale for each job.

5   *HRIS and job analysis*   HRIS programmes exist (as part of the reward management features of HRIS) that can analyse jobs and produce job descriptions automatically from the information provided.

In most situations job design is about changing jobs that already exist perhaps as the result of the introduction of new equipment, or an attempt to improve productivity, or as the result of high labour turnover, or simply to cut costs. The design of totally new jobs (perhaps resulting from opening a new factory or department) does exist but to a lesser extent. According to Snell and Bohlander (2007) there are four general factors that will influence the approach adopted to job design. These are:

1   *Organisational objectives*   The tasks, duties and responsibilities that are 'allocated' to the job and determine what it is supposed to achieve or deliver to the organisation.

2   *Industrial engineering considerations*   These relate to the way the job is to be carried out (work methods) and the efficient use of labour and work processing (productivity).

3   *Ergonomic considerations*   This aspect seeks to capture the physical and mental capabilities (and limitations) of workers in the design of a job.

4   *Behavioural considerations*   This aspect seeks to capture the attitudinal and behavioural capabilities of workers in attempting to encourage discretionary and corporate citizenship behaviours.

There are a number of approaches to job design including:

* *Simplification and job engineering*   This is an approach seen in many production and assembly line jobs. The classic problems of job simplification include monotony, boredom, a high labour turnover, alienation, and a lack of commitment. Such an approach minimises the cost of labour (low skilled work); makes resourcing easier (limited skills

needed by applicants); minimises training times (few skills needed); and maximises productivity (short work cycle times lead to high repetition frequency, a fast pace of work and few errors).

- *Job rotation* This approach to work organisation accepts that simplified jobs provide the most efficient method of work. However, it also recognises the effects of boredom and monotony on employee commitment and productivity levels. The solution to this is to combine two (or more) simplified jobs into a pattern of work rotation. Job rotation does not have to be based on a daily cycle; it could be weekly or monthly.

- *Job enlargement* This approach seeks to overcome the weaknesses in job simplification and job rotation by adding more tasks into a job to form a larger more meaningful one. It effectively adds a wider range of similar duties to create an enlarged job. The potential advantage is that the perceived meaningfulness of the work is increased for the employee as a result of the broader range of tasks involved. The major problem with enlargement is that it is frequently restricted to simple assembly line jobs, which even when enlarged remain relatively small jobs. Consequently, the benefits to employees quickly dissipate and the job becomes monotonous once again.

- *Job enrichment* This requires accountability and responsibility be added to a job in some way or another. It is a process intended to integrate responsibility and control over the tasks performed by the employee. Herzberg (1968, 1974) identified six forms of enrichment:

1 Accountability – provide a level of responsibility and support for employees that require them to accept accountability for their actions and performance.
2 Achievement – provide employees with an understanding and belief in the significance of their work.
3 Feedback – superiors should provide feedback to employees on their performance and work activities.
4 Work pace – employees should be able to exercise discretion over the pace of work that they adopt and also be able to vary that pace.
5 Control over resources – employees should have high levels of control over the resources needed to perform their duties.
6 Personal growth and development – opportunities should be found to encourage employees to acquire and practise new skills and develop themselves through their work.

Another approach to job enrichment was proposed by Hackman and Oldham (1980). They suggested that there were five core job dimensions, which in turn produce psychological responses, which in turn produce work and personal outcomes such as level of motivation, performance and job satisfaction, etc. This they termed the job characteristics model of job enrichment. Taking each of the five core job dimensions in turn:

1 *Skill variety*   A well designed job should contain a wide range of activities requiring a broad range of skills and talents from the employee. The broader the range of skills required the more significant the job will be to both the employee and employer.
2 *Task identity*   This element is about the degree to which the employee undertakes a complete job.
3 *Task significance*   The importance of the job is often reflected in its degree of impact on the lives or work of other people.
4 *Autonomy*   This reflects the degree of freedom for a worker to schedule and adapt work methods. Autonomy makes the individual responsible for their actions, thus providing a sense of ownership.
5 *Feedback*   This allows an employee to know how well they are doing in the eyes of others; it also provides an indication of how effectively they fit into the organisation.

- *Socio-technical job design*   Research has demonstrated that the social and technical aspects of work need to be integrated into a unified job design, in addition to being undertaken in an economically viable way. This invariably results in a form of work group-based approach to job design, of which the autonomous work group is perhaps the best known. The job to be done (or a specific aspect of operational activity) is effectively sub-contracted to a work group which then decides for itself how to undertake it. The notion of teamwork is now firmly entrenched into the design of work within many modern organisations and is also firmly grounded in this perspective on job design.

See also: *career management; competency; contract of employment; employee empowerment and engagement; high performance working; job evaluation; organisational structure; performance appraisal; performance management; reward management; succession planning and talent management*

job, job analysis and job design

163

BIBLIOGRAPHY

Hackman, J.R. and Oldham, G.R. (1980) *Work Redesign*. Reading, MA: Addison-Wesley.

Herzberg, F. (1968) 'One more time: how do you motivate employees?', *Harvard Business Review*, January–February: 53–62.

Herzberg, F. (1974) 'The wise old Turk', *Harvard Business Review*, September–October: 70–80.

Martin, J. (2005) *Organisational Behaviour and Management* (3rd edition). London: Thomson Learning.

Snell, S. and Bohlander, G. (2007) *Human Resource Management* (International student edition). Mason, OH: Thomson South-Western.

Job Evaluation

> *Job evaluation represents a process by which job descriptions can be used to identify the rank order (or relative magnitude, or relative worth) of jobs in an organisation.*

One of the key aims for job evaluation is to ensure that, 'non-discriminatory job evaluation should lead to a payment system which is transparent and within which work of equal value receives equal pay regardless of sex.' (Equal Opportunities Commission, 2003). Employees subject to a job evaluation scheme need to understand how it works and how the results were arrived at in order to have any confidence in it and to avoid conflict. Equally, there exists a legal requirement to be able to demonstrate (if challenged) that whatever pay structure is in place within an organisation it does not discriminate between jobs (or job holders) on the basis of sex.

There are a number of approaches to job evaluation but the two basic variations are the so-called analytical and non-analytical approaches. The analytical approach seeks to analyse each job (usually based on a job description) under a number of factors (such as effort, skill and decision making). There are two variations of this type of approach, points rating and analytical factor comparison:

- A points rating scheme would comprise a number of factors (such as effort, skill and decision making). These factors would be defined following an analysis of the type of work involved, the requirements necessary to carry it out, and the need to avoid discrimination. For each factor a range of points would be identified based on the significance of that factor and the scale of difference within the job family.

- An analytical factor comparison scheme would begin with the identification of a grade structure along with a profile of the characteristics of typical jobs in each grade based upon factor definitions. Role profiles, using the same factor definitions would be produced for each job to be evaluated. These would then be used to match jobs with the pre-determined grade profiles, thereby identifying the most appropriate grade for each job.

The non-analytical schemes as the name implies are whole job assessment approaches and do not rely on a detailed analysis of the job content, although job descriptions might be used to inform the decision-making process. This approach creates a job 'worth' hierarchy based on the perceived value of the 'whole job', but in doing so does not involve a detailed analysis of the job. There are three main job evaluation approaches under the non-analytical category:

- *Job ranking* This approach sorts the jobs into a rank order from the smallest to the largest, based on an understanding of the main purpose of each job.
- *Paired comparisons* This approach requires each job to be directly compared to each other job and scored as to whether it is superior or inferior to it in terms of its 'value' or 'size'. The larger job would be scored at two points, the lower at zero points. If the jobs are of equal size then they would be scored at one point each. At the end of the exercise the points for each job would be totalled and the higher the number of points the greater the size of the job.
- *Job classification* This approach starts with a grade structure, defines the type of work appropriate to each grade, and then each job is allocated into the relevant grade based on an interpretation of the nature of the job compared to the grade definition.

There are other approaches to job evaluation, including:

- *Proprietary schemes* These are schemes that have been designed by firms of specialised management consultants who specialise in reward system design. To make use of these schemes it is necessary to buy them from the specialists concerned. Usually as part of the package they would assist with the implementation of the scheme within the particular organisational context. The most widely used of these is the Hay Group Job Evaluation Method.

- *Market pricing* This approach usually starts with a job family and seeks to identify what the appropriate market rates are for that particular type of job. For example, for accountancy jobs a salary survey would be carried out which would identify the range of salary levels paid for particular types of accountant. That information could then be used to design a salary structure for accounting jobs within the company seeking to do so. In its pure form it pays no attention to internal relativities, nor is it a form of job evaluation.

It is possible for computers to assist with the process of job evaluation. One approach is grounded in job analysis and is effectively an extension of that process in which the job evaluation 'rules' from a points rating scheme are used by the computer to interpret the job analysis results and 'calculate' the final job evaluation score. Another approach combines both job analysis and evaluation into one process. It requires the job holder and perhaps their superior to sit down at a computer and work through a list of pre-determined questions aimed at identifying information that the program can convert directly into a job evaluation score. The advantages of using computers in job evaluations are that a consistency of scoring is guaranteed (the same input will always produce the same result) and once developed it would be much quicker to use than relying on a committee to discuss and judge each job. However, such systems can lack transparency (people can't 'see' the program) and it removes an area for joint involvement among managers and employees in 'creating' the rank order of job worth.

Armstrong and Stephens (2005: see Chapter 10) identified a 15-stage plan for the design and implementation of a points factor job evaluation scheme. The major stages are:

1 *Decide to develop a scheme* This decision can arise as the result of a number of influences.
2 *Prepare a detailed project plan* The steering group for the project should identify and agree the key stages and timescales for the project as well as agree on how they should monitor progress, work with the design team, and decide/agree on any outcome.
3 *Select, brief and train a design team* The steering group should appoint a design team that would be given the task of developing an

appropriate job evaluation system for the organisation and recommending the results back to the steering group for formal approval and recommendation to the senior managers/Board for their formal acceptance.

4 *Formulate a communications strategy* Once it is known that a new job evaluation exercise is to be undertaken, employees (and managers) are likely to regard that as a signal that they will get a (substantial) pay rise. Consequently, it is necessary to have an effective communications policy that seeks to inform, update and manage expectations from the first announcement of the project to the final implementation communications.

5 *Identify and define factors* This is the first stage of work for the design team. They need to analyse and explore the jobs involved in the project (one of the decisions taken by the steering group). Over time the creation of appropriate factors and their definitions will emerge.

6 *Define factor levels* This stage of the process involves decisions about the number of levels to be created within each factor. This question can only be answered based on a thorough understanding of the jobs in question along with the factors under consideration.

7 *Select and analyse test jobs* It is at this stage that the first test of a possible system becomes possible. Test jobs in this context are usually termed 'benchmark jobs'.

8 *Test a basic factor plan* Once identified and available for use it should be possible to begin to test the factors by trying to evaluate the benchmark jobs. The testing of the job evaluation factors and levels using benchmark jobs will begin to identify problems and difficulties with the factor choice and definition and so an iterative process of refinement and/or replacement can be undertaken.

9 *Develop a scoring model* At this stage points are added to the factor levels in order to convert the job into a numerical score.

10 *Decide on the weighting of factors* Next come decisions about the relative weighting of factors. Factors can be equally weighted, or they can have a weighting applied to them – for example, decision making might be weighted as having double the points when compared to the skills required factor.

11 *Prepare a full factor plan* As a result of the testing and refinement carried out in stages 8, 9 and 10, it should be possible (with some confidence) to prepare a final draft job evaluation scheme.

12 *Test the full factor plan* This would involve a full-scale test of the proposed job evaluation scheme with the benchmark jobs (perhaps with other jobs added to the process to provide further assessment

opportunities). It might even be possible (or practical or desirable) to train and use a different/new job evaluation panel in this test in order to provide fresh eyes and experience to the process – the design team are likely to be so familiar with the various drafts and tests that they may not 'spot' the obvious! Even at this stage there is the possibility and opportunity to change the design of the job evaluation scheme or the scoring mechanisms if the results of the test are not satisfactory.

13   *Computerise*   This involves the conversion of the intended job evaluation scheme to a computerised system.

14   *Test the computerised scheme*   This would involve a re-run of the test carried out in stage 12. It is possible that the process of computerisation has not been done correctly.

15   *Apply and implement*   At this stage the design group would formally present their conclusions and job evaluation system to the steering group for approval. This can be a useful safeguard and provide a fresh set of eyes and perspectives in relation to the project and outcomes. It also allows management and unions (if present and involved) one final opportunity to pull out of the project with some ability to save face and avoid major conflict should it be necessary from their perspective; or to engage in some final negotiation that might 'tweak' a scheme in some way or another to avoid problems after its implementation. Remember at this stage there is still no talk of money being attached to the outcome of the job evaluation process – it remains a rank order of jobs only.

The next stages in the process involve the design of a grading structure and the application of pay to each grade. These will be discussed subsequently in the appropriate sections on reward management and salary structure.

See also: *competency; discrimination, diversity and equality; employee relations and conflict; job, job analysis and job design; reward management; total reward; trade union/employee representation; wage structure*

BIBLIOGRAPHY

Armstrong, M. and Stephens, T. (2005) *A Handbook of Employee Reward Management and Practice*. London: Kogan Page.

Equal Opportunities Commission (2003) *Good Practice Guide – Job Evaluation Schemes Free of Sex Bias*. Manchester: EOC.

key concepts in human
resource management

Knowledge Management

> *The management of the knowledge available to an organisation from all possible sources in a way that enhances its value by allowing the effective sharing and use of existing knowledge together with its manipulation – resulting in the creation of new knowledge. The effective management of knowledge is intended to produce a benefit for the organisation, employees and other stakeholders.*

The above definition is reasonably clear in that it identifies that knowledge is something that can be managed in the service of the organisation and its stakeholders. As such it implies that knowledge is a resource or commodity that is as amenable to management direction and decision making as one of the resources that are available to serve the organisation's interests. There are the specified information paths that are determined by policy and business practice. For example, customer orders are collated and disseminated to appropriate departments according to rules set out in company procedures. However, these aspects of information flow represent only a small proportion of the total information circulating within a company at any point in time. There will be information about job vacancies, financial results, and forthcoming training courses for example. On top of all of that information there will be the inevitable gossip, rumour, idle chit-chat and thousands of other pieces of relevant and indeed irrelevant information (and misinformation) that circulate around every workplace all of the time. Information is the very lifeblood of an organisation, carrying with it all manner of necessary items of value (and occasionally malevolent rubbish that can do harm) to every corner. The need is for those seeking to manage knowledge to be able to separate out any information and data that would be definable as 'knowledge' from that which is irrelevant for that purpose.

Newell et al. (2002) identified two different approaches to understanding knowledge within an organisational context: the structuralist perspective – knowledge is something that people and organisations possess; and the process perspective – knowledge contains strong social practice and dynamic dimensions. The structural perspective understands knowledge as 'things' that can be articulated and in that sense are static and objective, whereas the process perspective regards knowledge as based on the interactive social processes of 'knowing' and 'action'. In short, because we as human beings behave and function in a social world our 'knowledge' is what allows us to relate to, and behave in, that world. From that perspective although some of our knowledge is explicit much of it is tacit and a substantial part of that will always remain so, being resistant to articulation or codification. Nonaka (1996) called this 'aspect knowledge' and suggested that it was just as important to organisational success as the formally classified and captured forms of knowledge. For example, imagine trying to write a training manual for driving a car that would allow a trainee to pass a practical driving test without the need to have any actual driving practice. It is the tacit knowledge gained from the actual experience of driving a car in controlled and supported conditions on a road that builds up the level of capability to demonstrate someone's competence during a test. It is generally suggested that although information and communication technology has a role to play in managing knowledge in an organisational context, much knowledge management is achieved through management of people and interactions between them. Several writers suggest that knowledge management strategies also need to be grounded in the concept of wisdom (usually defined as knowledge with a long shelf-life) compared to data (which represent information with a short shelf-life).

The intention of knowledge management is to inform, integrate, and use what is known to create a launch-pad for the development of new understandings and opportunities for the benefit of stakeholders and the organisation. Writers such as Lank (2002) have suggested that new organisational roles are emerging as organisations seek to understand and manage knowledge more effectively. It is interesting in relation to the earlier discussion that the following roles are very much explained in terms of the structural perspective on knowledge. The process perspective to knowledge does not make an appearance in the explanation. The roles identified by Lank are:

- *Knowledge architects* Senior strategic roles responsible for the determination of knowledge that is critical to the organisation; how it should be captured; how it should be shared; how people should be trained in knowledge management; and how they should be rewarded for collaboration and knowledge sharing.

- *Knowledge facilitators* People with these roles are responsible for finding ways of facilitating knowledge flow through communication media, indexing, and library and internal consultancy services.
- *Knowledge aware people* These are the users and contributors to the knowledge system.

There are also other perspectives on knowledge that need to be understood in relation to its management within an organisation. Knowledge is a basis for the acquisition of (and holding onto) power within organisations, a 'fact' that has long been understood by ambitious, politically-minded individuals across time. Knowledge, both explicit and tacit, can be treated as a commodity. Just as with any other commodity, knowledge can be stored, sold, bought, traded, and stolen. It can also be grown, developed, and harvested just like any crop. Access to knowledge can give an individual (or group) a real or potential advantage. That is why so much organisational activity is invested in market and competitor intelligence. It is also an aspect of internal organisational functioning that leads people to hoard information, keeping it to themselves or using it to achieve a personal advantage (or the disadvantage of others). It is against that background that knowledge management seeks to capture and facilitate knowledge to the benefit of all. Tranfield et al. (2003) described knowledge management in relation to innovation projects within an organisation as consisting of three phases: discovery, realisation, and nurture. These they then developed into an innovation model consisting of eight stages: search, capture, articulate, contextualise, apply, evaluate, support and re-innovate.

Scarbrough and Carter (2000) identified a number of different approaches to knowledge management and suggested the HR implications of each:

- *Best practice approach* This approach seeks to encourage employees to co-operate with knowledge management initiatives and to actively share knowledge with each other and management.
- *Knowledge work approach* The identification of key knowledge workers and the management of both them and the knowledge that they need/use. This may involve HR initiatives such as motivation, reward, incentive scheme design, job design, level of supervision, and career management.
- *Congruence approach* Seeking to align HR practices and policies with knowledge management strategies by encouraging team working, co-operation with management objectives, culture change and maximising contribution.

- *Human and social capital approach*   This approach seeks to achieve effective knowledge management through a focus on the adoption of management values by all employees through training and culture change processes, etc.
- *Learning approach*   This approach involves the creation of networks of learning communities amongst mutually dependant co-workers and also the adoption of elements from the learning organisation model

There are two basic strategies for managing knowledge:

- *Codification*   This approach seeks to capture knowledge formally and to codify it in a form and location that would be easily accessible to other people within the organisation and across time. Procedures, databases, electronic indexing, and storage media are relevant to this approach. This is closely linked to the structural perspective.
- *Personalisation*   This approach is linked to the process perspective and regards knowledge as something tied to the individual (or group) who develop and create it. Much of the knowledge available is tacit in form and so may be difficult to articulate, or the individuals may need to be persuaded and encouraged to offer it to others within the organisation.

Trust is an issue that has significance for knowledge management. At the 'hard' end of the spectrum, knowledge will be regarded as something that is explicit and capable of capture and codification – trust having a minimal impact on the process. The capture and codification of knowledge would be dependent on the ability of specialists and managers to identify 'knowledge' from a range of sources and then determine the way to store and disseminate it. The process perspective (what might be termed a 'soft' approach) takes the view that employees must be encouraged to co-operate and give their contribution of largely tacit knowledge willingly, thereby requiring trust to exist. Newell and Swan (1999) suggested that two forms of trust were significant for knowledge management:

- *Goodwill trust*   This form of trust requires the giver to trust that the receiver will not use the contribution against their interests. That assessment of trust can of course arise at the personal or organisational level. So the giver must trust both the individual receiver and also the organisation that allows the receiver to claim the right to be so.

- *Competence trust*   This form of trust requires the giver to believe that the receiver has the relevant skills and competence to be able to use the knowledge wisely and effectively. This can sometimes be found when a graduate trainee is placed alongside an experienced employee as part of their training/induction. It is not unusual to find that the more experienced employee resents the idea that they should 'show them the ropes' and thus hand over their hard won experience and knowledge to someone who as a consequence will rapidly progress to a more senior level than the 'giver'.

See also: competency; data protection; employee development; employee empowerment and engagement; high performance working; learning organisation; management development; organisational culture; organisational development (OD) and change; strategic HRM; succession planning and talent management

BIBLIOGRAPHY

Lank, E. (2002) 'Head to head', *People Management*, 8 (4): 46–49.
Newell, S. and Swan, J. (1999) 'Trust and interorganisational networking', *Human Relations*, 53 (10): 1287–1328.
Newell, S., Robertson, M., Scarbrough, H. and Swan, J. (2002) *Managing Knowledge Work*. Basingstoke: Palgrave.
Nonaka, I. (1996) 'The knowledge creating company', in K. Starkey (ed.), *How Organisations Learn*. London: International Thomson Business Press.
Scarbrough, H. and Carter, C. (2000) *Investigating Knowledge Management: Research Report*. London: CIPD.
Tranfield, D., Young, M., Partington, D., Bessant, J. and Sapsed, J. (2003) 'Knowledge management routines for innovation projects: developing a hierarchical process model', *International Journal of Innovation Management*, 7 (1): 27–50.

knowledge management

Labour Turnover

A term used to describe the number or percentage of employees who have left, had their employment terminated, been made redundant, died or retired during a specified period of time. There are usually separate indices calculated for each of the main categories of separation.

The simplest measure of labour turnover is:

$$\frac{\text{Total number of leavers over period}}{\text{Average total number employed over period}} \times 100 = \text{percentage wastage rate}$$

In its most basic form the figures used represent the total numbers who left in the period (usually one year) and so the figure produced does not differentiate between voluntary and involuntary separation. However, many organisations use that basic measure and so it allows for a comparability (benchmarking) between various indices and organisations. It is also possible to produce separate measures of particular categories of leaver such as those who left voluntarily in order to better understand employee attitudes about staying with the organisation.

It is also possible to calculate the level of employee retention through a stability index which indicates the proportion of experienced employees (the number who have stayed more than one year). The calculation is as follows:

$$\frac{\text{Number of employees with more than one year's service}}{\text{Total number of employees in post one year ago}} \times 100 = \text{percentage stability}$$

We are also able to explore various other aspects of employee retention and turnover through such devices as:

- *Cohort analysis* This tracks a particular group of people who can be described as a cohort. Graduate trainees who started in a specific year or factory workers doing the same would be possible cohorts. Graphs showing the survival of numbers from the cohort can be drawn up which would show the numbers staying across the years.

- *Half-life analysis* This is a particular form of cohort analysis in which the time taken for half the cohort to leave the organisation is determined and used as a basis for comparison across cohorts

Bevan et al. (1997) suggested that it was possible (and desirable) to create a risk assessment based on people who may leave the organisation and the potential impact that would have on it. They developed a four cell matrix based on two measures:

- Likelihood of an individual leaving?

  o High
  o Low

- Impact on the organisation?

  o High
  o Low

The four cells that resulted from that combination of questions and answer were:

- *High in terms of likelihood and High in terms of impact* This they categorised as the 'Danger zone', which implies that action needs to be taken to retain the individuals so designated.
- *High in terms of likelihood and Low in terms of impact* This they categorised as 'Thanks for all you've done', which implies that there is no real reason to try and retain the individual so designated.
- *Low in terms of likelihood and High in terms of impact* This they categorised as requiring a 'watching brief', which implies that whilst no immediate action to retain the individual is necessary that could easily change and so careful handling is necessary if they are to be retained as important to the future success of the organisation.
- *Low in terms of likelihood and Low in terms of impact* This they categorised as 'No immediate danger', which implies that no immediate action to retain the individual is necessary.

There is always a question over what an acceptable, expected, or appropriate level of labour turnover should be and unfortunately that is an almost impossible question to answer as many possible variables are active in any situation that can influence leaving decisions. The main reasons that people leave their existing jobs include:

- The induction crisis – inadequate recruitment, poor induction, and being lied to or misled about the job or other aspects of working in the company can lead people to resign very soon after starting work.
- The attraction of a new job at the same or a similar level – some aspect of a new job may simply be more attractive than the existing job. Even doing the same job for the same reward but in a different organisation and with different colleagues can seem attractive at times.
- Promotion or career development opportunities being provided by another organisation that are not available with the current employer.
- The lack of training or career development opportunities within the current organisation.
- The prospects of higher pay or a superior benefit package (more holidays, a bonus, etc).
- Dissatisfaction with some aspect of the existing job, colleagues, management, or organisation.
- The existence of poor, ineffective, or aggressive management style or policies, procedures, and practices.
- Personality clashes or interpersonal conflicts with colleagues and co-workers.
- The creation of expectations during recruitment that are not delivered creating resentment and a feeling of being cheated, misled, or lied to.
- The existence of poor working relationships with colleagues, subordinates, or managers.
- The existence of poor or ineffective HR policies, procedures, and practices.
- Employees continually assessing the organisation's direction and future prospects in order to judge how they fit into that predicted future.
- Personal reasons including family commitments, changes in circumstances, and relocation.
- Following the offer of early retirement, or when other entitlements become available.

- Ill health which can result in an individual having to leave their current job or employer.
- Death in service.
- Dismissal for reasons associated with conduct, capability, or legal bar.
- Dismissal for redundancy.
- Dismissal for some other reason (fairly or unfairly) and potentially subject to a Compromise Agreement or an Employment Tribunal claim.

The reasons that people give for leaving an organisation are often only partially true. Exit interviews although widespread can be notoriously unreliable for many reasons. For example, it may be conducted by someone who may be subsequently asked to write a reference for the departing employee; the departing employee may seek re-employment with the organisation in the future; or they may not want the true reason to be known. Generally people are reluctant to openly criticise their managers, colleagues or the organisation, preferring instead to provide vague, general, conventional or expected reasons for leaving. The 'induction crisis' refers to the reasons behind employee turnover in the first few days, weeks, or months of employment. Equally, expectations with regard to promotion, status, responsibilities, career development, wage/bonus levels, and many other facets of the work on offer are often raised during the recruitment process, leading people to accept jobs which will sooner or later result in disappointment, frustration, and disengagement.

In terms of whether or not a particular level of labour turnover is a problem several factors have to be considered. For example, in situations where it is easy to quickly find and train new employees at little cost, it is possible to sustain effective organisational functioning despite a high turnover. Conversely, where skills are scarce, when recruitment is expensive, or where it takes a long time to fill vacancies, high labour turnover is likely to be a problem. Some level of employee turnover can benefit an organisation (for example, if a poor performer is replaced by a more effective employee or when new people bring new ideas into the organisation – often referred to as acquiring 'fresh blood'). It can also help to offset the need for redundancy or short-time working/layoffs if there are some voluntary departures (termed 'natural wastage').

The cost of replacing a leaver can be estimated by multiplying the cost of recruitment by the turnover rate for specific categories of leaver or jobs.

The following represent the major categories of cost to take account:

- Administration of the resignation/termination.
- Cost of any settlement necessary to effect a separation.
- Recruitment costs (including advertising, agency costs, staff time, etc.).
- Selection costs (including interview costs, travel expenses, assessment centre costs, etc.).
- Administration of the recruitment and selection process.
- Cost of doing the work during the period in which there is a vacancy.
- Cost of any 'golden hello'.
- Induction training for the new employee.
- Loss in productivity during the vacancy and induction period.
- Savings in salary and related costs during the vacancy.

From the above list it will be obvious that at least one of the items included is actually a saving – wages will not be paid to an employee during the gap between someone leaving and the next job holder starting. However, there may be some extra costs arising if temporary workers or overtime are needed to cover the work that would otherwise be done during the 'gap'. Some of the costs are also difficult to identify as (for example) HR staff will simply be diverted from another resourcing activity to that of the specific vacancies (opportunity costs). However, the higher the level of turnover the greater the volume of HR time that will be needed to facilitate resourcing and so it is a relevant cost to include. Other opportunity costs will be more difficult to justify as distinct entries. For example, line managers may not be able to identify what they might have done with the time saved if a particular resourcing activity were not necessary. Less than 3 per cent of respondents to the CIPD (2008a) survey were able to provide figures relating to the estimated costs of labour turnover. Figures that were produced suggest that the average cost per employee was £5,800, rising to £20,000 for senior managers or directors.

There is a range of things that organisations can do that would be expected to have an impact on the level of labour turnover and a number of employee retention strategies are covered in the appropriate section below.

See also: benchmarking; discipline and grievance; employee assistance programme; employee relations and conflict; flexibility; human resource planning; incentive schemes; organisational culture; performance management; quality of working life and the psychological contract; resourcing/retention; reward management

BIBLIOGRAPHY

Bevan, S., Barber, L. and Robinson, D. (1997) *Keeping the Best: A Practical Guide to Retaining Key Employees*. London: Institute of Employment Studies.

CIPD (2008a) 'Recruitment, retention and turnover'. Annual Survey Report. London: CIPD. Available at www.cipd.co.uk (last accessed November 2008).

CIPD (2008b) 'Employee turnover and retention'. *Factsheet* (revised August). Available at www.cipd.co.uk (last accessed November 2008).

Learning Organisation

> *The facilitation of learning for all employees and the constant transformation of the organisation in response to that new knowledge and ability. The term is intended to capture the ability of an organisation to focus on the individual learning that occurs within it and to capture the benefits available through it in shaping the way in which customer needs are met effectively and in a commercially successful manner.*

It was Pedler et al. (1989) who began the discussion about what a learning organisation might be. They described it in terms of the facilitation of learning for all employees and the constant transformation of the organisation in response to that new knowledge and ability, in effect suggesting that organisations could adapt to new understandings based on a learning process similar to that experienced by people. The concept requires that organisations should adapt to accommodate the developing capabilities of the humans within it.

However, there are several problems with this apparently simple idea. The first is how can organisations as such learn? Organisations do not have a life or existence separate from the people that work in them. So the only way that an organisation can learn is through the collective acquisition of this by all employees and then the conversion of that learning into actions, procedures, practices, and behaviour. This is similar to aspects of the discussion of knowledge management earlier in relation to explicit and tacit knowledge, etc. Marquardt and Reynolds (1994) identified a number of characteristics associated with learning organisations:

- Embraces uncertainty and change.
- Has a holistic, systems based view of the organisation.
- Encourages risk-taking and experimentation.
- Has a culture of high trust, feedback and disclosure.
- Encourages empowerment at all levels.
- Links employee self-development to the development of the organisation.
- Encourages managers to act as mentors, coaches, and facilitators.
- Has an organisation-wide vision that is shared with all levels of managers and employees.
- Seeks to create new knowledge as part of its competitive strategy.

The main characteristics of a learning organisation are generally identified as including:

- Managers accepting responsibility for the identification of their own training needs and setting challenging learning goals.
- The provision for all employees of regular performance reviews on learning achieved.
- Encouragement for managers to identify and provide job/work-based learning opportunities for both employees and themselves.
- Encouragement of a questioning attitude to the accepted ways of doing things within the organisation.
- The acceptance that, when learning, some mistakes are inevitable, but also requiring that individuals learn from them.
- Encouragement of on-the-job training and other learning activities.

Salaman (2001) was very critical of the notion that the learning organisation can exist in any meaningful way as the basic terms 'learning' and 'organisation' are essentially contradictory. He argued that the term 'organise' (the basis of organisation) implied that much can safely be forgotten (as a result of the reliance on system, function, specialism, procedure, routine and repetition) and that this in practice reduced variety. Variety in this context meant 'difference'. Learning, Salaman argued, implied an ability to 'disorganise' and increase 'variety' – the very opposite of organisation.

Individuals and groups that increase their learning (or knowledge) have a greater ability to 'do' things that they could not previously 'do'. As a result they are enabled to tackle a greater degree of work and decision making without reference to a manual, procedure, or guidance note. Such capability (competence) also increases the potential variety that can be achieved. Salaman, however, went on to argue that even with such difficulties the learning organisation concept has value because it should encourage managers to question how they engage with change and performance in relation to the nature of conventional organisational frameworks and processes to the benefit of all stakeholders.

Single and double loop learning are often associated with that of the learning organisation. The first loop reflects the learning involved in the acquisition of a skill – based on trial and error problem solving and involving learning how to make choices from a limited range of options. The second loop reflects the decision process in identifying what should be learned during the first stage in the process. This perspective on the learning organisation seeks to reflect the need to be able to link effectively both operational and strategic aspects of organisational activity through an integrated learning process. It is of little benefit for an organisation to seek to improve efficiency in order to meet current customer need, if that need is constantly changing. Equally, it is of little value in understanding the environment through the business strategy processes if that is not converted into actions at an operational level. Both approaches are needed. Subsequent writers added a third loop to the basic model and created triple loop learning:

1 *Single loop learning*   Learning at the operational level seeking to be able to develop ways of doing existing things more efficiently.
2 *Double loop learning*   This represents learning at the level of questioning why what is done is being done. The double loop goes on to seek answers to questions about 'doing different things'.
3 *Triple loop learning*   This level seeks answers to questions about the underlying purpose and principles of the organisation. For example, should the organisation be doing what it does in the way that it does in the place that it does and is its approach to social and other responsibilities most effectively achieved through its current business area and model?

Senge (1990) sought to bring together a number of themes (including double loop learning) as a way of creating a learning organisation. He identified five disciplines that he described as coming together to create an integrated approach to how organisations should learn. The disciplines that he identified are:

- *Systems thinking*   The systems perspective reflects the fact that everything associated with organisational activity is related to a greater or lesser extent by a complex web of mutually interactive and dependant relationships. Although there are different approaches to systems thinking, the principles that underpin Senge's views are based on systems dynamics:

  o That complex systems often produce unexpected and counter-intuitive outcomes.
  o In complex systems the links between cause and effect can be distant in time and space, making it difficult to identify patterns and determine causal relationships.
  o Complex systems are highly sensitive to some changes but remarkably insensitive to others.

- *Personal mastery*   Senge regarded this as a process of continually clarifying and deepening our personal vision and understanding of the world in which we live. Senge described this as the spiritual foundation of the organisation.
- *Mental models*   These reflect the assumptions or generalisations that we hold about people, the world, and how they interact.
- *Building a shared vision*   This reflects the view of the organisation and what it stands for as understood by the different stakeholders. In Senge's view, this cannot be imposed or based only on a management 'wish-list' of what everyone else is supposed to believe, agree with, or support. It should develop as a result of people working together and creating a sense of a shared understanding of the future and how to relate to it individually and collectively.
- *Team learning*   This describes situations in which the collective capability of the team is greater than the capability of individual team members. This occurs when the team 'learns' to interact in ways that build on the understanding of each individual in the facilitation of new understandings and ways of doing things.

Pedler et al. (1991) suggested that a learning organisation displayed 11 characteristics which could be categorised into five overarching themes. These are:

- *Strategy:*
  - A learning approach to strategy is necessary – the development and implementation of strategy represent an opportunity to question past actions and current understandings and so demonstrate learning in action.
  - The existence of policy making on a participative basis – the processes for strategy should involve all employees, customers, suppliers and others in the supply chain who might have a view or perspective.

- *Looking inwards:*
  - The creation of a widespread informating capability – this implies the widespread adoption of a technology capable of informing and empowering employees, so enhancing their understanding, learning, and capability to contribute effectively to the direction and development of the organisation.
  - The creation of formative accounting and control systems – the development and adoption of budgetary and other control systems that facilitate learning by people about the jobs they do and hence facilitate their ability to contribute.
  - The creation of an internal exchange basis for interdepartmental connectivity and functioning – this seeks to encourage an adoption of the internal customer model.
  - The creation of understanding and an acceptance of rewards linked to performance variability – a reward allocation should be recognised as potentially leading to different wage levels across the organisation and the resultant debate about why this is so encouraged in the spirit of openness, involvement, and development.

- *Structure:*
  - The creation of flexibility in job roles based on a need to match the requirements of internal and external customer demands and which encourages personal growth and experimentation among job holders.

- *Looking outwards:*

  o The use of internal and external boundary spanning roles to identify, collect, and disseminate intelligence and information for use within the organisation.
  o The creation of inter-company learning opportunities that could involve benchmarking exercises and perhaps creating product development, joint problem solving, and learning programmes with other organisations in the supply chain

- *Learning opportunities:*

  o The creation of a learning climate that should encourage some risk taking in seeking to learn from experience and questioning the status quo and received wisdom. Some mistakes should be tolerated as not all new ideas will work and often the most effective learning occurs when mistakes have been made.
  o Encouragement for the identification of self-development opportunities.

See also: benchmarking; competency; employee development; employee empowerment and engagement; flexibility; high performance working; human capital; knowledge management; management development; organisational development (OD) and change; performance management; quality of working life and the psychological contract; strategic HRM

BIBLIOGRAPHY

Marquardt, M. and Reynolds, A. (1994) *The Global Learning Organisation*. Burr Ridge, IL: Irwin.

Pedler, M., Boydell, T. and Burgoyne, J. (1989) 'Towards the learning company', *Management Education and Development*, 20, Part 1.

Pedler, M., Boydell, T. and Burgoyne, J. (1991) *The Learning Company*. Maidenhead: McGraw-Hill.

Salaman, G. (2001) 'A response to Snell. The learning organisation: fact or fiction?', *Human Relations*, 54 (3): 343–359.

Senge, P. (1990) *The Fifth Discipline*. London: Doubleday.

key concepts in human resource management

Management Development

The full range of training and development activities aimed at maximising the actual and potential contribution of a manager to the business over both the short and longer term. Some writers prefer the shorter form of attempts to improve managerial effectiveness through learning processes.

As a starting point the development of managerial competence and capability rather than what might be termed the technical elements of a job, for example computer skills, defines management development. However, some 'technical' development is necessary for all managerial jobs. For example, all professions and areas of work experience will change – HR managers need to be aware of developments in employment-related legislation even if they do not need know the detailed provisions that have changed. Equally, at some point in every manager's career they will be given responsibility for subordinates who work in different disciplines to those of the manager. For example, a sales person may be appointed to the post of sales and marketing manager and so will be exposed to the detail and activities of the marketing function for the first time. Although these are strongly related disciplines there are differences between them and so the newly appointed manager must quickly assimilate these and be able to operate effectively in both areas of work.

The CIPD (2008a) make the point that senior managers and directors often expect to be treated differently in relation to management development, partly because they will be more senior in status than the HRD professional responsible for their development. Also they are more likely to identify their development needs in terms of leadership rather than as conventional management development. Other 'factors' that differentiate senior management development activity include:

- *Numbers* The relatively small number of senior management positions in any organisation precludes the application of standardised development options.
- *Isolation* The relatively small number of senior management positions together with their responsibilities result in post holders being relatively

isolated (without a real peer group). Senior managers may lack the opportunity to talk to colleagues about what they regard as their strengths, weaknesses, and development needs. Isolation is difficult for more junior HRD staff to understand and can cause difficulties in identifying and providing suitable development.

- *Political skills* Senior management work contains a high level of political activity and the individuals achieving such senior posts need well developed political skills in order to survive. The provision of development in this area is a sensitive issue for most organisations, but it is a necessary skill for senior managers to develop.

Some writers suggest that different types of organisation will adopt different approaches to management development and that six levels of what might be termed 'maturity' in relation to the provision of management development can be detected:

1 *No systematic management development* Often there is a reliance on individuals to seek out and undertake their own management development.
2 *Isolated tactical management development* Management development that takes place is in response to problems or events.
3 *Integrated and co-ordinated structural and development tactics* Management development based on a need to develop careers and prepare people for promotion or an unfolding business event.
4 *A management development strategy which implements corporate policy* This approach implies a degree of planning in relation to management development in that it is intended to meet managerial needs arising from the business strategy.
5 *A management development strategy input to corporate policy formulation* This approach provides feedback into business strategy development. The development of a business strategy can benefit from an understanding of the current and evolving managerial capability.
6 *Strategic development of the management of corporate policy* This represents the full integration of management development and a business strategy activity.

Mathis and Jackson (2008: 311) identified a number of sources of experience-based management learning that could be categorised under three headings:

- *Job transitions* These include moving to new jobs, dealing with problems at work, dealing with new people as subordinates or colleagues, and changes to job responsibilities. Each of these sources of development arises as a result of changes to the job of a manager and in turn this forces the individual to develop new ways of working with people.

- *Challenges*   These include being involved in a project as part of the development or introduction of change or another aspect of organisational activity such as cost reduction, a productivity improvement, or the development/introduction of new products, etc.
- *Obstacles*   These can include a bad job context (such as the existence of a hostile employee relations climate, taking over from a weak or ineffective manager, or working in a very political culture), working for a difficult boss, working for demanding customers, hostile or unsupportive colleagues, wider economic or trading conditions.

Mathis and Jackson (2008) also suggested that the outcomes from the above three learning sources could contribute to the following lessons that managers needed to learn:

- *Setting agendas*   This includes taking responsibility for managing their responsibilities and setting goals and objectives for themselves and their teams.
- *Handling relationships*   Managing people is also about managing colleagues, peers, superiors, customers, suppliers, and other external contacts.
- *Management values*   Understanding what differentiates successful and appropriate management behaviour from that which is not appropriate or effective.
- *Personality qualities*   Developing the necessary personal and psychological characteristics to be able to deal with the inevitable chaos, ambiguity and stress associated with managerial jobs.
- *Self-awareness*   Understanding one's personal style of leadership and other preferred behaviour/working patterns and how these might impact on others (and hence create reciprocal behaviour patterns) in the work environment.

The CIPD (2008b) propose that only when such informal opportunities are captured and brought within some type of formal process should they be regarded as management development. However, to restrict it like this limits the definition of management development to those processes undertaken within a formal company process and ignores self development. Given that individuals are now expected to take an increasing level of responsibility for their own development and career management activities this perhaps represents too narrow a focus. According to the same source, management development includes:

- Structured informal learning with work-based methods aimed at structuring the informal learning which will always take place.
- Formal training courses of various kinds, from very specific courses on technical aspects of jobs to those on wider management skills.
- Education, which might range from courses for (perhaps prospective) junior managers or supervisors at NVQ Level 3 to Master of Business Administration (MBA) degrees.

There are a number of methods for management development, all with advantages and disadvantages relative to their intended purpose and the context within which this will be carried out. These include:

- *Coaching.*
- *Counselling* This is particularly relevant for individuals experiencing motivation or self-confidence issues that might respond to this form of intervention.
- *Mentors.*
- *Project work* This involves working in cross-functional teams on particular projects. It provides exposure to different functions, ways of thinking and of doing things, as well as providing an opportunity to learn about different parts of the organisation.
- *Action learning* This approach capitalises on the fact that many people learn most effectively by doing things. It achieves that intention by making participants focus on solving live issues from their working situations. It also represents a team activity in that members set out to define and then solve a problem (or improve/change a situation) by trial and error approaches involving a series of iterations.
- *Secondments* This provides development for an individual through a job in another organisation for a defined period (perhaps for a year). It also provides a way of broadening experience and of forcing the individual to leave their comfort zone by having to experience different ways of doing things.
- *Performance and development reviews* Many performance management systems have evolved into a process that is intended to explore both performance and development issues.
- *Development centres* The purpose of a development centre (as compared to an assessment centre) is to focus on opportunities for

individual development and identify promotion potential and opportunity.

- *Succession planning* This involves one or more successors being identified for key and senior posts within an organisation. Career moves and/or development activities would be planned and offered to identified successors in order to prepare them to be able to perform effectively at a more senior level.
- *Formal training courses* In many organisations formal training courses may be provided at transition points such as when appointed to a first management job or appointed to the Board of Directors. Such development programmes can be designed and delivered by in-house specialists, at local university business schools, by training consultancies, or by freelance trainers supporting in-house specialists. Outdoor development is sometimes used for team building purposes as part of these offerings and involves groups of people being brought together at an outdoor specialist provider's location and might include building rafts, paint-balling, or mountain climbing, etc.
- *E-learning and blended learning* E-learning uses computer technology to deliver training. It is useful when large numbers of people have to be exposed to the same material, and where flexible access is useful in that it allows people to work through the material at their own pace and in their own time (or at a time convenient to their working activities). It is a form of learning that has limitations in management development activities (in relation to the type of people, knowledge and information that it suits), but when combined with other approaches (i.e. a blended learning approach) it can be useful.

See also: assessment/development centre; career management; competency; employee development; high performance working; performance management; succession planning and talent management

BIBLIOGRAPHY

CIPD (2008a) 'Developing senior managers'. *Factsheet.* (revised January 2008). Available at www.cipd.co.uk (last accessed January 2009).
CIPD (2008b) 'Management development'. *Factsheet.* (revised February 2008). Available at www.cipd.co.uk (last accessed January 2009).
Mathis, R.L. and Jackson, J.H. (2008) *Human Resource Management* (12th edition). Mason, OH: South-Western.

management development

189

Negotiation

> Negotiation broadly reflects a process of difference reduction through the forming of agreements between individuals and groups who have mutually dependent needs and desires. A more formal definition of negotiation envisages it as a process by which one party obtains what they want from another party who wants something in return.

In an organisational context negotiation is most apparent in the employee relations field or when commercial contracts are being arranged. However, negotiation has a much broader significance in organisational activity. For example, one manager may seek to influence, persuade, or gain agreement from other managers for a particular course of action and in doing so will engage in a form of negotiation. Another example might involve a boss and subordinate agreeing priorities of a range of projects and objectives as part of their performance review. Therefore, many employees and managers are involved in negotiations in one form or another for a significant proportion of their time at work.

Beardwell et al. (2004: 469) identified two approaches to what they termed as collective bargaining (meaning negotiating within an employee relations context):

- *Distributive bargaining*   This reflects a win-lose approach to negotiation in which the 'things' being negotiated are envisaged to be a limited resource and the process is intended to determine an appropriate share for each group participating. The most frequently used analogy for this approach is that of cutting a cake. Once a piece of cake is cut and allocated then it cannot be available to any other party or play any other role within the negotiation. Such an approach is combative in that it encourages the negotiating strategy of fighting over one point, winning it (or conceding it) and then moving on to the next point. It takes each point in the negotiating agenda as separate entities and does not consider the overall balance, theme, or effect on the deal created.
- *Integrative bargaining*   This reflects the win-win approach to negotiation in that it seeks to create an overall outcome that can maximise the benefits to all parties. It rejects the limited resource approach of

key concepts in human resource management

distributive bargaining by deliberately adopting a problem-solving approach and seeking to achieve mutual gains in areas of common interest for all parties in the process. Such an approach is collaborative in that it seeks to establish trust and mutual respect and encourages the open and willing sharing of information in order to create outcomes that allow all parties to achieve outcomes of benefit.

In extreme cases, the tactics employed by individuals using a distributive bargaining approach can be aggressive in order to maximise the chances of a win on each point as they move through the list. There are many aggressive tactics that can be used in pursuit of this approach, including:

- *Probing*   Before a meeting starts and then during it, probing for information of value without giving anything away about their own position.
- *Get before you give*   Seeking to gain something before conceding anything, often by using the argument of a need for the other side to demonstrate 'good faith' and of being serious in seeking an appropriate outcome.
- *Emotion*   The use of tone of voice, temper, and other body language signals to create emotion in the process.
- *Good guy/bad guy*   The 'reasonable' speaker follows the 'aggressive' and 'unreasonable' one and builds on the advantage gained through a threat of more aggression to follow.
- *Poker face*   An ability to manage their body language and verbal cues allows the fighter to cloak their feelings and intentions.
- *Managing the minutes*   The person who writes the minutes of a meeting is in a strong position to shape/slant the official record.
- *Understanding, not agreement*   One side may claim to understand the other's position throughout the negotiations, only to fail to accept that an agreement has been reached at the end of the process. This approach encourages the party being 'set-up' to think that progress is being achieved and so to relax. When this failure to accept the agreement becomes apparent it throws them into a panic and encourages last minute concessions to be made – usually not in the best interests of the party making them – which was the intention right from the start.
- *Getting upstairs*   Demanding to go over the head of the negotiating team to talk to the 'real' boss is a threat that can be used to great effect. No one wants their boss think that they are incapable and so it can encourage concessions in order to reach a settlement. From the employee representative point of view, allowing managers to talk

negotiation

directly to employees might undermine their power base and again concessions might be made unwisely.

- *Forcing* There are various forms of force that can be used. Threats of a work to rule, a go slow, strikes, lockouts, etc. are sometimes voiced.

These fighting tactics described here are intended to gain and retain control of the process. There are various ways in which such tactics can be dealt with, but essentially it comes down to remaining in control of one's temper, emotions, content, and process. Another feature of negotiation is that of conflict. It is always possible for arguments to arise and for tempers to be lost in the heat and stress of discussions. However, it arouses conflict which can result in a failure to make progress in reaching an outcome that can form the basis of an agreement between the parties. There are a number of ways of minimising the risk of conflict arising and approaches to dealing with this once it has arisen, according to Torrington et al. (2005: 673–4):

- *Avoidance* This approach ignores the problem on the basis that most problems causing conflict will simply disappear as time and the negotiations move forward.
- *Smoothing* This approach to conflict seeks to 'patch up' any rift through calming actions to get beyond the 'problem' occurrence. It might include calls to stay loyal to the objectives of the negotiation; seeking to calm things down by reference to past events where problems have been overcome; or putting that issue aside for another meeting and moving on to another issue; or calls to stick together as a team or show support for the organisation.
- *Forcing* This can work in the short term if the power balance is favourable to the party/individual seeking to force the others. However, it invariably leads to resentment and a desire to seek revenge in some form or other when the opportunity presents itself.
- *Compromise* This approach seeks to avoid conflict by adopting the middle ground. It represents the best-worst solution to any situation.
- *Confrontation* This approach requires the parties to confront the problem. It requires an acceptance by them that there exists a difference of opinion and interest (with the danger of conflict) which can only be resolved by exploring the issues in some depth and from all perspectives. By so doing the parties can seek to develop an accommodation of the differences that exist in whatever solution is agreed. This approach should deliver a greater level of satisfaction among the parties that their objectives have been recognised as far as it is possible to do so within the eventual outcome and agreement.

The tactics that negotiators are likely to adopt during a negotiation will depend on a number of factors, including:

- *The preferred style of the individuals involved*   This reflects the usual patterns of negotiating behaviour, communication, and problem solving adopted by the individuals involved in the process.
- *The relative power balance between the parties.*
- *The degree of change involved in the topics covered by the negotiation*   A negotiation involving a 5 per cent reduction in the working week would be likely to result in a different approach compared to one involving staffing cuts of 25 per cent and a pay reduction of 20 per cent.
- *The willingness of the parties to accept change*   If one or more parties in a negotiation is unwilling to accept change or is only prepared to accept minor levels of it, then it is likely that a difficult and fraught negotiation will result.
- *Previous encounters*   The experience gained from previous meetings and negotiating encounters builds a pattern of expectation as to what to expect the next time.
- *Environmental and contextual influences*   Changes in the political party forming the national government, economic condition, trading difficulties, etc. can all have an impact on the background to a negotiation.
- *The expectations of and pressure from the constituents of the negotiators*   Negotiators do not usually act on their own or as an autonomous body; they will represent and act on behalf of their constituents to whom they must report and seek ratification and acceptance of the agreement reached.
- *Training and experience in negotiation*   Better trained and experienced participants result in a more effective process.
- *The dynamics of the process*   People are not machines that function at peak effectiveness all of the time. Personality clashes, feeling unwell, pressures and stress form other aspects of their job or outside of work and can all have an effect on the dynamics of a negotiation process.

There are many different approaches to a negotiation and Fisher and Ury (1986) termed their approach 'principled negotiations'. This model requires negotiators to concentrate on four elements within a negotiation process:

- *Separate the people from the problem*   It is the issues at the core of the negotiations that are important, not the people negotiating them. Personal likes, dislikes, friendships, etc. can all get in the way of the process and prevent a clear focus on the issues to be negotiated. By

negotiation

forcing attention away from the individual and onto the issues, the negotiators should be able to focus on creating solutions.

- *Focus on interests, not positions* All parties will have interests relevant to the negotiation but these may not be reflected in their stated positions at the start of the process. For example, a trade union may demand a 10 per cent pay rise, longer holidays, and an improved pension scheme (their position). But their actual 'interests' (which are unstated but underpin the claim) may include having secure, well paid, and interesting jobs, with the availability of flexible working and family friendly policies in order to enhance the quality of their working life and the work-life balance opportunities for staff. By identifying these 'interests' and focussing on them it should encourage mutually acceptable real benefits to the long-term benefit to all parties to be created.
- *Invent options for mutual gain* In business (particularly the HR field) there is usually no need to adopt a win-lose approach to negotiation as it is almost always possible to create options for mutual gain. For example, in negotiations over pay, the discussions need not only be about profit and cost. It is possible that an increase in pay can be self-funding to a significant degree if conditions regarding flexibility, productivity, and co-operation can be met.
- *Insist on objective criteria* The measures of success or failure need to be judged against objective criteria. This aspect of the negotiation process is about answering the question about whether or not the deal was a good one. 'Objective criteria' means it should be evaluated independent of the interests of one side or the other.

The authors recognise that not every negotiator will follow or subscribe to these principles and they identify a number of tactics for dealing with such situations. These include knowing what the alternatives to an agreement might be.

See also: contract of employment; downsizing, reorganisation, outsourcing and redundancy; employee relations and conflict; interview; performance appraisal; reward management; trade union/employee representation

key concepts in human resource management

194

BIBLIOGRAPHY

Beardwell, I., Holden, L. and Claydon, T. (2004) *Human Resource Management: A Contemporary Approach* (4th edition). Harlow: Pearson Education.

Fisher, R. and Ury, W. (1986) *Getting to Yes: Negotiating Agreement Without Giving In.* New York: Penguin.

Torrington, D., Hall, L. and Taylor, S. (2005) *Human Resource Management* (6th edition). Harlow: Pearson Education.

Organisational Culture

Culture is a difficult term to define in ways that are clear and unambiguous. One way of defining it is in terms of the acquired and conventionally accepted ways of thinking and behaving among a group or society. Another often quoted definition is the way we do things around here. However it is defined, culture reflects the ideologies, shared philosophies, values, beliefs, assumptions, attitudes, expectations, and norms of an organisation.

Schein (1985) identified six dimensions that he suggested reflected the composition of culture within an organisational context. These are:

- *Behavioural regularities*   The regular, routine patterns of behaviour in a particular context.
- *Dominant values*   The beliefs held by specific groups and organisations.
- *Norms*   The general patterns of behaviour that all members of a particular group would be expected to follow.
- *Rules*   Unlike norms which may be unwritten and informal, these represent specific instructions and requirements about what must be done in specific circumstances and which direct much human behaviour at work.
- *Philosophy*   These represent the underlying beliefs that people hold about human beings and how they function in relation to work.
- *Climate*   The physical location, design, and layout of buildings together with the facilities within them and the style of management, dress codes, etc. are among the factors that all help to create the atmosphere or climate within the organisation.

Trice and Beyer (1984) identified culture as a way of providing common meaning for a particular group containing four categories:

1   *Company communications*   This provides the mechanism by which culture is described, communicated, and reinforced across time. It

includes the stories, myths, legends, folk tales, and symbols that constantly circulate.

2   *Company practice*   This reflects the culture in operation by demonstrating and reinforcing its importance. It includes the rites, rituals, and ceremonial activity that demonstrate the cultural norms and values.

3   *Common language*   This category reflects the learning and use of a common language by a particular group. This serves to separate group members from non-members, as well as providing 'local' knowledge (a context specific, form of communication).

4   *Physical culture*   This reflects the features that represent the tangible nature of a culture. It includes the artefacts and layout associated with the way that the business wants to portray itself.

Johnson et al. (2005) developed the foregoing ideas further into what they termed a cultural web. They proposed that each of the following elements combined and interacted to create this web forming the particular culture in any specific context:

- *Routine behaviour*   This reflects the normal patterns of behaviour in a particular context which determine how people behave towards each other, superiors, subordinates, and customers, etc.
- *Rituals*   These reflect the formal and informal events and activities that the organisation and individuals choose to celebrate and thus emphasise what it values.
- *Stories*   These reflect the antics of heroes, villains and other personalities that reflect aspects of the culture of the group who perpetuate the stories.
- *Symbols*   The logo, uniforms, status symbols, etc. used by an organisation all reflect aspects of the way that the organisation or group want to be seen by those inside and outside.
- *Power structure*   The way that power is exercised and by whom can differ depending on the actual culture in place.
- *Control systems*   What is controlled and how it is measured reflect what the organisation values and sees as important.
- *Organisational structure*   This reflects who reports to who and how activity is compartmentalised and directly shapes behaviour in the consequent pattern of activity.
- *Paradigm*   This reflects the overarching element of the web in that it seeks to describe the way that the organisation goes about what it does and why it does this.

One of the most frequently quoted models' culture was explained by Handy (1993). It offered four distinct forms or type of culture:

- *Power culture* Typically everything revolves around a key person. All important decisions are made by the key person and they exercise absolute authority. Common examples of this type of culture would be found in small organisations run by an owner/manager
- *Role culture* Typically this type of culture is based on the existence of procedure and rule frameworks to guide and direct all aspects of the business. It is hierarchy and bureaucracy that dictate how this type of organisation functions.
- *Task culture* This type of organisation depends for success on the expertise of the individuals within it. Typically project-based organisations such as consultancy and civil engineering would adopt this cultural framework.
- *Person culture* Based on an individual but this should not be confused with the power culture. The person culture allows different people to become the key player depending on the circumstances. A consultancy practice and barristers' chambers are used by Handy to illustrate this cultural framework.

Deal and Kennedy (1982) identified the existence of what they termed a strong culture – one where almost all group members supported it or one based on the deeply held values and beliefs of a significant proportion of the group. A weak culture by comparison was not strongly supported or rooted in the value systems of the group. They identified four categories of culture based on the approach to risk and the speed of feedback coming from the environment on decision making (each could be strong or weak in nature):

- *Work and play hard culture* Often found in cohesive groups that 'attack' both work and play enthusiastically. This category would typically be found in organisations with low risk but rapid feedback loops, for example, hotels or fast food restaurants.
- *Process culture* Focussed on systems and procedures as success depends on attention to detail. Found in low-risk environments with a slow feedback response, for example local government and large insurance companies.
- *Macho culture* Often found in situations involving high risk and rapid feedback. Success comes from the ability of the key person to achieve

across the full range of business activity. Might be found in small entrepreneurial organisations and specialised consultancies.

- *Bet your company culture* The focus is on the technical skill to 'get it right' within overall guidelines. The risks can be very high but the feedback is slow in coming. For example, spotting the latest trend in computer or gaming technology far enough in advance so that the hardware and software are developed in time to 'ride the wave'. In this culture it is the very survival of the company that is being gambled on getting 'it' right.

Culture is generally thought of as a unifying or integrating mechanism binding people together within an organisation. However, it is also possible to see culture as a differentiating feature within organisational life. Organisations comprise many different groups – departments, work teams, friendship groups, social groups, professional groups, and so on. Therefore it is perhaps overly simplistic to talk of a single culture in an organisation. Perhaps it would be more accurate to describe an organisation as consisting of a number of cultures that will have a number of common features, but also some differences that somehow combine, coalesce, and integrate to form an overarching culture for the organisation. From this perspective it becomes necessary to consider the possibilities of disunity and even conflict as part of the cultural reality. Some cultures might even be hostile to the dominant culture. For example, following a company take-over individuals may feel that their previous achievements and contribution are being undervalued in the new company and this can cause resentment to develop. This can in turn become self-reinforcing in that it isolates these individuals from the new dominant groups and also increases the perceived value of belonging to a counterculture among the disaffected.

It has been argued that culture cannot be managed/changed easily because it forms an integral part of an organisation's fabric. Alternatively the following six-step programme has been proposed as a means by which to change culture:

- Identify the existence of any external forces that would encourage a culture change.
- Identify the existence of any internal forces or individuals that would encourage a culture change.
- Identify any significant pressure on the business that would encourage a culture change.

- Identify key stakeholders, champions and opinion formers and ensure that they buy-into the need for a culture change.
- Develop the means and processes for implementing the new culture.
- Develop and implement a range of action plans intended to change the old culture.

There are a number of difficulties with this model of culture change. It is based on a rather simplistic view of what culture is; it takes no account of multiple cultures (counter- and sub-cultures for example); power; politics and control mechanisms are also ignored within the specific organisational context. Perhaps culture could be 'manipulated' or 'nudged' or 'pushed' in certain directions over time. However, it could also be amenable to major and significant change in times of crisis when survival is at risk – which provides a reason to concentrate the attention and level of co-operation of everyone on saving the organisation and jobs. Consequently, managers (guided by HR specialists) should take an active interest in this and the degree to which it could be created in a way that makes the running of a business easier and more effective. Easier and more effective in this context means that the acceptance and internalisation of management's intentions, goals, and ways of thinking by employees would reduce the cost of operations because the entire organisation would be focussed on delivering customer satisfaction in the ways envisaged by management. However, that does assume that management knows best – a big assumption!

See also: benchmarking; bullying and harassment; discrimination, diversity and equality; employee empowerment and engagement; high performance working; learning organisation; organisational development (OD) and change; quality of working life and the psychological contract

BIBLIOGRAPHY

Deal, T. and Kennedy, A. (1982) *Corporate Cultures: The Rights and Rituals of Corporate Life*. Harmondsworth: Penguin.

Handy, C.B. (1993) *Understanding Organisations* (4th edition). Harmondsworth: Penguin.

Johnson, G., Scholes, K. and Whittington, R. (2005) *Exploring Corporate Strategy* (7th edition). Harlow: Prentice Hall.

Schein, E.H. (1985) *Organisational Culture and Leadership*. San Francisco, CA: Jossey-Bass.

Trice, H.M. and Beyer, J.M. (1984) 'Studying organisational cultures through rites and rituals', *Academy of Management Review*, 9: 653–669.

Organisational Development (OD) and Change

> *Organisational development, usually referred to as simply 'OD', is an approach to dealing with change which incorporates aspects of culture, working atmosphere, employee commitment, conflict, power, and politics in seeking to achieve organisational effectiveness for all stakeholders. As an academic discipline, it utilises ideas from the social psychology, sociology, psychology, and anthropology disciplines. It reflects the systematic application of behavioural science to the planned development of organisational strategies, structures, and processes for improving effectiveness.*

Cummings and Worley (2005) identified five features common to an OD intervention that differentiate it from other change management approaches. These are:

1 OD applies to changes in the strategy, structure, and/or processes of an entire system, such as an organisation or work group.
2 OD is based on the application and transfer of behavioural science knowledge and practice and is distinguished by its ability to transfer such knowledge and skill so that the system is capable of carrying out more planned change in the future.
3 OD is concerned with managing planned change in a flexible manner that can be revised as new information is gathered.
4 OD involves both the creation and the reinforcement of change by institutionalising change.
5 OD is orientated to improving organisational effectiveness by:

   o helping members of the organisation to gain the skills and knowledge necessary to solve problems by involving them in the change process, and
   o by promoting high performance including financial returns, high quality products and services, high productivity, continuous improvement, and a high quality of working life.

Robbins (1998) identified five key values that underpinned an OD intervention as:

1   That an organisation's culture should be based on trust, openness and mutual support for members.
2   That individuals should be treated with respect and dignity within the organisation.
3   That authority and control based only on position within the hierarchy are not usually effective.
4   That the people likely to be effected by change should be involved in its design and implementation.
5   That problems and conflict should be surfaced and addressed, not hidden or ignored.

The strands of theory and practice within OD include:

- *Encounter groups*   These are small unstructured groups of people who meet and, without a formal leader, given purpose or agenda, begin to explore aspects of the personal and interactive behaviour within the group, the intention being to create a basis through which members can connect with each other in a deeper and more meaningful way. Consequently they (the group) should be able to engage in participative change processes more effectively. This would be used as the first stage in a major teambuilding and group development project within a change programme.
- *Process consultation*   This is based on the use of an external consultant to help organisational members better understand problems and to facilitate a process allowing them to find acceptable, workable solutions. This is different to the usual approach to consultancy which is based on the consultant providing technical expertise in relation to the 'problem'. In process consultation the people experiencing the 'problem' are regarded as the 'experts' and the role of the consultant is to facilitate a process of understanding, learning, and ultimately, resolution.
- *Attitude and opinion surveys*   These provide a way for organisations to find out what employees think about their jobs, management, and working in the company. They can be designed and used in such a way that learning opportunities and improved understanding are created about what needs to be changed, as well as how, why, and in what way, so that it is dealt with more effectively.
- *Action research*   This reflects an active and iterative approach to learning about a situation and changing it. Action research is an

approach based upon a cyclical process that begins with research into an identified problem or situation. This in turn leads to the creation of conclusions and action plans in relation to the target 'problem'. Opportunities for further study and problem solving would be identified during the research process and also as a result of the implementation of the conclusions, which would begin the cycle again.

- *Planned approach to OD interventions* This reflects a seven-stage process as follows. However, it may be that in practice it is not a simple linear process from beginning to end as reflected in these seven stages. For example, several iterations of stages 2, 3 and 4 of the model might be necessary in order to impact on the 'real' problem. The stages are:

  1 Scouting – this stage involves exploration between the client and consultant on the nature and scope of any proposed intervention.
  2 Entry – this stage involves creation of agreement and support among all the parties involved for a consultancy relationship and involvement in the process.
  3 Diagnosis – this stage involves identification of the problem and the objectives as understood by the client, together with identification of the resources available to deal with the project.
  4 Planning – this stage involves the objectives for the intervention and how it will be undertaken to be identified. Areas of resistance to the change will also be identified at this stage.
  5 Action – this stage reflects the implementation of the actions determined in the previous phase to be achieved.
  6 Stabilisation and evaluation – this stage reflects the 'fixing' or 'locking' of the new state into the usual behaviour and other routines of the organisation and its members.
  7 Termination – this stage represents the closing down of the OD project and the withdrawal of the consultant.

- *Quality of working life* The quality of working life (QWL) movement has a number of features that can be of use, including the use of teamwork and seeking the improvement of interpersonal and intergroup relationships.
- *Strategic change* Strategy (or what is sometimes called vision) generally seeks to integrate the resources and efforts of an organisation into a common, unified and planned purpose. The change aspect of strategy arises as a result of the need to integrate activity into a cohesive whole. This can involve the need to change the structure, job design, systems, or operating procedures in order to achieve the cohesion required by a strategy.

OD has been criticised for a number of reasons, for example it assumes that incrementalism provides the best way to achieve change (by relatively small, frequent changes). However, not all situations will allow the time for this – a crisis situation might require an immediate and major change be undertaken. For example, a company faced with the unexpected appearance of a new competitor offering an improved product or service may not have the time or financial resources to wait for an OD approach to identify a solution. Also individuals or groups may resist any change (even if they have been involved) for many reasons, perhaps as a consequence of being disadvantaged by the outcome. Individuals might not be able to influence the analysis of situations or the direction of change even if they are actively involved in the process and might seek to slow down or disrupt the process itself. Involvement can expose but not necessarily solve problems. Compromise may only identify the best-worst option and so not fully resolve the underlying problems and seeking to persuade those with strongly opposing views may only serve to crystallise attitudes and harden a resolve to resist. A weakness in the traditional OD approach to change is a lack of any reference to power as an integral part of the process. Recognising this, Schein (1969) made several suggestions for including power and politics in OD interventions: for example, identifying powerful stakeholders and gaining their support and attempting small projects first to gain credibility. Stephenson (1985) suggested the following tactics be included in a change process which should minimise the risk of power or politics having an adverse impact on it:

- *Simple first* Begin with small projects that are more likely to succeed. That should create confidence in the process and encouragement to tackle more complex issues.
- *Adaptation* Flexibility in modifying changes during the change process and based on unfolding knowledge, understanding, and experience (an action research-type approach) improves the chances of success.
- *Incorporation* The incorporating of 'things' from an existing situation into a changed situation provides a degree of continuity and stability. That in turn reduces stress and threat levels and so is likely to increase the level of acceptance.
- *Structure* Attitudes can influence the structural aspects of change, or vice versa. So try to change attitudes before a change is introduced, say through training. Conversely, it is also possible to change attitudes through making physical changes to the way that work is done.

- *Ceremony* Management can send very clear messages on what behaviour and attitudes about change are valued and rewarded as a result of the way that such events are recognised.
- *Assurances* Whatever assurances and guarantees that managers provide about the consequences of a planned change it is the previous experience of employees about these that will influence future responses.
- *Timescales* It is often argued that the more time is available for making change the more likely it is to be successful – because it allows for more thinking and planning, etc. Conversely, crisis situations can become a focus for successful change as these concentrate the minds of everyone on what is important – usually a continued income and employment.
- *Support* Change often causes people to feel stressed and under threat as a result of losing control, the familiar, having to acquire new ways of working and skills, etc. The provision of support during these times can help people make the necessary adjustments and also minimise the level of resistance.
- *Transition* Changing from what has existed to what will exist means that there are three different contexts active at the same time: the old situation, the desired situation, and the transitional situation. All three will overlap during the change and until the new situation becomes firmly established this can create uncertainty, ambiguity, and complexity – all of which must be managed.
- *Unexpected* Preparation for the unexpected can be done and not all are hostile to change.

The CIPD (2007) identified some key areas for HR involvement in change projects as being:

- Involvement at the initial stage in the project team.
- Advising project leaders on skills available within the organisation – identifying any skills gaps, training needs, new posts, new working practices, etc.
- Balancing out the narrow/short-term goals with broader strategic needs.
- Assessing the impact of change in one area/department/site on another part of the organisation.
- Being used to negotiating and engaging with various stakeholders.
- Understanding stakeholder concerns to anticipate problems.
- Understanding the appropriate medium of communication to reach various groups.
- Helping people cope with change, performance management, and motivation.

See also: benchmarking; employee empowerment and engagement; employee relations and conflict; high performance working; knowledge management; learning organisation; management development; organisational culture; performance management; quality of working life and the psychological contract; teamworking

BIBLIOGRAPHY

CIPD (2007) 'Change management'. *Factsheet*. Available at www.cipd.co.uk (last accessed January 2009).
Cummings, T.G. and Worley, C.G. (2005) *Organisation Development and Change* (8th edition). Mason, OH: South-Western Publishing.
Robbins, S.P. (1998) *Organisational Behaviour: Concepts, Controversies and Applications* (8th edition). Englewood Cliffs, NJ: Prentice Hall.
Schein, E.H. (1969) *Process Consultation: Its Role in Organisational Development*. Reading, MA: Addison-Wesley.
Stephenson, T. (1985) *Management: A Political Activity*. Basingstoke: Macmillan.

Organisational Structure

> *The most basic definition of organisational structure is that it is the way in which the departments, functions and sections are arranged to allow the organisation to achieve its business objectives. Traditional approaches to structure emphasised the task aspects of the work being undertaken in the organisation intended to reinforce the hierarchical control and segmented responsibilities.*

The most common forms of organisational structure found include:

- *Entrepreneurial structures* Typically found in a small organisation with the owner usually playing an active and dominant role in running it. In this form of organisation, management and decision making are largely inseparable from the personal preferences of the owners.
- *Product-based structures* In such organisations the product or service produced becomes the focus for the arrangement and 'organisation' of

the people and other resources. In a large organisation each product type would form a separate unit within the overall business. Product-based structures are advantageous when there is a need to get close to customers and the company offers a range of products, each serving a specific market.

- *Process-based structures* Sometimes called the functional approach, such organisations would typically be 'organised' according to the manufacturing or service activities involved. For example, a university would 'organise' around academic and other departments such as business, chemistry, physics, maths, etc., personnel, finance, accommodation and estates.

- *Matrix and project-based structures* The matrix approach represents an attempt to integrate both functional and product responsibilities into people's activities. For example, on large-scale construction projects civil engineers would report professionally to the chief civil engineer for their company (in head office) whilst reporting on a day-to-day basis to the manager in charge of the construction project. The possible difficulties with the matrix structure include:

  o Complexity of operation – it could add complexity to an existing complex organisational structure, particularly in very large organisations.
  o Split accountabilities – with more than one boss and split accountabilities involved it can be difficult for managers and employees to determine priorities.
  o Increased political opportunity – it becomes easier for an employee to play one boss off against the other or for a boss to 'blame' someone else when things go wrong.
  o Lack of clear focus – split responsibilities allow for a lack of focus, possibly resulting in things not being done as or when they should be.
  o Requires specific skills – working for more than one boss increases the pressure on individuals and they need resilience, more skills, appropriate personality characteristics, and training to be able to work in this type of environment.
  o Change process – developing a matrix structure will involve changing from a more traditional model for most organisations. The change together with the time and resources required can create difficulties in their own right.

- *Flexible and flatter organisations* The flexible firm is based on the idea that an organisation should be capable of easily adapting itself to the dynamic circumstances that it will experience. That is extensively covered in the flexibility section (p. 124) and so will not be developed here. As an approach it has led many trade unions to talk of the increasing casualisation of work. However, employees (perhaps with key or readily transferable skills or simply because of personal preference) can benefit from the associated freelance (or multi-employer) working.

Flatter organisations are those with relatively few levels between the most senior and the most junior jobs. The hope is that with fewer levels a closer focus on the needs of the customer and a speedier decision-making response can be achieved. In creating a flatter organisation more needs to be changed than the removal of layers of jobs. Removing levels and people and expecting those remaining to absorb the consequences is a recipe for disaster. Systems, procedures, and working practices need to be adapted to cope with and facilitate the new situation if it is to work successfully.

- *Virtual and federal organisations*   The virtual organisation means an organisation that is capable of delivering more than its resources would allow. For example, an alliance including suppliers, competitors and specialists in design, engineering, and finance could be used to achieve a specific outcome that could not be achieved by any individual member but from which each would ultimately benefit. One risk in this type of approach is that of providing potential competitors with contacts, commercially sensitive information, or expertise. Also, a failure to manage the relationship effectively could lead to the collapse of a venture. The federal organisation is the combining of separate organisations under a common identity for a specific purpose.

- *International organisations*   There is a wide range of different types of international activity all of which can influence the type of structure adopted. For example, there is franchising, acting as an agent for a type of product or service, direct or joint investment, and the multi-national organisation. There are a number of ways in which international activities can be incorporated into the organisation. For example:

  o An international division – the creation of a separate business unit within the company.
  o Product-based business units – the grouping together of international activity by product type.
  o Geographic business units – each geographic location would contain either a product, process, or some other structural arrangement.
  o Functional structure – this approach retains the functional structure irrespective of location.

- *The holding company* This framework (in pure form) is one in which the group head office is a company which owns (fully or partly) a number of separate businesses (subsidiaries) which are companies in their own right. Technically each subsidiary could adopt any one of the frameworks described in this section. In its basic form a holding company acts as an investment fund or a banker to the group. It would look to acquire businesses that could create a synergy within the group and would divest itself of those companies that did not fit or deliver a profit potential.

It was writers such as Weber (1947) and Fayol (1916) who first began to articulate ideas about structure and its form and significance for the people who worked in them. Weber wrote about bureaucracy. He compared the benefits achievable through bureaucracy to be as those gained through machine-based manufacturing. He recognised the potentially deleterious effect on the workers of the approach, but he thought that it was a necessary state of affairs that resulted from the need for organisational performance. Fayol identified a number of principles that he suggested impacted on the structure of an organisation which later writers developed into classical management theory. These included the division of work into compartments and the unity of command, principles which are still relevant today. Kanter (1983) described segmentalism as the 'boxes' within bureaucratic organisations. By comparison she suggested that successful organisations demonstrated an entrepreneurial spirit. The structural dilemma emerges because classical design creates task-based efficiency through segmentation, often on the basis of function. But as a consequence of segmentation there is a need for activity and effort to be integrated in order to deliver the whole product or service.

Bureaucracy seeks this through procedure and work routines, but at the cost of responsiveness. Innovative organisations seek to deal with this dilemma by adopting other structural approaches.

Bolman and Deal (1994: 95) suggested that organisational structure can be considered as part of a theatrical performance because it represents, 'an arrangement of space, lighting, props, and costumes to make the organisational drama vivid and credible to its audience'. The authors argued that the structure of an organisation creates a stage for performances to be carried out for the benefit of particular audiences. It provides the framework for the actors (employees) to deliver a controlled performance within a defined script (involving procedures and roles). The significance of structure from this perspective is that it provides a framework for how the organisation wishes itself to be understood by those who come into contact with it as the result of how it 'organises' the roles and actions of those within it.

The contingency model (of structure) suggests that a broad range of factors influence the structural arrangement of an organisation. It provides a useful way of explaining the diversity in organisational design that exists in practice. The model suggests that the external and internal forces acting on the organisation are interpreted by managers and the results of that understanding would then be filtered through capability, etc. The result of that process would produce a structure specific to that organisation and its context at a particular point in time. The main influencing factors in this approach are:

- *External contingency factors*   For example, the activities of competitors, the industry in which the organisation operates, the location, will all impact on the structural arrangements adopted.
- *Internal contingency factors*   For example, the knowledge base, the level of bureaucracy, the production technology, and the size of the organisation.
- *Managerial perceptions and objectives*   For example the future direction and strategy of the organisation, the scale and location of operations, the culture and management style.
- *Organisational capability, will, and politics*   The organisation needs to have the capability and will to achieve its desired objectives in a particular way. The political realities within the organisation must also be taken into account when considering structural arrangements.

Quinn and Cameron (1983) proposed that an organisation goes through four lifecycle phases over time:

- *Entrepreneurial phase*   This first phase begins with the creation and early years of an organisation and would be typified by little formal control and an emphasis on survival.
- *Collectivity phase*   With growth, this phase emerges when it becomes more difficult for the owner/manager to control all aspects of the business and delegation/functional development becomes necessary.
- *Formalisation phase*   This phase occurs when the organisation becomes mature, stable, and predictable in its activities and processes. This would be achieved through the development of rules, procedures, meetings, and improved communication.
- *Elaboration phase*   This phase occurs when the organisation recognises the need to fight stagnation. It would seek change that was aimed at the

encouragement of innovation and an increase in motivation and performance, etc.

Cameron et al. (1988) added a fifth to that list:

- *Organisational decline* Two forms are suggested: absolute and relative decline. Relative decline is a result of stagnation and lethargy arising from the organisation's passivity towards the competitive environment, allowing the markets and competitors to move ahead of the organisation.

Whetten (1980) identified four options for dealing with possible organisational decline:

- Generating new ways of interacting with the market involving a continual adjustment of the organisation in retaining its position. This should be the most effective of the options identified.
- Reacting by taking the view that decline is a temporary change and that existing approaches' procedures can meet the needs of a situation if control is exercised more thoroughly.
- Defending by attempting to match the organisation to the new situation, usually through cutbacks across a broad range of costs.
- Preventing by seeking to influence the environment, perhaps through involving mergers and acquisitions, marketing, PR and lobbying initiatives.

See also: benchmarking; downsizing, reorganisation, outsourcing and redundancy; employee empowerment and engagement; expatriation and international management; flexibility; job, job analysis and job design; learning organisation; organisational development (OD) and change; strategic HRM

BIBLIOGRAPHY

Bolman, L.G. and Deal, T.E. (1994) 'The organisation as theatre', in H. Tsoukas (ed.), *New Thinking in Organisational Behaviour: From Social Engineering to Reflective Action.* Oxford: Butterworth–Heinemann.

Cameron, K.S., Sutton, R.I. and Whetten, D.A. (1988) *Readings in Organisational Decline: Frameworks, Research and Prescriptions.* Cambridge, MA: Ballinger.

Fayol, H. (1916) General and Industrial Management, trans. C. Storrs (1949). London: Pitman.

Kanter, R.M. (1983) *The Change Masters.* London: Allen & Unwin.

Quinn, R.E. and Cameron, K. (1983) 'Organisational life cycles and some shifting criteria of effectiveness: some preliminary evidence', *Management Science,* 29: 33–51.

Weber, M. (1947) The Theeory of Social and Economic Organization, trans. M.A. Henderson and T. Parsons. New York: Oxford University Press.

Whetten, D.A. (1980) 'Sources, responses and effects of organisational decline', in J. Kimberly and R. Miles (eds), *The Organisational Life Cycle.* San Francisco, CA: Jossey Bass.

Performance Appraisal

This reflects an assessment process that seeks to assess the overall capabilities and potential of an individual or team based on past and current work behaviour and performance. This can be measured against a number of criteria, but is usually intended to address an employee's achievements compared to what they were expected to achieve.

For some jobs it is relatively easy to measure performance, but for others it can be very difficult. For example, an employee working on a machine-paced assembly line will deliver a good performance if they keep up with the pace of the line. On the other hand, how can the performance of a chief executive be measured when it can take several years for the results of their efforts to become apparent? Bratton and Gold (2003: 251) identified a number of purposes for the use of appraisal, including:

- To improve individual performance.
- To improve motivation and morale.
- To clarify expectations and reduce ambiguity about performance achievement.
- To determine the size of reward.
- To identify training and development requirements and opportunities.
- To improve communication between boss and subordinate.
- To select people for promotion and career development.
- To aid career management.
- To identify any need for counselling.
- To identify a need for disciplinary action.
- To set goals and targets.

However performance appraisal is done it involves a review of past behaviour and achievements. Whilst that is necessary to consider the causes of good and bad outcomes, its only real value is to seek improvement in future performance. In essence the purpose of any form of performance appraisal simple, and it is to find answers to the following questions:

- What went well?
- What went not so well (or badly)?
- Why?
- What can be done to maintain and encourage those behaviours that reflect good performance?
- What can be done to improve future performance and contribution in those areas where weakness or problems have been identified?

Although the underlying purpose of a performance appraisal appears simple based on the above list, life is very rarely that simple or easy. For example, some of the questions that may arise as a result of the above list include:

- What does 'went well' mean and how does this relate to performance? Who decides – the line manager may have a different view of what went well compared to a customer or colleague of the individual being appraised?
- The same point can be applied to the question about what 'went not so well' means and how that relates to performance?
- What if the employee being appraised does not agree with the appraiser's view about their performance?
- Can employees be expected to deliver good performance all day every day?
- Is a mistake the same as poor performance?
- What level of performance does the basic wage or salary entitle the employer to expect/require from the employee?
- If managers, other employees, colleagues, customers or suppliers disrupt or cause changes or problems in the work activities of the appraisee should this reflect on the assessment of the performance of the appraisee?
- Given that virtually all employees work within a structured system of interconnected work activity, can the performance of any individual be meaningfully assessed?
- Does the performance of an individual actually matter as long as they play an effective part within their work group and the group overall performs effectively?

The CIPD (2008) suggest, 'The performance appraisal or review is essentially an opportunity for the individual and those concerned with their performance – most usually their line manager – to get together to engage in a dialogue about the individual's performance, development and the support required from the manager. It should not be a top down process or an opportunity for one person to ask questions and the other to reply. It should be a free flowing conversation in which a range of views are exchanged'. The same source identifies five key elements of the performance appraisal as:

1 *Measurement* Performance should be assessed against agreed targets and objectives.
2 *Feedback* The start of the process involves providing the individual with information on what the manager regards as the key aspects of their performance and progress.
3 *Positive reinforcement* There should be an emphasis on what was done well and constructive criticism about what might be improved.
4 *Exchange of views* The discussion should encourage a frank and open exchange of views about what has happened, the causes of it, how appraisees can improve their performance, the support they need from their managers to achieve this and their aspirations for their future career.
5 *Agreement* The aim should be to achieve a joint understanding and hopefully agreement between the boss and subordinate about what needs to be done to improve performance and to deal with any performance-related issues raised during the course of the discussion.

To that list of five, could be added another two:

6 It should also be expected that future performance expectations should be discussed along with times and dates for any review meetings to examine progress.
7 Obtain and review prior to a meeting the necessary records informing the assessment of performance and also during and after the meeting the creation of records about the appraisal process and the outcomes. For example:

   – *Objectives and targets* Information from the last appraisal about what these were and any subsequent information about their achievement and the reasons for failure or a low performance.
   – *Competence* Information about the job role and its requirements and also whether the individual is performing below, at, or above the requirements of it.

performance appraisal

- *Training* Information on any training the individual has under-taken during the review period and what training or development either the boss or individual thinks appropriate for the future.
- *Actions* Information on any actions that were deemed necessary during the last review period and the notes from any review or progress meetings and also in relation to any actions deemed necessary by either the boss or the individual during the next review period.

Although logically performance appraisal has benefits for both employer and employee as outlined above, there can often be problems and difficulties in realising those benefits. Snell and Bohlander (2007: 334–6) brought together a number of sources to identify the major causes for a lack of effectiveness in appraisal systems within organisations. These include:

- Inadequate preparation on the part of the manager.
- Objectives not clear to the employee.
- Manager may not be aware of full range of actual employee behaviours in carrying out their job.
- Performance standards may not be clear.
- Inconsistency in rating performance between raters assessing performance.
- Rating personality rather than performance.
- The presence of the halo or horns effect – this means that either one good (or one poor) result influences the judgement about all other activity.
- Tendency among managers to avoid discussing difficult or 'bad' news or conflict.
- Politics, personal preferences, and likes/dislikes influencing judgements.
- Lack of follow-up or support after appraisal meeting.
- Job description being out of date and/or unrealistic expectations about what the employee should be doing.
- Managers and/or employees feeling that little or no practical benefit will result from the process, perhaps as a result of previous failures to action or follow-up on outcomes.
- Some appraisal systems combine judge (determining the appraisal score) and helper (finding ways to improve future performance) roles for the manager and this cannot be easily achieved.

There are a number of possible people who will have a view on the performance of any individual in a work context. They can be combined to produce what is termed a 360 degree appraisal and include:

- Self.
- Superior.
- Peers.
- Suppliers.
- Customers.
- Subordinates.
- Team members.

The factors against which performance will be measured will vary depending upon a number of factors, including type of job, level of seniority, scheme design, and industry. However, a number of factors are found in many appraisal schemes including:

- Job knowledge and capabilities – ability to perform all the duties associated with the job.
- Productivity – level of work outputs.
- Performance against targets – achievement of objectives previously set.
- Quality of work – level of consistency in output quality and attention to detail.
- Adaptability/flexibility of the worker – ability to cope with change and a wide range of work activity.
- Interaction with colleagues – communication and team working.
- Attendance and time-keeping record.
- Attitude to work – level of commitment, motivation and enthusiasm.
- Judgement and use of resources – the planning and organising of work.
- Management – leadership and related qualities.
- Originality of thinking and initiative in problem solving.

There is a wide range of methods that can be used separately or in combination to appraise performance including:

- *Rating scales* These approaches involve the predetermination of a number of factors against which performance will be evaluated and the identification of a 'quantity' measure of performance for each one.

- *Behaviourally anchored rating scale (BARS)*   Similar to standard rating scales but based on factors that reflect behaviours identified as necessary for the achievement of high performance in the job in question.
- *Ranking and forced distribution methods*   These seek to compare the performance achievement between all the employees being considered. In its simplest form, ranking seeks to provide a list of all employees from the highest performer to the lowest performer. Forced distribution seeks to categorise all employees into performance bands based on set proportions in each band.
- *Critical incidents*   Assessing performance using this approach requires the boss to identify important events (critical incidents) that demonstrate effective and ineffective performance by the individual. These would then form the basis of the discussion about performance during the appraisal review.
- *Essay approach*   This approach simply presents the boss with a blank sheet of paper and requires them to describe in their own words the performance of the subordinate. This would then be discussed with the individual during the appraisal meeting.
- *Management by objectives*   This approach involves the identification of key tasks, projects and other objectives that the individual has to achieve during the review period. At the end of that period the achievement of each objective would be used to identify the performance implications.

See also: assessment/development centre; behaviour management; benchmarking; career management; competency; employee development; employee empowerment and engagement; high performance working; incentive schemes; management development; performance management; succession planning and talent management

BIBLIOGRAPHY

Bratton, J. and Gold, J. (2003) *Human Resource Management: Theory and Practice* (3rd edition). Basingstoke: Palgrave Macmillan.

CIPD (2008) 'Performance appraisal', *Factsheet* (revised January 2008). Available at www.cipd.co.uk (last accessed February 2009).

Snell, S. and Bohlander, G. (2007) *Human Resource Management* (International student edition). Mason, OH: Thomson South-Western.

Performance Management

The term 'performance management' refers to any management process intended to control, direct, and increase the performance of employees working in an organisation. More directly it is usually taken to refer to the system through which organisations set work goals, determine performance standards, provide performance feedback, determine training and development needs, and possibly distribute rewards related to performance.

The starting point for any discussion about performance management is to consider how much work it is reasonable to expect an employee to do under normal circumstances. This is not new as around 1890 F.W. Taylor developed what he termed 'scientific management' and introduced it into the companies in which he was working. His approach involved using work study techniques to identify what he termed the 'one best way' of carrying out a job. He then used incentive payments to motivate employees to follow the specified work method. His initial attempts were successful in that workers increased their earnings, productivity increased, and costs reduced. However, his success was short lived and he was dismissed by his employer as the level of unrest at the introduction of his methods grew. But in the longer term the use of work study techniques flourished, particularly in manufacturing organisations. They were in common use until the 1990s when technology largely reduced the role of people in factories to that of machine minders or forced them to work on machine-paced activities over which they had little direct output-related influence.

Motivation theory also has a significant part to play in performance management in that high performance can be directly equated with what is usually described as motivated behaviour. So the underlying intention of motivation theory is to explain what factors or forces act on the behaviour and attitudes of an individual in order to encourage them to deliver more output. For example, perhaps employees could be motivated to use training and development activities as a way of improving their performance. There are many motivation theories and it is not possible to explore them all in this section and so only one will be outlined in this context for illustrative purposes.

Locke (1968) developed what is called a goal theory model of motivation, based on the notion that people's objectives play a significant part in formulating their behaviour patterns. The model is based on a linear process that begins with the desires or wants that an individual has, which in turn convert into the goals that they set themselves. For example, I want a new car means that I set myself the goal of earning enough money to pay for one. That in turn means that I would be likely to focus my behaviour on ways to earn more money. If the organisation that I work for can provide me with the opportunity to earn additional money then I would be motivated to deliver what they wanted in return. Although the example used refers to the ability to earn extra money that is not the only relevance that goal theory has for performance management. For example, it is the basis for many performance appraisal systems that offer employees who meet the performance standards expected by management the opportunity to be rewarded with a higher salary, career development opportunities, or promotion depending on the design of the system and links with other HR and career processes. There are a number of features associated with this model of motivation which have implications for the objective setting and feedback aspects of performance management and can significantly influence the likelihood of a positive outcome being achieved. These include:

- The more specific the objective the more likely it is to be achieved.
- The completion requirement (finish date) should be specific.
- Objectives that are difficult to achieve are more likely to be achieved than easy ones.
- Objectives should be SMART – standing for setting objectives that are specific, measurable, attainable, realistic and time bounded).
- The approach is based on what Lawler (1995) called the line of sight. The 'line of sight' begins with the effort delivered by the employee, leading to job performance; in turn leading to results being achieved; leading to those results being measured; and resulting in the reward being obtained by the employee.

The use of objectives in performance management does have limitations. For example, what level and form of subordinate involvement in setting objectives are necessary to achieve positive results? How is the behavioural impetus of the employee maintained once the objectives have been agreed and the performance period is underway? Some jobs are not amenable to objective setting (factory jobs for example). With an unpredictable and changeable operating environment being the norm these days, objectives might be expected to change frequently during a review period. This makes it difficult for individuals to maintain their performance on specific objectives over an extended period and hence might also impact on the rewards obtained. Objective setting is also largely an individual level process, but most tasks within an organisation will require groups of people to work co-operatively to achieve them. This too might be expected to impact on the achievement of objectives and the rewards obtained as a result of the performance delivered – for example, I might perform well but be let down by team colleagues or vice-versa.

Performance management is generally regarded as a continuous process rather than a discrete event which should be owned and driven by line managers rather than HR. The reasons that line manager ownership becomes significant can be understood when the full range of factors that impact on individual performance are identified. Some of the major areas of influence on performance include:

- *Corporate objectives*   Appropriate and clear corporate objectives that are well communicated throughout the organisation make it easier to deliver a high performance because everyone knows what is expected of them and the effect that their efforts have on the whole organisation.
- *Clarity of personal objectives*   If the objectives to be achieved at a personal level are not clear then employees will not know what they are trying to achieve and will not be able to deliver them with any certainty or regularity.
- *Work environment*   This refers to the physical circumstances in which the work takes place. For example, the level of technology, methods of work used, and equipment provided are obvious examples.
- *Management structure and style*   The approach adopted to how management of the business is to be organised and carried out can enhance or inhibit the contribution of employees and also enhance the level of performance achieved.
- *Organisational culture*   The type of culture that exists can either encourage high performance working or inhibit it.
- *Job design*   The ways that the work is organised into 'chunks' of activity called jobs can have a significant effect on the level of performance that can be achieved.
- *Competency*   The competencies that individual employees posses. This also reflects the resourcing processes along with its training and development provision.

- *Job performance* This relates to any differences between the meaning of performance within the performance management system and what it means to the employee.
- *Willingness to perform* Group influences, career prospects, rewards available and management style are among the influences that can impact on attitudes and the willingness of an individual to deliver performance to management's expectation.
- *Employee relations climate* The working relationships between employees and management can significantly impact on productivity and performance.
- *Intrinsic rewards* Intrinsic rewards are those that accrue to job holders as a direct result of the job itself. Well designed and organised jobs that provide employees with a sense of doing something of value and significance can also impact on performance.
- *Extrinsic rewards* These are generated from outside of the job itself, the most obvious example being bonus schemes in which pay is based on output.

Another approach to performance management found in many organisations over recent years is based on the concept of competencies often defined as the behavioural dimensions that affect job performance. This encourages personal development as the basis of future performance enhancement. The CIPD (2007) survey identified the most popular terms found in competency frameworks:

- Communication skills.
- People management.
- Team skills.
- Customer service skills.
- Results-orientation.
- Problem solving.

Another approach to performance management emerged from research carried out by the CIPD in association with the International Labour Organisation (part of the UN) which suggested that high performance working (and hence what should be managed in performance terms) should contain the following items (Stevens and Ashton, 1999):

- Market success (achievement of organisational objectives).
- Innovation in quality and customer satisfaction (product or service differentiation).

- Demonstrating a customer and continuous improvement focus.
- Widespread use of self-managed work teams.
- Viewing the workplace as a source of added value.
- Establishing clear links between training, development, and organisational objectives.
- Demonstrating support for organisational and individual learning.

See also: benchmarking; employee development; employee empowerment and engagement; employee relations and conflict; Human Resource Management (HRM) and personnel management (PM); high performance working; learning organisation; management development; organisational culture; performance appraisal; reward management; strategic HRM; total reward

BIBLIOGRAPHY

CIPD (2007) *Learning and Development: Annual Survey*. London: CIPD.
Lawler, E. (1995) 'The new pay: a strategic approach', *Compensation and Benefits Review*, July/August: 14–22.
Locke, E.A. (1968) 'Towards a theory of task motivation and incentives', *Organisational Behaviour and Human Performance*, 3: 157–189.
Stevens, J. and Ashton, D. (1999) 'Underperformance appraisal', *People Management*, Institute of Personnel and Development (15 July): 31–32.

Psychometric and Other Tests

Broadly speaking, psychometric tests allow the identification and measurement of particular characteristics (such as ability, aptitude, attainment, intelligence or personality) of individuals. They provide systematic scoring and administration in order to allow comparison between the testee and the population against which the test has been validated.

The main categories of test include:

- *Personality*   Personality inventories seek to identify the characteristics and form of the individual's personality using a particular model or theory of what personality means.
- *Aptitude*   Aptitude tests seek to assess the individual's potential to learn to do a new task and so they attempt to predict a future value to, and performance in, the organisation.
- *Ability*   Ability tests seek to measure either general or particular types of intelligence. For example, numerical, verbal and logical reasoning; problem-solving skills; the ability to accurately and quickly identify mistakes.

The CIPD (2008) suggested that organisations increasingly use psychometric testing to identify and develop future leaders and to obtain information about predicted employee behaviour in different circumstances. It also suggests that the growth of technology has allowed online testing to become a very popular approach to the testing process. This approach is particularly useful in the recruitment of graduates or when high numbers of applicants are expected. Findings from the CIPD annual resourcing survey indicate that the levels of psychometric test usage were:

- General ability tests – used by 41 per cent of responding organisations.
- Personality/aptitude questionnaires – used by 35 per cent of responding organisations.
- Specific skills tests – used by 48 per cent of responding organisations.

The argument for psychometric testing is that it can provide an independent means of assessing individual characteristics that should allow for a more effective match between the person and job. The argument against them is based on the idea that it is not possible to categorise human characteristics in such standardised terms and that to understand each individual a more holistic approach is necessary. There are many individual theories of personality. For example, Hans Eysenck (1965) developed what he called personality types based on two scales of introversion-extroversion and stable-unstable; Raymond Cattell (1965) developed the sixteen personality factor questionnaire (16PF) based around 16 personality factors that his research had suggested existed; the 'big five model' brought together many of the existing nomothetic ideas and identified the most common five characteristics as:

- *Extraversion*   Ranging from outgoing and assertive at one extreme, to reserved and quiet at the other.

- *Emotional stability* Ranging from secure and self-assured at one extreme, to anxious and depressed at the other.
- *Agreeableness* Ranging from co-operative and trusting at one extreme, to quarrelsome and hostile at the other.
- *Conscientiousness* Ranging from dependable and responsible at one extreme, to unreliable and disorganised at the other.
- *Openness to experience* Ranging from imaginative and broad-minded at one extreme, to disinterested and closed-minded at the other.

There are different ways of interpreting the results of psychometric tests. Some tests have predetermined results obtained form a range of populations and against which the performance of an individual taking the test can be compared. For example, a test may be used to measure a range of personality characteristics of successful chief executives. The purposes of such a test would be to determine the degree to which a particular candidate being considered for a chief executive position had the necessary or desirable personality characteristics to succeed in the job. Other tests (again personality tests will serve as an example) simply measure how much of a particular feature an individual possesses. For example, the scale of extraversion and introversion from the big five personality model outlined above would simply seek to measure where along that continuum the individual would fall. This reflects an attempt to build up a profile of the individual rather than compare them against population norms.

The development, administration and interpretation of test material are skilled jobs and require appropriate training. To that end the British Psychological Society has developed a range of test-related training certificates that can prepare people for those roles. The CIPD (2008) suggest that before using a test, users should consider:

- The intended purpose for test use and whether it is appropriate to use a test for that purpose. Essentially asking the question of whether the test will provide any relevant information that cannot be obtained (or is not already available) through other sources.
- Identify if there are sufficient trained resources available to carry out testing appropriately and effectively.
- Tests being used for selection purposes should be relevant to (and aligned with) the relevant job/person specification.
- Who will choose the tests to be used and on what basis will such decisions be made?
- The stage of a decision-making process that tests should be used needs to be determined.

- How any equal opportunities issues have been identified and dealt with.
- How test results will be used and the weight that they will be given in the decision-making process.
- What the policy on confidentiality relating to test results will be, who will have access to the results for what purpose, and how the results will be stored, all need to be identified.
- Company policy and provision for giving feedback to those who have been tested need to be clear and applied consistently.
- Ensure that test copyright obligations are complied with.

The same source also suggests that test administrators should ensure that individuals receive:

- Advance notice that they will be required to take tests.
- Advance notice of the duration of tests and whether this is significant in the interpretation of the results.
- Adequate time for them to make any practical arrangements to enable them to take the tests.
- Access to an appropriate environment free from interference in which to take the tests.
- Adequate information in advance about the requirements of each test they will be asked to complete, and the opportunity to raise any queries they have before the testing process begins.
- Information on the arrangements for feedback on test results.

The CIPD (2008) propose that before deciding which tests to use the following questions should be satisfactorily answered by the test providers:

- How reliable is the test and how consistent is it as a measure?
- How valid is the test and does it really identify the attributes or skills which the supplier claims?
- What evidence can suppliers provide that their tests do not unfairly disadvantage certain groups?
- Will the test seem appropriate to those taking it and what have previous reactions been to this test?
- Has the test been used effectively in similar circumstances?
- Are the norms provided by the supplier for comparative purposes up to date and appropriate for the user's requirements? Do the norm results apply to a sufficiently representative mix of occupations, gender, or ethnic groups to allow a fair comparison with the user's group?

- Is the method of test evaluation and scoring appropriate to the purpose for which the test will be used?

As should be obvious from the foregoing discussion, the basis of a psychometric test is that the responses given by the testee can be interpreted as an indication of an underlying characteristic. Therefore, a test is claimed to be valid if it measures what it claims to measure and the questions asked obtain responses that can discriminate between those people with the underlying characteristic and those without it. In practice a test needs to be valid and reliable in a number of ways, including:

- *Face validity*   Does the test appear to measure what it sets out to measure?
- *Predictive validity*   Does the test predict future events? A test would have predictive validity if high-scoring individuals were successful in the job for which the test was being used, while low-scoring individuals were not.
- *Construct validity*   Does the test relate to an underpinning theory related to the theme of the test?
- *Test/retest reliability*   Does the test produce the same score when it is administered on two different occasions?
- *Alternative form reliability*   Does the test produce the same results when it is presented in two or more different forms?
- *Split half reliability*   Does the test demonstrate internal consistency? Splitting the test into two halves (or trying different combinations of question) and comparing the results from each variation measures this form of reliability.

Psychometric tests go through a considerable development process before being accepted as usable for general application. The process of test development can be summarised as:

- The initial ideas for a test often emerge from a practical need, for example, assisting personnel managers to identify the most appropriate job applicants.
- The development of appropriate test items is a creative process. Many items generated will be unsuitable for any number of reasons, chiefly that they do not contribute to measuring the intended characteristics.
- The final forms of the test are developed and the administration arrangements designed. Attempts to prevent 'faking' an answer are built into the test.

- The 'standardisation' and 'norming' process – the populations for whom the test is intended will be identified and statistically valid test scores collected for them.
- At this stage, the data will be subjected to the various reliability and validity analyses described earlier. This is done in order to establish the credibility and value of the test for the users.

See also: assessment/development centre; career management; employee development; interview; management development; resourcing/retention; succession planning and talent management; teamworking

BIBLIOGRAPHY

Cattell, R. B. (1965) *The Scientific Analysis of Personality.* Harmondsworth: Penguin.
CIPD (2008) 'Psychological testing'. *Factsheet* (revised August 2008). Available at www.cipd.co.uk (last accessed February 2009).
Eysenck, H. J. (1965) *Fact and Fiction in Psychology.* Harmondsworth: Penguin.

Quality of Working Life and the Psychological Contract

Quality of working life represents an approach to management that seeks to enhance the dignity of workers, improve an organisation's culture, and also improve the physical and emotional wellbeing of employees. The psychological contract refers to the broad range of expectations in terms of rights, obligations, privileges, and duties which although not part of the formal contract of employment can have a major influence on the behaviour of both managers and employees.

QoWL activity tends to be concentrated into eight areas of working life experience (Walton, 1973):

- *Reward*   The pay and benefits obtained from work should be above the minimum needed for an acceptable standard of life and should also be equitable.
- *Health and safety*   The working environment should be designed and run in such a way that minimises and eliminates any adverse effects of danger and pollution that might impact on the physical, mental, and emotional state of employees.
- *Job design*   The design of jobs should enable the needs of the organisation for production and also the individual's desire for satisfying and interesting work.
- *Job security*   Employees should not have to work under the constant threat of a loss of their job, career, or income.
- *Social integration*   The elimination of anything that could lead to individuals not being able to associate with groups to which they belong. This implies the elimination of discrimination and individualism, with the encouragement of the formation of teams and social groups.
- *Protection of individual rights*   The introduction of procedures aimed at guaranteeing the rights of employees at work.
- *Respect for non-work activities*   Respect for the activities that people engage in outside of work. This includes a recognition of the impact that work activities might have on aspects of an individual's private life.
- *Social relevance of work*   This implies the adoption of initiatives by management to increase employee understanding of the organisation's objectives and of the importance of their part in the achievement of these.

QoWL initiatives have enjoyed mixed results, partly as a result of the complexity of the internal and external issues involved, for example the economic climate can either be hostile or favourable to the security of employment aspects of QoWL. The activities of other organisations can also influence employee perceptions about the actions of their own employer, for example, the arrival in an area of a new employer offering better terms and conditions of employment. The wider social environment and attitudes can also influence events. For example, the changing role of fathers in accepting the need to become more active in the upbringing of their children whilst at the same time managing their careers.

NFER (2009) have developed a psychometric test to measure QoWL. This can be completed either via a computer-based questionnaire or through a paper and pencil questionnaire. The questions in both forms of the test are designed to measure the strength of response in relation to the following seven scales. These scales the test developers found were most significant in reflecting the QoWL experienced by the respondent. The seven scales used within the test are:

- The type and level of support obtained from the immediate manager.
- Freedom from work-related stress.
- Salary and additional benefits.
- Job satisfaction, challenge, use of skills and autonomy.
- Relationships with work colleagues.
- Involvement and responsibility at work.
- Communication, decision making and job security.

The individual taking the test gives their answer based on a five-point scale (ranging from 'strongly agree' at one end of the range to 'strongly disagree' at the other). The responses are then input into the computer-based software which analyses them and produces a report of the scores for each scale of measurement, which in turn gives an overall description of the perceived quality of working life. The report produced highlights both areas for improvement and also those areas reflecting positive QoWL issues. The value of tests such as these is that they provide an opportunity to measure the degree to which QoWL is being achieved in the perceptions of the employees themselves, not just the extent to which managers think that it is being achieved. The potential problem and difficulty with them is the certainty that the scales of measurement actually reflect QoWL factors. There is no single set of factors that everyone would agree reflects the meaning of QoWL. For example, Ellis and Pompli (2002) identified a number of factors contributing to job dissatisfaction and quality of working life among nurses, including:

- Poor working environments.
- Resident aggression.
- Workload.
- Unable to deliver the quality of care preferred.
- Balance of work and family.
- Shiftwork.

- Lack of involvement in decision making.
- Professional isolation.
- Lack of recognition.
- Poor relationships with supervisor/peers.
- Role conflict.
- Lack of opportunity to learn new skills.

Some of the above factors are the same or broadly similar to those identified in the NFER scales above, but what of the others? Some could be put down to the particular context of nursing; others might reflect similar scales to those in the NFER but expressed differently; and others might be categorised differently in the NFER test. Consequently there is no easy answer to the question of which view of QoWL is correct, or even the most accurate!

The psychological contract reflects the unwritten but nevertheless powerful implicit expectations and obligations that come to exist between the employer and employee. In a real sense the psychological contract is what actually makes the organisation function on a day-to-day basis. Constant reference to the formal contract of employment, the company rule-book and procedure manual is impractical on a day-to-day basis and so the psychological contract provides a basis for a practical application of the rights and obligations of both parties in the working relationship. Both the formal and psychological contract are under constant pressure to change from both parties in the employment relationship. From the employee side there is the social and economic pressure to gain more 'rewards and benefits' in the widest sense of the term in order to enhance the standard and quality of life achieved as a result of being employed. From the employer side there exists the ever-present imperatives to maximise productivity and reduce cost in order to maximise profits and remain competitive. Guest and Conway (2002) suggest that the quality of the psychological contract is heavily influenced by:

- The extent to which employers adopt effective people management practices.
- The employees' sense of fairness in the determination of how they should behave in carrying out their duties and the level of trust in their employer and belief that they will honour the 'deal' between them.

They also suggest that a positive psychological contract will increase levels of employee commitment and satisfaction and also encourage an improved business performance.

The psychological contract is largely based on personal working relationships between boss and subordinate as each has a need to find ways of adapting to the demands, needs, expectations and expectations of the other whilst at the same time achieving their own objectives. Whilst the psychological contract as so far described functions at an interpersonal level, it will also contain elements of the broader organisational level of implicit expectation for both employers and employees (for example, the employee expectation of being given opportunities for development and the employer's expectation that employees will be flexible in relation to work volume and content). It is not always within the gift of an immediate line manager to influence the organisational-level aspects of the psychological contract, but the line manager is inevitably the first one to become aware of, and potentially suffer any negative consequences of, any employee perceived breach of it. As the labour market changes so do the expectations of employees and this influences what they will accept and expect from their employers. The CIPD (2009) report showed how performance management practices are being used to move away from a situation in which job security and career progression exist, to one where a sustained high performance and level of commitment will determine a continuation of employment. This represents a top-down imposed change which can leave employees disenchanted and concerned about the fairness and accuracy of the process and produce feelings of anger and betrayal together with eroding trust.

Bratton and Gold (2003) put forward that there are three important features associated with the psychological contract which will challenge managers in their desire to achieve high performance organisation status. These are:

- *Organisations do not communicate with one voice*   Because the employment relationship is based upon a personal relationship between boss and subordinate many psychological contracts exist.
- *It reaffirms the notion that the employment relationship is based on exchange*   This emphasises that one good turn creates an expectation for a return of the favour. Research quoted by the authors' shows that managers frequently do not keep their promises about

these expectations and so the basis of the psychological contract degrades over time.

- *The psychological contract is based upon a mixture of the social and economic context; leadership; communication and human resource practice* The psychological contract is therefore based on the complex interplay between many forces and factors and can easily fail if these are not all mutually supportive.

There has been much debate over recent years about whether the psychological contract has changed, the argument being that both individuals and organisations now want and expect different things from each other. Young people (often referred to as generation X) are said to take responsibility for their own careers and development and to want interesting work and high rewards from their current employer. Organisations are said to seek flexible, innovative people who may not want to stay in the long term but who will work hard and flexibly whilst they are there. The new psychological contract is said to be (CIPD, 2009):

- *Employees promise to* work hard; uphold company reputation; maintain high levels of attendance and punctuality; show loyalty to the organisation; work extra hours when required; develop new skills and update old ones; be flexible, for example, by taking on a colleague's work; be courteous to clients and colleagues; be honest; come up with new ideas.
- *Employers promise to provide* pay commensurate with performance; opportunities for training and development; opportunities for promotion; recognition for innovation or new idea; feedback on performance; i nteresting tasks; an attractive benefits package; respectful treatment; reasonable job security; a pleasant and safe working environment.

The same source suggests that the psychological contract may have implications for organisational strategy in a number of areas, for example:

- *Process fairness* People want to know that their interests will be taken into account when decisions are taken; they would like to be treated with respect; and they are more likely to be satisfied with their job if they are consulted about change.

- *Communications*   An effective two-way dialogue between employer and employees is a necessary means of giving expression to employee 'voice'.
- *Management style*   In many organisations, managers can no longer control the business 'top down' – they have to adopt a more democratic, consultative, involving style.
- *Managing expectations*   Managers may have a tendency to emphasise positive messages and play down more negative ones. Managing expectations by not being overly optimistic, or giving half promises that might not be realised, and especially when bad news is anticipated, will help to avoid undermining the psychological contract.
- *Measuring employee attitudes*   Employers should monitor employee attitudes on a regular basis as a means of identifying where action may be needed to improve aspects of the psychological contract or its health.

See also: benchmarking; compliance/commitment; contract of employment; employee empowerment and engagement; employee relations and conflict; high performance working; labour turnover; learning organisation; organisational culture; resourcing/retention; strategic HRM; total reward

BIBLIOGRAPHY

Bratton, J. and Gold, J. (2003) *Human Resource Management: Theory and Practice* (3rd edition). Basingstoke: Palgrave Macmillan.

CIPD (2009) 'The psychological contract'. *Factsheet*. Available at: www.cipd.co.uk (last accessed March 2009).

Ellis, N. and Pompli, A. (2002) 'Quality of working life for nurses', *Research Report*. Commonwealth Dept of Health and Ageing, Canberra.

Guest, D.E. and Conway, N. (2002) *Pressure at Work and the Psychological Contract*. London: CIPD.

NFER (2009) Available at http://www.nfer.ac.uk/research-areas/pims-data/summaries/ qwl-development-of-a-quality-of-working-life-measure.cfm (last accessed 20 March 2009).

Walton, R.E. (1973) 'Quality of working life: what is it?', *Sloan Management Review*, 15: 11–21.

Resourcing/Retention

Resourcing is the process of bringing into an organisation personnel who will possess the appropriate education, qualifications, skills and experience for the post(s) offered. Retention is about those policies and practices that encourage and create positive working conditions and an environment that encourages employees to stay with the company in the longer term.

Resourcing broadly covers three main areas of HR activity:

- *Recruitment* This stage of the resourcing process is about identifying and bringing forward an appropriate pool of potentially appropriate candidates from which a specific selection of the individual will be chosen for the next stage in the resourcing process. As such it consists of a number of distinct features:

  o Identification of a vacancy – people leave a company for many reasons (creating potential vacancies) and new posts are created (perhaps as the result of changes in business activity) all the time.

  o Labour markets – having identified the need to fill a vacancy it is necessary to then think about where likely candidates will be found. That involves understanding the labour markets appropriate to the position(s) involved. In some cases these may be internal to the company, or these can be external. There are many possible external labour markets and these will differ depending upon the type of job. For example, some jobs will attract people living locally to the company whereas others may involve very specialised skills and experience meaning that potential candidates may be currently based in any part of the world.

  o Advertising – this aspect of the resourcing process is about accessing the appropriate labour markets in order to bring the opportunity to the attention of as many potential applicants as possible. The aim being to attract enough high calibre applicants but not so many average or inferior candidates that they 'swamp' the selection process.

o Documentation – a range of documents is necessary for any resourcing process, including: role and person specification; advert; vacancy/advert authorising and sign-off approvals; use of CVs or standard application forms; staff handbooks and any relevant contracts/agreements; application tracking log; standard letters covering the stages of the process; and shortlisting criteria.

o Initial sifting – once the applications are available to the company it will be necessary to somehow grade the applications so that eventually three 'piles' emerge. The three piles are definitely interview; possibly interview; and reject. Sifting is a critical stage in the process and can be difficult if there are a large number of applications or alternatively very few applications. The aim should be to identify an objective method of differentiating between candidates in relation to the requirements of the job in question without bias or discrimination creeping into the process either deliberately or accidentally.

• *Selection*   This represents a two-way process and is as much about the applicant selecting the organisation as it is about the organisation selecting the applicant. It has been argued that from the organisation's perspective there are three levels of 'fit' that are being evaluated during the selection process;

o Fit with the organisation.
o Fit with the department and team.
o Fit with the job itself.

There are many selection methods that can be involved individually or in combination as part of a selection process. The choice of methods will depend on many factors including appropriateness, the numbers involved, and time and cost. They include the following list of methods:

o Application form or CV.
o Interviews.
o Self and peer assessment.
o Telephone interviews.
o Psychometric testing.
o Group methods and assessment centres.
o Work tests and portfolios.
o References.
o Other methods such as handwriting analysis.

- *Appointment* The final stage of the selection process should be the identification of the chosen applicant(s) for the job(s) being filled. In an ideal world the chosen individual would be contacted with a formal offer of employment, they would accept and a starting date would then be determined. However, an individual may reject an offer, or may do so if they cannot agree suitable terms and conditions of employment, or at any time before starting work, or even shortly after starting work (the induction crisis). Equally things can change for the company and it may find itself in a position of having to withdraw the offer of a job. In that sense it represents a 'dangerous' time for both parties and as a consequence it is likely that both will have some contingency plans. For example, many organisations will seek to delay notifying applicants who narrowly missed out on being offered the job so that they have the possibility of making one of them an offer if necessary. However, this can only last for a few days as applicants will be sensitive to any delay in notification and so will become aware that they were 'second best' with all that is implied by such a perception! On the other hand, applicants may continue with any outstanding applications and only make a decision when they feel it necessary to make a binding commitment. So failure in the selection process can occur at the final stages and in extreme cases could mean that it becomes necessary to re-advertise the position and begin the process again.

Another major area of decision making in the resourcing process is in relation to the role of agencies or consultants. Such providers claim to offer a professional, cost effective and efficient service. They can advertise using the company details or anonymously if it is a sensitive recruitment situation. The possibilities include:

- Assistance with the creation, layout and placing of adverts.
- Assistance with the creation of role and personnel specifications.
- A resourcing service involving taking the role brief; developing a person specification; advertising; and drawing up a shortlist for selection.
- Additional services could include psychometric testing and initial interviews.

Having appointed an individual to a position it would be hoped that they would become an effective member of the organisation and that they would wish to remain with it. Clearly situations might arise when either party realises that they have made a mistake and would seek to end the employment relationship as quickly and painlessly as possible. However, in most cases an extended period of mutual benefit could be envisaged and retention becomes the area of HR policy and practice that is intended to be the means of achieving that. *Labour Market Trends* (2001) identified that job tenure (length of service) ranged from 6 per cent of the workforce who had been in their current job for up to three months; 21 per cent who had held their job for between two to five years; and 19 per cent of the workforce who had done so for between ten to twenty years. People leave organisations for many reasons and equally organisations release people for many reasons as well. These include:

- Increased income.
- Better job/career prospects or promotion.
- Change in type of work.
- To gain experience.
- Change in industry.
- Family/career responsibilities.
- To work fewer hours or change the work pattern.
- Dissatisfaction with current job/company/working conditions.
- To escape poor working relationships with boss and/or colleagues.
- Retirement.
- Death or serious illness.
- Family or company moving location.
- Company closure or redundancy.
- Change in company fortunes.

Some of the common staff retention strategies include:

- *Managing expectations about the job, company and prospects for career development* If the experience of the job and working in the company does not match what the employee has been led to expect then it is likely that they will quickly become dissatisfied and seek alternative employment.
- *Reward* Most individuals would say that they are worth more money and would take it if it were offered. But in practical terms the feeling of being paid fairly and equitably can go a long way to helping employees to feel valued by the employer.
- *Induction* Induction is about 'converting' a new recruit into an effective member of the organisation as quickly and effectively as possible.

Starting a new job in a new organisation is a stressful and daunting prospect. If the induction process is missing or not effective then the new person will feel lost, unsure of their role, and an outsider.

- *Work-life balance and family friendly HR practices*   People have many responsibilities in this area including child care, elder care, or family commitments, that will make it difficult to accept the traditional working patterns. It can also include voluntary and other activities and commitments that people acquire over the course of their lives that require a different work-life balance to be adopted by both parties to the employment relationship.

- *Training and development*   These aspects of retention seek to capture the desires of most individuals to develop and grow in relation to their work and careers.

- *Good management*   The higher the quality of line management the more effective will be many aspects of operational activity, including the degree to which employees feel 'connected' to the organisation and valued by it, so aiding retention.

- *Avoid 'presenteeism'*   This working environment is one where people feel 'pressured' or 'obliged' to work longer hours than necessary because they are frightened to refuse, or through a desire to impress management.

- *Job and organisational design*   Boring, monotonous, meaningless work is less likely to hold the interest of employees much beyond the need for an income.

- *The use of confidential attitude surveys*   These include questions about the intention to leave and questionnaires sent to former employees on a confidential basis around six months after their departure.

- *Career development*   This maximises opportunities for individual employees to develop their skills and careers.

- *Employee relations policies*   Employee involvement and participation in decision making within the company represents ways in which individuals can have a 'voice', contribute to, and gain an understanding of issues that they would not normally have exposure to.

- *Defend*   This is an interesting suggestion from the CIPD (2008), the idea being to try and prevent penetration by headhunters and anyone seeking to poach staff. The same source suggests keeping internal e-mail addresses confidential, training telephonists to spot calls from agents and to avoid giving them any useful information, refusing to do business with agents who have previously poached your staff, and entering into pacts with other employers not to poach one another's staff.

- *Employer of choice*   This (along with a good employer brand) implies that people will actively seek employment with the company and also people are more likely to want to stay with such an employer.

See also: *assessment/development centre; benchmarking; benefits; career management; discrimination, diversity and equality; employee development; employee empowerment and engagement; flexibility; human resource planning; interview; labour turnover; performance management; psychometric and other tests; reward management; strategic HRM; succession planning and talent management; total reward*

BIBLIOGRAPHY

CIPD (2008) 'Employee turnover and retention'. *Factsheet* (revised August 2008). Available at www.cipd.co.uk (last accessed November 2008).

Labour Market Trends (2001) 'Length of time continuously employed by occupation and industry', *Labour Market Trends*, February.

Reward Management

> The meaning of reward management is the design, creation and management of the salary, wage, incentive and benefits arrangements within an organisation. Put more formally, Armstrong and Stephens (2005: 3) define it as, '... concerned with the formulation and implementation of strategies and policies the purpose of which are to reward people fairly, equitably and consistently in accordance with their value to the organisation and to help the organisation to achieve its strategic goals'.

Traditionally the aim of reward systems was to attract, retain, and motivate staff. However, in more recent times, the traditional view has changed as it has been recognised that individuals are attracted, retained, and motivated by a wide range of financial and non-financial rewards and that these can change over time depending on a range of influences including the personal circumstances of employees. This change in perspective has resulted in the total reward approach to pay which places the broadest definition possible on the 'rewards' available as a result of working for a particular organisation. Today reward management is essentially a matching process – seeking to match employee wants and desires with the organisation's ability to meet these expectations in the most cost-effective way and in a manner that supports business objectives both collectively and individually, whilst meeting the legal, social, and ethical obligations that exist.

The CIPD (2009) suggest that with regards to reward strategy (the basis of reward management policy and practice):

> It is important to establish a reward strategy which clearly articulates the aims of the various reward elements, integrates them in a coherent way and tells employees what they can expect to receive and why. This strategy needs to be written, communicated and understood throughout the organisation. It is the yardstick by which reward elements are measured and evaluated and manages the expectations of all employees. Without an articulated reward strategy, the various elements will at best seem like individual initiatives and at worse employees will be left to form their own opinions about what the organisation is trying to achieve.

The range of objectives that generally reflect what employers and employees seek from the company reward system include:

Employer objectives	Employee objectives
1 That the pay levels used within the company reflect the prestige and status of the organisation within the business and local community.	To maximise the purchasing power that can be achieved from the sale of labour by the individual.
2 That the pay levels and other rewards should enable the recruitment of the best people in a competitive labour market.	That the pay level is 'felt fair' by the recipient relative to the scheme criteria and perceived social value of the job.

(Cont'd)

reward management

Employer objectives	Employee objectives
3 That the use of elements within the reward package should facilitate management control of operational processes.	That the pay level is 'felt fair' by the recipient relative to the perceived pay level of others both inside and outside the organisation
4 That the design of the reward system should encourage high performance and motivation among employees.	To obtain a reasonable share of wealth created from work undertaken.
5 That the reward system should not add a level of cost to the business that inhibits competitive trading.	That the pay reflects the degree of recognition that the employer has for the contribution of the employee.
6 That the elements in the reward package should underpin an acceptance of change in employee behaviour and job activity.	That the composition of the pay package should reflect the broader needs and aspirations of the employee at that particular stage in their life.
7 That the outcome from the reward system should be predictable and allow expenditure planning by employers.	That the outcome from the reward system should be reasonably predictable to provide stability in income and allow expenditure planning by employees.

For many employers reward represents the single most significant cost of doing business. Consequently there is a strong pressure on management to minimise the total cost of labour and also the unit labour cost (a measure of productivity). Incentive elements within the total reward package represent some of the major levers available to managers in seeking to direct employee behaviour in ways appropriate to the achievement of business objectives. Reward also has significance in conveying messages to the wider business and other stakeholder communities about how the organisation wants to be seen and regarded in relation to the value that it places on its employees and how its approach to the management of people should be viewed. From the employee perspective the reward package impacts directly on the standard of living and life-style of the individual and their family in the short- and long-term (a pension, for example, is frequently

key concepts in human resource management

described as deferred salary), but it also represents a measure of status and success in social terms. The reward package holds a social and psychological significance for both parties which adds to the complexity of design.

In reward management practice there are a number of specific themes that form the backbone of this aspect of HR activity. These are based on Armstrong and Stephens' (2005) work and each will form the basis of the subsequent discussion:

- The determination of job values and relativities.
- Grade and pay structures.
- Rewarding and reviewing contribution and performance.
- Reward management for special groups.
- Employee benefits and pension schemes.
- Reward management procedures.

- *The determination of job values and relativities*   There are many ways in which the relative value or job magnitude for a particular set of tasks can be determined. The options include:

  o Job family structures group jobs together into 'types' or families (managerial, technical, sales, accounting for example) with appropriate 'grading' mechanisms being developed for each. The individual structures may then be aligned within a common pay framework.
  o Job evaluation, which is discussed in a specific section elsewhere and so will not be developed further here.
  o Market pricing, which seeks to identify appropriate market rates of pay (based on salary surveys) for each family of job.
  o Equal value, where the legislation requires that reward systems are non-discriminatory and equal pay reviews are one way of seeking to ensure that bias does not creep into reward design or practice.

- *Grade and pay structures*   It then becomes necessary to create a job magnitude hierarchy and link it to money in some way or another. The options include:

  o Grade structures – having identified a hierarchy of job magnitude it then becomes necessary to create some form of grade structure to form the basis of a wage structure.
  o Narrow or broad-bands structures – narrow bands group jobs based on small variations on job value thereby creating a large number of grades. Broad-banding on the other hand uses a small

number of wage bands to encourage flexibility in work activity. There are advantages and disadvantages associated with each.

  o Spot rate or wage bands – spot rates provide everyone in a particular grade with the same wage. Wage bands mean that different wages can be paid to individuals undertaking the same job. That requires pay progression policies to be developed in order to justify individual rates of pay.

- *Rewarding and reviewing contribution and performance*   These days contribution and performance are key features in the design and management of reward systems. The options around this aspect of reward design include:

  o Incremental progression – the existence of a number of steps from the minimum to the maximum wage for a grade. Progression through the increments could be based either on annual progression or acceptable performance.

  o Performance progression – managerial discretion could decide an individual's position within the grade based on relative performance (compared to others) and budget constraint, which may incorporate the annual cost-of-living review. It would also be possible to link a performance rating with progress through the grade by using a pay matrix.

  o Competency pay – this is based on the view that people should be paid for the level of competence that they demonstrate in relation to their work.

  o Incentive schemes – there are many incentive schemes possibilities including group or individual incentives, a profit share, or share options.

- *Reward management for special groups*   This aspect of reward management covers a wide range of people and jobs within organisations. For example, senior managers, directors, expatriate workers, and sales personnel all have a particular complexity in their work that makes the need to give a careful consideration to their reward schemes essential.

- *Employee benefits and pension schemes*   The benefit package that an employer provides is intended to support the general wellbeing of the individual and in some cases their immediate family. The benefits package is in addition to the wage or salary payments made to the individual and represents a significant element within the total cost of labour for the employer. Not all organisations offer all benefits and some benefits are only available to senior people within the company.

- *Reward management procedures*   Pay levels are never static for long and there is a need to monitor market trends and adapt company policy and practice in light of the information collected. Most organisations will engage in salary surveys on a regular basis in order to determine market trends. This together with general economic data and company financial position allows company pay policy to be determined.

Other key elements in the reward management process are the role of line managers, trade union or employee representative body in relation to consultation, involvement, and collective bargaining over reward aspects of the employment relationship. Decisions about cost-of-living pay rises and the possible links to any performance awards also need to be clear. A key concept within reward management is that of 'felt fair' – a term used to mean that something should be 'felt to be fair' by the people subjected to the system or policy – if acceptance is to be achieved and problems avoided. Something that is not 'felt fair' will create resentment and a negative response somewhere along the line.

See also: benchmarking; benefits; competency; contract of employment; employee relations and conflict; Human Resource Management (HRM) and Personnel Management (PM); high performance working; incentive schemes; job, job analysis and job design; job evaluation; negotiation; performance management; strategic HRM; total reward; trade union/employee representation; wage structure

BIBLIOGRAPHY

Armstrong, M. and Stephens, T. (2005) *A Handbook of Employee Reward Management and Practice*. London: Kogan Page.
CIPD (2009) 'Pay and reward: an overview'. *Factsheet* (revised March 2009). Available at www.cipd.co.uk (last accessed April 2009).

reward management

Statutory Bodies (ACAS; Central Arbitration Committee (CAC); Employment Tribunals; Health and Safety Executive (HSE); Equality and Human Rights Commission (EHRC); Low Pay Commission)

> *The term statutory body means an agency established in law and intended to have a significant degree of influence over matters pertaining to its sphere of influence. Another term used to describe such bodies is non-departmental public body (NDPB). In practice these are bodies established by the UK parliament but in such a way that they operate at arm's length from the government of the day and ministers.*

1   The Advisory, Conciliation and Arbitration Service (ACAS)
    This is an independent body charged with the responsibility to seek to improve employee relations and resolve disputes between employers and employees. Most of the following information is taken from the ACAS website (www.acas.org.uk) and related official publications.

ACAS is managed by a council which reports to Parliament and is made up of leading figures from business, the unions, independent members and academics. The ACAS Council is responsible for determining the strategic direction, policies and priorities of ACAS and for ensuring that its statutory duties are carried out effectively. ACAS employs approximately 750 staff based in 11 main regional centres throughout England, Scotland and Wales, with its head office in London.

The range of services offered by ACAS and against which performance is reported each year includes (based on 2007–08 data):

- *Conciliation in collective disputes* (including the arrangement and facilitation of mediation and arbitration). ACAS dealt with about 900 cases involving conciliation and 47 for arbitration and mediation.
- *Conciliation in employment tribunal cases* (individual rights disputes). Some 203,000 claims were received with between 53–85 per cent of cases presented being settled or withdrawn as a result of conciliation.
- *Workplace projects to improve workplace employment relations*. In 2007–08 over 230 projects were started.
- *Advisory meetings to discuss and offer advice.* These involved some 1,900 meetings.
- *Training.* This was intended to raise awareness on how good employment practice can improve organisational performance (some 2,500 sessions).
- *National helpline.* This offers advice to anyone who calls (around 885,000 calls).
- *Mediation services.* Promoting internal mediation intended to deal with cases before they are presented to employment tribunals.
- *Diversity and equality services.*
- *The publication of codes of practice and advisory booklets.*

2   The Central Arbitration Committee (CAC)
An independent body with statutory powers to adjudicate on the statutory recognition (or derecognition) of trade unions for collective bargaining purposes. It would hear cases referred to it by either party where there has been a failure to reach agreement voluntarily. Most of this information is based on the CAC website (www.cac.gov.uk).

In addition, there exists a statutory role for the CAC to determine disputes between trade unions and employers over the disclosure of information necessary for collective bargaining purposes, and in resolving complaints under the following regulations:

- The Information and Consultation Regulations 2004.
- The European Public Limited-Liability Company Regulations 2004.
- The Transnational Information and Consultation of Employees Regulations 1999.

The procedure to be followed in claims for recognition is clearly laid out in appropriate legislation and regulation. It is broadly as follows.

If the CAC receives an application for recognition from a trade union it must first decide whether or not it can accept the application. The CAC does this by applying a number of admissibility tests laid down in the relevant legislation. These include identifying whether or not the trade union has 50 per cent of the workforce from its proposed bargaining unit in membership and whether or not a majority of workers in the proposed bargaining unit would be likely to support recognition of the trade union. If the CAC decides that it can accept the application on the basis of the previous questions, and if the bargaining unit proposed by the trade union has not been (or cannot be) agreed with the employer, the CAC must then decide whether or not the proposed bargaining unit is appropriate. The CAC would answer that question by considering whether or not the proposed bargaining unit is compatible with effective management. If the CAC concludes that a different bargaining unit would be a more appropriate one, then it must next consider whether or not the original application by the trade union remains valid. It does this by reapplying the original tests or questions to the bargaining unit that the CAC has determined as appropriate.

Where the CAC decides the application remains valid and over 50 per cent of the appropriate bargaining unit are members of the applicant union, the CAC may declare the union should be recognised. Alternatively, where the CAC is satisfied that the interests of good industrial relations require it, a secret ballot can be required of the parties to determine the actual level of union membership. If the CAC is not satisfied that the applicant union has majority membership in the appropriate bargaining unit, the CAC must always arrange for a ballot to be held before deciding whether or not to grant recognition. Where a ballot is held, the CAC is required to order recognition of the trade union where a majority of participants in the ballot, and at least 40 per cent of the workers in the appropriate bargaining unit, vote in favour. Where the CAC issues a declaration granting recognition, or where a semi-voluntary agreement has been concluded, the parties have 30 days to negotiate and agree a bargaining procedure. If no agreement can be reached, even with CAC assistance, the CAC will determine the procedure to be used.

In certain circumstances the CAC is able to declare a union de-recognised where the employer or workers in the bargaining unit make such a request and the relevant statutory provisions have been complied with.

3   Employment tribunals

The jurisdiction list in the Employment Tribunals website lists about 63 separate areas of employment-related events that can lead to claim being made to a tribunal for resolution. Not all of them relate directly to employer actions or behaviour towards an employee (or potential employee). For example, there is provision for an individual to make a claim that the Secretary of State make a redundancy payment following an application to the National Insurance Fund for such a payment (in cases involving the insolvency of the employer). However, the majority of cases relate to issues such as unfair dismissal; sex discrimination; victimisation on the grounds of sex, marriage or transgender; equal pay; or a failure to consult in cases of redundancy, etc.

There were changes to the Employment Tribunal's Rules of Procedure which affect how to make and respond to a claim and these came into effect on 6 April 2009. Any claim will not be accepted by a tribunal unless it meets certain conditions:

- It must be on an approved form provided by Employment Tribunals.
- By law, a claimant must include the specified information.
- The claim must also usually be received by the tribunal office within three months of the effective date of termination.
- To make a claim of unfair dismissal it is necessary to have worked continuously for the employer for a minimum of one year. Exceptions include dismissal for being involved with a trade union, maternity reasons, etc.

When a claim is accepted by the tribunal the claimant will be notified and a copy of the claim will be sent to the company and also ACAS.

When the company respond (on a form supplied to them by the tribunal office) a copy is also sent to the claimant and to ACAS. An ACAS Conciliation Officer will contact both parties in order to assess the likelihood of a compromise or settlement being reached without the need for a full tribunal hearing. If either or both parties appoint a representative to act on their behalf then all correspondence would be sent to them and it becomes their responsibility to keep their client informed as to progress, etc. If the ACAS conciliation process succeeds then the case would be settled (or withdrawn). If that does not happen then the case would go forward to be listed for hearing by a tribunal. In the new rules and procedures there are strict timescales by which all of these stages and processes must be done. If an employer refuses to respond then the tribunal can go ahead and make a ruling on the case based on the claimant's evidence alone. In certain circumstances (usually on a point of law) it is possible for either party to appeal a decision to the Employment Appeal Tribunal (EAT) and subsequently to the higher courts of appeal.

4   Health and Safety Executive (HSE)

A booklet produced by the HSE (2008/09) sets out that the main purpose of health and safety at work is intended to prevent people from being harmed by work or becoming ill by taking the right precautions in advance and providing a satisfactory working environment, a simple objective that can prove difficult and complicated to achieve in practice. Inspectors from the HSE or from a local authority have inspection and enforcement powers depending on the nature of the organisations as follows:

- HSE inspectors for factories, farms, and building sites.
- Local authority inspectors for offices, shops, hotels, catering and leisure facilities.

The main legal obligations placed on employers are:

- To protect the health and safety of staff and other people (such as customers and members of the public) who may be affected by workplace activity.
- To appoint a competent person to help the organisation meet its health and safety responsibilities.
- To write a health and safety policy identifying who does what, when, and how in relation to health and safety.
- To make the workplace safe and eliminate or control risks to health.

- To ensure plant and machinery are safe and that safe systems of work are set and followed.
- To ensure articles and substances are moved, stored, and used safely.
- To provide adequate welfare facilities.
- To give workers the information, instruction, training, and supervision necessary for their health and safety.
- To consult workers on health and safety matters.
- To display a health and safety poster providing the specified information, or provide employees with a booklet containing the same information.
- To understand the system for reporting work-related accidents, diseases, and near-miss incidents (RIDDOR).

Penalties for breaches of health and safety legislation can be severe up to and including two years imprisonment and unlimited fines if a case is tried in the Crown Court.

Risk assessment helps to identify the risks that matter – those with the potential to cause significant harm to individuals, customers, other stakeholders, or the business. The relevant legislation does not require the elimination of all risks, but to protect people 'so far as is reasonably practicable'. A risk assessment involves three things:

- The identification of hazards – that is, anything that could cause harm in the workplace or to do with the product or service offered by the organisation.
- The determination of the level of risk that exists.
- The determination of the seriousness of the harm that could result.

HSE (2008–09) sets out a simple risk assessment process that is intended to identify the existing risks and the necessary steps to avoid, manage and control them. It involves a number of steps as follows:

- Step 1: Identify the hazards.
- Step 2: Decide who might be harmed and how.
- Step 3: Evaluate the risks and decide on precautions.

The booklet suggests that when controlling risks the following principles should be applied, preferably in the following order:

o Try a less risky option.
o Prevent access to the hazard.
o Organise work to reduce exposure to the hazard.

- o Issue personal protective equipment.
- o Provide welfare facilities.
- Step 4: Record the findings and implement them.
- Step 5: Review the risk assessment and update if necessary on a regular basis.

The basic processes and principles of HSE enforcement are:

- Organisations and the people in them will be offered information and advice, both face to face and in writing, on health and safety matters. An inspector may also warn that, in their opinion, there exists a failure to comply with the law.
- Where appropriate, inspectors may also serve improvement and prohibition notices, withdraw approvals, vary licence conditions or exemptions, issue formal cautions (England and Wales only), and they may also prosecute (or report to the Procurator Fiscal with a view to prosecution in Scotland) where serious breaches have been identified, or where advice is blatantly or wilfully ignored.

5   Equality and Human Rights Commission (EHRC)
This body brought together a range of previous 'equality' based provision surrounding employment including sex, race, and disability discrimination. According to its website (www.equalityhumanrights.com), the EHRC sees its job as being 'To create a fairer Britain and a society without prejudice, to raise awareness of your rights and implement an effective legislative framework for the future'.

Clearly this remit is much broader than that of employment rights, although these represent a fundamental aspect of its work. As a statutory body it has the responsibility to protect, enforce, and promote equality across the seven areas specifically covered by legislation (age, disability, gender, race, religion and belief, sexual orientation, and gender reassignment). Each of these issues has an obvious association and link with the world of work and consequently HR policy and practice. However, the EHRC has a particular role in such matters based on a legislative requirement which at best represents a relatively narrow and particular interpretation of diversity.

From the employer's perspective the EHRC has identified the following as the major areas in which discrimination can arise. They each represent a major area of HR policy and practice, with perhaps the last one representing a broader-based facilitation role bringing together a range of other areas of management in seeking to match what the organisation needs to do in order to successfully accommodate an individual with particular needs:

- Recruitment and job advertisements.
- Pay, benefits, and workplace conditions.
- Pregnancy, maternity, and parenthood.
- The requirement to make reasonable adjustments for disabled employees.

From an employee perspective, the process of raising a complaint would be through the normal internal company procedures and thereafter if the issue were not resolved satisfactorily by a claim to the Employment Tribunals.

6   Low Pay Commission

The Low Pay Commission (LPC) was set up under the National Minimum Wage Act 1998 to advise the government about the national minimum wage. It undertakes the following activities (taken from its website (www.lowpay.gov.uk/lowpay/index.shtmb)):

- Extensive research and consultation.
- The commission of research projects to be carried out by others.
- Analysing relevant data and actively encourage the Office of National Statistics to establish better estimates of the incidence of low pay.
- Carrying out surveys of firms in low-paying sectors.
- Consulting with employers, workers, and their representatives.
- Taking written and oral evidence from a wide range of organisations.
- Conducting fact-finding visits throughout the UK to meet employers, employees and representative organisations.

In general terms, most HR practitioners will have little or no direct contact with the Low Pay Commission. However, the effects of the research activity and recommendations made to government will have a significant impact on HR work and policy. The national minimum wage is announced by the government each year and represents the lowest wages that can legally be paid by any employer. As such this serves as a benchmark against which many pay policy and practice decisions will be made. Equally the minimum wage is enforceable in law and so there are penalties and consequences for not applying the necessary requirements.

See also: employee relations and conflict; Human Resource Management (HRM) and Personnel Management (PM); Strategic HRM; trade unions/employee representation

BIBLIOGRAPHY

ACAS (2008) *ACAS Annual Report and Resource Accounts 2007/08*. London: The Stationery Office.

Central Arbitration Committee (2008) *Annual Report 2007–08*. Available at http://www.cac.gov.uk/cac_2_annual_report/Final%20CAC%20Annual%20Report%20 07-08.pdf (last accessed June 2009).

Employment Tribunal (2009) *Making a Claim to an Employment Tribunal*. Available at http://www.employmenttribunals.gov.uk/Documents/FormsGuidance/New_Making_ a_Claim.pdf (last accessed June 2009).

HSE (2008–09) *An Introduction to Health and Safety: Health and Safety in Small Businesses. What you Should Know About – Where to get More Information*. Available at http://www.hse.gov.uk/pubns/indg259.pdf (last accessed June 2009).

http://www.acas.org.uk
http://www.cac.gov.uk/
http://www.employmenttribunals.gov.uk/index.htm
http://www.employmentappeals.gov.uk/index.htm
http://www.equalityhumanrights.com/
http://www.hse.gov.uk/riddor/
http://www.lowpay.gov.uk/lowpay/index.shtml

Strategic HRM

Strategic HRM is often described as a process of aligning human resources and human behaviour more closely to the strategic and operating objectives of the organisation. Strategic HRM is about the alignment of people activity as closely as possible with the direction, purpose, and objectives of the organisation in order to achieve a competitive advantage.

Business strategy is sometimes described in terms of the application of a specific approach to understanding what the future holds and thereafter deciding on how the business should position itself relative to that 'known' future. However, it would be too simplistic to take that as the only view as there are many different possibilities for how strategy should be determined, if indeed it can be determined at all. For example, there is debate about the degree to which any decision-making process can be truly rational; there is the political dimension to human activity; the nature of information and data which can also be problematic. Strategy appears to provide a measure of certainty in an uncertain world and it can be argued that by imposing an apparent order on a chaotic reality a misleading view of the inherent complexity and randomness of the environment results. However, such arguments aside, there are four main perspectives on business strategy means and how it should be used to shape the direction and activities within an organisation:

- *Classical or rational-planning approach* Based on a formalised and rational decision-making process. Key stages include a comprehensive analysis of the external and internal environments, followed by the evaluation and selection of strategic options, followed by the planning and implementation of actions intended to achieve the selected strategies. This approach to strategy has been criticised as too mechanistic and providing an unrealistic reflection of how commercial and business success can be achieved.
- *Evolutionary approach* This is based on the idea that markets are too fluid and competitive to engage in extensive strategising and too unpredictable to outguess. It represents an opportunistic approach in which the markets dictate what will 'work' and what won't and it is the job of managers to respond in a timely manner and to maximise appropriately the commercial advantage from opportunities as they arise.
- *Processual approach* It has been argued that strategy development tends to be fragmented, evolutionary, and largely intuitive, based on small incremental steps. This was further developed by Mintzberg (1987) who recognised that planned strategies sometimes don't always become realised strategies. Thus an iterative, circular process could emerge in which planned strategies are impacted on by environmental forces to create emergent strategies.
- *Systemic approach* Human activity (including strategy) occurs within a particular social context, carried out by people who are individually and collectively shaped by cultural, language, political, social, family, friendship, education, and work organisations in the locations that they

originate from and work within. Consequently, any strategy developed will be directly or indirectly influenced by those forces.

Whatever the organisation's view of strategy, HR specialists should be trying to ensure that the HR policies align with, support – and possibly even shape – business strategy. The range of possible links between business and HR strategy, according to Torrington et al. (2005) include:

- *Separation* This level represents a minimal level of connection between business and HR strategic thinking and planning within the organisation.
- *Fit* At this level the HR function is allowed access to the business strategy outcomes and allowed/encouraged to develop appropriate HR strategies to support it.
- *Dialogue* This level recognises that possible strategic benefits can be achieved by allowing a dialogue between the HR and business strategy specialists during the business strategy development process.
- *Holistic* This level of relationship goes beyond dialogue and recognises the need to integrate HR and business strategy if success is to be achieved. Business strategy retains the lead role but recognises that it can only be developed effectively if the HR dimensions are integrated into it.
- *HR driven* Here the HR strategy is allowed to shape the business strategy. This level accepts that a significant part of business strategy rests on the current and future people capabilities.

There are four main models of strategic HRM that have emerged through the academic literature:

1 *Best practice model* Based on Guest's (2002) prescriptive model of HRM which identifies the following HR policy objectives:

  - Integration of HR into the strategic planning process.
  - Commitment of employees to the organisation and high performance working.
  - Flexibility in the organisational structure and the use of employees through multi-skilling.
  - Quality in goods and services is achieved through the employment of high calibre employees who can offer high performance and work flexibility and are committed to the organisation.

2 *Contingency model* The most appropriate approach can only be determined in relation to circumstances. It identifies two aspects of circumstances that need to be identified:

- The degree of 'fit' between HR and business strategy.
- The degree of 'fit' or integration across HR policies and practices.

3 *Harvard model* Developed by Beer, Spector, Lawrence, Mills and Walton, this has similarities with both the best practice and contingency models. It recognises that there are situational factors that impact on the HR strategy choices that exist, but is prescriptive in that it envisages a predetermined set of HR outcomes that would be universally valued.

4 *Resource-based model* This is based on the view that people are just one of the resources available to an organisation that need to be harnessed into a cohesive whole in delivering the desired strategy. It emphasises the achievement of competitive advantage through the development of human capital, not just the alignment of HR with business strategy. It suggests that for a competitive advantage to be achieved through the people resource it must be capable of meeting four criteria:

- Valuable – The use of the people resource must add value to the process (provides differentiation with competitors).
- Scarcity – Because there is a limited supply of any resource people must be found and 'used' with care and thought to extract maximum value from them in creating a competitive advantage.
- Inimitable – To achieve a real and sustainable competitive advantage it should not be possible for competitors to copy a resource or its use, including the contribution and role of people.
- Non-substitutable – To create a unique contribution it should not be possible to substitute one resource with another. For example, it is relatively easy to replace people with technology, but technology is relatively 'copyable' and it is the way that it is linked with other resources (such as people) that can provide a competitive advantage.

There is a wide range of HR strategies that will exist in most organisations. For example, there may be strategies in relation to diversity, equality in pay matters, or in relation to high performance working. But these in themselves are not strategic HRM, the overall framework intended to determine the nature, form, and delivery of the individual strategies. Boxall and Purcell

(2003) argued that strategic HRM is concerned with understanding the relationship between HRM and organisational performance, in the process pointing out that HR strategy is not the same as strategic HR plans. Strategic planning represents a formal process identifying and prescribing how, what, where, and when things will be done. The CIPD (2009) argue that a number of writers consider strategic HRM and human capital management as identical, this argument being that both rest on the assumption that people are assets rather than costs, the importance of adopting an integrated and strategic approach to managing people and that people management is a concern for all the stakeholders in an organisation not just an HR function. They go on to argue that the concept of human capital management complements and strengthens the value available from strategic HRM by:

- Drawing attention to the significance of 'management through measurement', the intention being to establish a clear line of sight between HR interventions and organisational success.
- Providing guidance on what to measure, how to measure it, and how to report on the outcomes from it.
- Underlining the importance of using measurement to demonstrate that HR policy and practice are delivering superior results and to identify the direction in which HR strategy needs to go.
- Reinforcing the need to base HRM strategies and processes on creating value through people.
- Defining the link between HRM and business strategy.
- Strengthening the view that people are assets rather than costs.
- Emphasising the business partner role for HR practitioners.

See also: employee development; employee empowerment and engagement; employee relations and conflict; Human Resource Management (HRM) and Personnel Management (PM); high performance working; human capital; knowledge management; learning organisation; quality of working life and the psychological contract; succession planning and talent management; total reward; trade union/employee representation

BIBLIOGRAPHY

Boxall, P. and Purcell, J. (2003) *Strategy and Human Resource Management*. Basingstoke: Palgrave Macmillan.

CIPD (2009) 'Strategic human resource management'. *Factsheet* (revised May 2009). Available at www.cipd.co.uk. (last accessed June 2009).

Guest, D. (2002) 'Human resource management, corporate performance and employee wellbeing: building the worker into HRM', *Journal of Industrial Relations*, 44(3): 335–59.

Mintzberg, H. (1987) 'The strategy concept I: five Ps for strategy', *California Management Review*, Fall: 11–24.

Torrington, D., Hall, L. and Taylor, S. (2005) *Human Resource Management* (6th edition). Harlow: Prentice Hall.

key concepts in human resource management

Succession Planning and Talent Management

> *Succession planning is about finding people with the right skills and experience to fill more senior jobs. In its simplest form it is about ensuring that the 'run over by a bus' eventuality does not have a major effect on the ability of an organisation to continue to function effectively. It is related to talent management in that it seeks to ensure that the organisation has a stream of people flowing through it who are capable of meeting the need for talent at every level.*
>
> *Talent management is also sometimes referred to as human capital management. It can be taken to mean the integration of HR policies and practice aimed at maximising the contribution from all employees. However, it can also be taken to mean the HR policies and practices associated with the attraction, selection, retention, development, and career management of those people identified as critical for the future success of the business.*

CIPD (2009a) suggests that because organisations differ in size, scope, and type it is difficult identify a single model of succession planning. However, usually succession planning covers only the most senior jobs in the organisation in relation to short-term and long-term possible successors for these posts. The latter group are in effect on a fast-track, and are developed through job moves within various parts of the business. This focus on the most senior posts means that, even in large organisations, only a few hundred people at most and at any given time will be subject to succession planning processes. This makes the process more manageable. That said, however, many large organisations will attempt to operate devolved models in divisions, sites, or countries where the same or similar processes are applied to a wider population. It is also where the links with talent management and the broader employee and management development processes become more apparent.

In today's flatter and less hierarchical organisations there are fewer opportunities for vertical promotion and so more career development and succession planning is based on what might be termed 'talent management'. This is to both retain and encourage those with considerable capability to rise to the highest levels and to see their longer-term prospects as aligned with the current employer. The same source points out that these days there needs to be a high degree of openness and visibility included in succession planning processes in order to demonstrate and capitalise on diversity and equality as key HR and business objectives. The relationship between the number of existing employees as compared to the number of outside applicants for senior positions is also a difficulty for any succession planning process. It is easy to adopt resourcing policies that rely too heavily on either category of applicant with consequences for the organisation and those that work within it. Appointing too many outsiders to senior positions might help to bring in new ideas and so on, but this also runs the risk of sending a signal to existing employees that they are not considered worthy of promotion and so they may lose their motivation and support for the organisation. Promoting too many people from inside the organisation presents the danger of stagnation, accepting the status quo, not introducing new ideas, and also of not finding the best applicant for a particular post.

Succession planning involves many of the planning, resourcing, and development activities that are covered extensively elsewhere in this book and so this will not be repeated here.

The CIPD (2008) identified a range of forces acting on the competitive, organisational, and employment environments that are creating an increased focus on the so-called war for talent and talent management. They found four categories of force acting on the situation:

- *External context* This includes factors such as increased globalisation, government policy, and technology.
- *Organisational context* This includes employee engagement, line manager roles and capability, HR policy and practice, business strategy, resourcing, succession planning, and employment patterns.
- *Workforce (supply) factors* This includes demographic trends, diversity, work-life balance, and labour sources.
- *Employers (demand) factors* This includes workforce flexibility, 'employer of choice' practices, competition for labour, and skills shortages.

The same source suggested that the value of a tailored, organisation-wide talent management process is that it provides a focus for an investment in human capital and places the subject high on the corporate agenda. It can also contribute to other strategic objectives, including:

- Building a high performance workplace.
- Encouraging a learning organisation.
- Adding value to the employer of choice and branding agenda.
- Contributing to diversity management.

A strategic approach to talent management can therefore provide a host of benefits that will interact with and support other areas of HR activity. Also identified is a four-stage cyclical process for talent management involving attracting talent, developing talent, managing talent, and evaluating talent. In general terms, the specific practices and policy areas associated with talent management are covered across other relevant sections of this book. Mathis and Jackson (2008: 292) identified a number of key areas of HR strategy as relevant to talent management, including:

- Creating and maintaining an organisational culture that values individuals.
- Identifying the future needs of the organisation and how to develop individuals to fill those needs.
- Developing a pool of talented people who are capable of meeting future job requirements.
- Establishing ways of managing and conducting HR activity that will encourage and support talent development.

The HR function can expect to consider the following issues when looking at international talent management (CIPD, 2009b):

- Managing the talent pipeline, where employers are trying to recruit 'ahead of the curve' to engage individuals with particular skills and aptitudes, bearing future business needs in mind.
- Developing relationships with universities and business schools to secure future talent from a known resource.
- Using global IT systems to create databases of internal talent pools.
- Creating skilled and competent teams of recruiters in different geographies.

- Managing recruitment suppliers on a global basis, introducing speed, cost, and quality controls, the use of preferred partners and branding messages, and ensuring audit trails to protect against legal issues associated with global diversity.
- Using e-enabled job boards and websites to attract and select applicants and to convey messages about the employer brand worldwide (see the CIPD factsheet on e-recruitment).

See also: assessment/development centre; benchmarking; career management; competency; compliance/commitment; employee development; employee empowerment and engagement; Human Resource Management (HRM) and Personnel Management (PM); high performance working; human capital; human resource planning; knowledge management; learning organisation; management development; performance management; resourcing/retention; strategic HRM

BIBLIOGRAPHY

CIPD (2008) 'Talent management: an overview'. *Factsheet*. Available at www.cipd.co.uk (last accessed July 2009).

CIPD (2009a) 'Succession planning'. *Factsheet*. Available at www.cipd.co.uk (last accessed July 2009).

CIPD (2009b) 'International recruitment, selection and assessment: an introduction'. *Factsheet*. Available at www.cipd.co.uk (last accessed July 2009).

Mathis, R.L. and Jackson, J.H. (2008) *Human Resource Management* (12th edition). Mason, OH: Thomson South-Western.

> *Most people will work in conjunction with other people to some degree. But that is not to say that every collective work activity represents a teamwork activity. For example, employees who all travel to work on the same bus or train are in a 'collective process', but they would not be a 'team' in the conventional sense. A team is usually defined as a small, cohesive group who will interact and influence each other and perceive themselves as a social entity through focussing on a common task.*

The term 'team' is often used interchangeably with that of 'group', but a distinction has been suggested based on performance achievements. For example, Katzenbach and Smith (1993) suggested the existence of the following hierarchy of performance-based groups and teams:

- *Working group*   Individuals working collectively to a limited degree. Performance largely reflects the efforts of individuals.
- *Pseudo-teams*   A collection of individuals who could achieve a higher performance if they worked in a more integrated and effective way.
- *Potential teams*   In this category individuals seek out ways to integrate more effectively.
- *Real teams*   This category is committed to the common purpose and develops appropriate ways of working to achieve it.
- *High performance teams*   This category has all the characteristics of real teams but also encourages personal growth and going beyond performance expectations among members.

The CIPD (2008) proposed the following as the most common types of team found in organisations (although also recognising that different terminologies and variants exist). Normally, teams are internal to an organisation and so are made up of people from that employer. Sometimes however teams from different employers are combined in

teamworking

261

relation to a specific task or project (for example, teams on major civil engineering or construction projects or teams which include customers and suppliers). The most common forms of team include:

- *Production and service teams* These would be expected to have a relatively long life-span, providing an ongoing product or service to customers or the organisation.
- *Project and development teams* These would be dedicated to a particular objective and have limited life-spans and a clear set of short-term objectives. They are often cross-functional, with members selected for the contribution their expertise can make.
- *Advice and involvement teams* Members would not usually devote a great deal of time to these team activities and once the team has achieved its objectives it would usually be disbanded.
- *Crews* For example, an airline crew may be formed from people who rarely work together but through prior training clearly understand their respective roles.
- *Action and negotiation teams* These have well-developed processes and clear objectives as a result of regularly working together (perhaps surgical or legal teams).
- *Virtual teams* These often work in separate buildings or even in different countries. Managing such teams is particularly difficult, not least because remote working can exacerbate misunderstandings.
- *Self-managed teams* These are also referred to as semi-autonomous or fully autonomous teams depending on the degree of self-management in the team. They reflect teams where much of the decision making is devolved to team members.

The same source suggested that the introduction of teamworking needs 'skilful management and resources devoted to it, or initiatives may fail'. They also identified the benefits of teamworking (from an organisational perspective) as:

- To improve productivity.
- To improve the quality of products or services.
- To improve the customer focus.
- To speed up the spread of ideas.
- To respond to opportunities and threats and to fast-changing environments.

- To increase employee motivation.
- To introduce multi-skilling and employee flexibility.

The same source identified benefits from the employee perspective as:

- Greater job satisfaction.
- Increased levels of motivation.
- Improved learning.

So far the discussion has focussed on teams and groups that would be created and would function formally within an organisation. Such groups and teams would be generally referred to as formal groups. However, there are also informal groups that exist within all organisations. These serve a number of functions, usually described as having either friendship or interest purposes. Such groups would never appear on an organisation chart or a company document and membership would be voluntary. However, the significance in terms of their impact and effect on organisational functioning is frequently understated. Many things will get done on the basis of such informal groups and networks. Hofstede (1984), for example, refers to a marketplace bureaucracy in his analysis of culture and structure. In such an organisational form individuals will depend more on the personal relationships that exist to get things done than on formal reporting relationships. It is about the trading of support, often outside the formal work arrangements and processes for mutual advantage – representing a instrumental approach to work, based on a 'You help me this time and I will help you in the future', type of approach to work.

In extreme cases informal groups can become a matter of concern for an organisation if they become overly influential or powerful. Some writers refer to such groups as becoming a shadow organisation, reflecting something sinister and potentially damaging to the host organisation. But there is still an inevitability about the formation of informal groups and, if 'used' appropriately, they can be of value to management. For example, the grapevine can provide a useful means through which to communicate information around the organisation. One of the earliest and most influential research studies into the effects of groups and teams on work activity was carried out in the late 1920s by Elton Mayo and a team of researchers at the Hawthorne Works of the Western Electric Company in the USA (see Roethlisberger and Dickson, 1964). The key findings to emerge included:

- Informal groups inevitably form within formally designated groupings.
- Informal groups will not always match the groupings designated by management.

- Individuals at work are not simply motivated by pay and other tangible benefits.
- Informal groups will seek to manage their managers in order to influence their working environment.
- The rewards that an individual gains from membership of an informal group may be more significant and meaningful to that individual than any benefit that can be obtained from management
- Informal groups may seek to frustrate management's intentions and objectives.
- The groups to which an individual belong will have a significant influence on their behaviour and attitudes towards work.
- First-line managers and supervisors are subjected to strong and competing pressures for their affiliations from those above and below.
- Management has little or no influence on the establishment, form or membership of informal groups within the organisation.
- Informal groups can engage in activities that are against the interests of the organisation as a whole.
- People change their behaviour as a result of being treated differently and observed during research activities (this became known as the Hawthorne effect).

When groups and teams are formed the individuals have to become acquainted and form some sort of relationship before they can begin working effectively together. Tuckman and Jensen (1977) described a five-stage model of what they termed group development:

- *Stage 1: Forming* This is when individuals first meet and begin to get to know each other. Individuals also use this stage to make a personal impact on the group as the hierarchy and roles that will exist within the group begin to emerge.
- *Stage 2: Storming* With increased familiarity and formal structure emerging, individuals gain in confidence and so conflict begins to arise. Individual agendas begin to emerge as the group 'storms' its way towards the next stage.
- *Stage 3: Norming* Establishing the norms that will be applied within the group takes place next. Norms established are likely to include the behavioural standards of members (what is allowed within the group) and procedural rules (how the group should do its work).
- *Stage 4: Performing* Having established the norms the group is now able to operate effectively and begin to tackle the range of issues implied by its remit.

- *Stage 5: Adjourning*   Having achieved its remit many groups are then dissolved and members will go their separate ways. It often creates a period of reflection as members consider their work and achievements.

Groups are not guaranteed to successfully negotiate each of the five stages above. Also if individuals seek to include items from a hidden agenda in a group's activities it can become a major source of difficulty and friction if not dealt with effectively. Unresolved difficulties may be carried forward and could result in problems emerging in subsequent stages, or even the collapse of the group's ability to function at all. As a minimum, such difficulties are likely to result in a reduction in the level of effectiveness or member satisfaction within a group. Group dynamics refers to the patterns of behaviour and interaction within a group context. Some of the important features that influence how groups are likely to interact include:

- *Cohesion*   This reflects the attractiveness of a group to its members, shown in their motivation to play an active part in it and the degree of resistance to leaving it.
- *Risks and group decisions*   It has been suggested that groups take riskier decisions than individual members would be prepared to take (the risky shift phenomenon).
- *Groupthink*   Janis coined the term groupthink as a result of his studies of a number of military planning activities in the USA. Military planners were a highly cohesive group, very hierarchical in structure and membership – ideal conditions for creating the conditions that prevented critical discussion of important issues.

Belbin (1993) identified a number of team roles, which he argued had an important part to play in achieving effective group functions and interaction in relation to the objectives being sought. The existence of a balance of individuals with the requisite role profiles forms a complementary dynamic process rather than a destructive one. Belbin also made the point that large groups were inefficient and there was an optimal size of group membership. The roles identified by Belbin were:

- The plant.
- The resource investigator.
- The co-ordinator.
- The shaper.
- The monitor evaluator.
- The teamworker.

teamworking

- The implementer.
- The completer.
- The specialist.

Belbin (1981) described the attributes of successful and unsuccessful teams. 'Winning teams', as he terms them, have the following characteristics:

- An individual in the chair who is able to use the role to ensure an effective process.
- A strong plant – a creative and clever person, within the group.
- A good range of mental abilities among individuals within the group to complement the team role contributions.
- Wide team roles present within the group providing a measure of effective interaction and balanced decision making.
- A match between team roles and relevant work experience.
- The ability of the team to compensate for role imbalances and weaknesses.

See also: behaviour management; employee empowerment and engagement; flexibility; high performance working; human capital; job, job analysis and job design; learning organisation; organisational culture; organisational structure; performance management; quality of working life and the psychological contract; strategic HRM; total reward

BIBLIOGRAPHY

Belbin, M. (1981) *Management Teams: Why they Succeed or Fail.* Oxford: Butterworth-Heinemann.

Belbin, M. (1993) *Team Roles at Work.* Oxford: Butterworth-Heinemann.

CIPD (2008) 'Teamworking'. *Factsheet.* Available at www.cipd.co.uk (last accessed June 2009).

Hofstede, G. (1984) *Culture's Consequences: International Differences in Work-related Values.* Beverley Hills, CA: Sage.

Katzenbach, J.R. and Smith, D.K. (1993) *The Wisdom of Teams: Creating the High Performance Organisation.* Boston, MA: Harvard Business School Press.

Roethlisberger, F.J. and Dickson, W. J. (1964) *Management and the Worker.* New York: Wiley.

Tuckman, B. and Jensen, N. (1977) 'Stages of small group development revisited', *Group and Organisational Studies*, 2: 419–427.

Total Reward

> Total reward describes a reward strategy that incorporates components including learning and development, aspects of the working environment, into a 'total' benefits package. It brings together all types of reward direct and indirect, intrinsic as well as extrinsic. Each aspect of reward (base pay, contingent pay, employee benefit and non-financial rewards, including intrinsic rewards from the work itself) are linked together and treated as a coherent whole.

The core components of any reward system are the pay and benefits that most people would instinctively identify as their pay package. That includes:

- *Basic pay* This is the money that is paid as a consequence of an individual's job. It could be based on a job evaluation and would be earned as a salary, daily wage, weekly wage, etc.
- *Contingent pay* This refers to financial rewards linked to the performance, competence, contribution, or skill of individual employees. To complicate matters, such pay can be integrated into base pay or it can be paid as a bonus or an additional 'at-risk' payment. The 'at-risk' payment term implies that the payment can be taken away if certain conditions are not met by the employee: the employee must deliver the performance to qualify for extra pay.
- *Benefits* These generally refer to the range of additional 'things' (such as pension, sick pay, company car, etc.) that are provided by the employer to employees as part of their reward package.

This combination of pay and benefits is usually referred to as the total remuneration package. Some writers also refer to it as the transactional reward package, transaction in this context indicating the 'exchange' nature of the working relationship based on the contract of employment. In essence, work by the employee is 'exchanged' in return for payment being 'delivered' by the employer. The term 'total reward' incorporates a range of what are sometimes referred to as relational rewards, or non-financial intrinsic rewards. These include:

- *Learning and development* This represents the investment by the employer in the career-and work-related development of the employee.

It allows the employee to progress further both in terms of job level and career and not necessarily within the narrow confines of the same employer. Part of the psychological contract is that an employee will commit to investing their time and effort into the current employer as long as they provide the employee with a transferable capability.

- *The work experience* This covers a wide range of 'things' that relate to the physical, social, and psychological working environment. It relates to working conditions such as office decor, facilities quality, the facilities available, the opportunity to interact with colleagues and managers, the leadership style and the way that work is organised and controlled. It also embraces many of the features that would be associated with the quality of working life.

- *Achievement, recognition, responsibility, autonomy, growth* This covers benefits that accrue from the level of engagement, commitment, and corporate citizenship evident in a particular situation. For example, the achievement experienced by an employee from a job 'well done', by being allowed to contribute to problem solving or having their ideas accepted, the opportunities that an employee has access to as a result of being allowed and encouraged to grow, develop and apply their expanding range of competencies.

Total reward expands the conventional focus of reward strategy, policy, and practice by embracing the company culture together with a wide range of intangible and intrinsic 'benefits' that are intended to provide all employees with a voice in, and a stronger connection to, the organisation and its activities. In return the employer hopes to encourage the creation of an engaged and committed employee who will align their work behaviours and attitudes to those preferred by the employer and so deliver a high performance. An analysis of various total reward models by Thompson (2002) found that these were characterised by an approach which reflects the following themes:

- *Holistic* Provides a focus on the attraction, retention, and motivation of employees and their contribution to organisational success by incorporating a broad range of financial and non-financial rewards into the package.
- *Contingency approach* Total reward programmes designed in relation to the specific organisation's culture, structure, work processes, and objectives.

- *Integrated* Delivers innovative reward features that are well integrated with other human resource management policies and practices.
- *Strategic* Delivers the alignment of reward to business strategy.
- *People-centred* Total reward recognises that people are a key source of sustainable competitive advantage.
- *Employee based* Provides a focus for identifying and incorporating into reward systems what it is that employees value in relation to their work experience.
- *Personalised* Provides a flexible mix of rewards that are designed to meet individual employee needs in relation to their lifestyle, preferences, and life stage.
- *Distinctive* Provides a comprehensive and diverse set of rewards supporting the distinctive employer brand.
- *Evolutionary* This allows for incremental and evolutionary change in the range of benefits available and the way in which the total package is constructed.

New pay is another concept in the reward specialism that has connections with total reward in that it recognises the complexity of the organisational 'reality' in relation to functioning, purpose, operational activity, and human nature. In starting from this broader base, new pay seeks to offer guidance on how to shape reward decisions rather than offering specific design principles (Lawler, 1995). It is about seeking ways to enhance strategic effectiveness through reward practice. It is based around the following principles:

- Reward systems should be designed to reward results and behaviour consistent with organisational goals.
- Pay can encourage organisational change.
- The major emphasis in new pay is the introduction of variable pay (pay at risk if results are not delivered).
- New pay emphasises team as well as individual contribution.
- New pay allows employees to share financially in the organisation's success.
- Pay contains a very strong employee relations dimension, with employees having the right to influence the type of reward package adopted.

The CIPD (2009b) reported that over 45 per cent of all firms surveyed had or were in the process of implementing a total reward approach. The proportion doing so was larger among bigger private sector employers and lower in the public sector and among small firms. According to Thompson (2002), the benefits that flow from a total reward scheme are:

- *Easier recruitment of better-quality staff*   With the emphasis on the total working environment, development and reward, it is likely that a larger number of stronger candidates will wish to work for the organisation.
- *Reduced staff turnover*   Because of the overall benefit available from the current employer, fewer people will want to leave.
- *Better business performance*   The rise in commitment and motivation is likely to result in a high performance working environment. This in turn should result in a more certain and profitable long-term future for the organisation and its employees.
- *Enhanced reputation as an employer of choice*   The employer brand should help to 'win the war for talent' in reflecting the status of being a 'great place to work' and therefore an employer of choice – the place everyone wants to work.

Brown and Armstrong (1999) developed a model of total reward based on a four-cell matrix. The four cells were:

- *Transactional and individual rewards*   Pay including base pay, contingent pay, incentive pay, shares, and profit share.
- *Transactional and communal rewards*   Benefits including pensions, holidays, health care, and flexible working.
- *Relational and individual rewards*   Learning and development including training, development, performance management, and career management.
- *Relational and communal rewards*   Work environment issues including values of the organisation, leadership style, employee voice, recognition, job design, role development, responsibility, autonomy, quality of working life, work-life balance, and talent management.

They argued that the transactional rewards being financial in nature are what will attract and retain staff, but because they can easily be copied by competitors they don't provide the basis for a sustainable competitive advantage. It is the relational rewards that are non-financial in nature and can provide a distinctive dimension of the reward system that is very difficult to replicate by another organisation, particularly when integrated and combined with the transactional reward aspects of the total package.

In doing so the relational reward elements enhance the particular value of the transactional rewards available, creating a sustainable competitive advantage. Armstrong and Stephens (2005: 22–3) provided a ten-stage process for implementing a total reward scheme. The ten steps are:

1 Be clear what total reward means and the benefits available through it.
2 Define the transactional and relational rewards that are appropriate to the organisation.
3 Identify and document setting out how each total reward component can be developed and applied to the organisation.
4 Convince senior management of the benefits of a total reward approach.
5 Discuss with staff how a total reward approach would operate and benefit them.
6 Communicate to staff the details of the proposed scheme.
7 Plan and implement each element of the total reward scheme previously agreed.
8 Provide training for line managers who will have responsibility for the implementation and running of many of the total reward elements, particularly the relational ones.
9 Ensure that HR staff are available to provide encouragement, support, and guidance on the implementation and running of the total reward scheme and ensure its coherence between all the active elements.
10 Monitor the implementation and running of the total reward scheme so that any difficulties or problems are dealt with quickly and effectively and also ensure that the original objectives and intentions for the scheme are achieved.

The CIPD (2009a) suggested that total reward is not without its problems. For example, how and where the line should be drawn between allowing employees a choice in relation to personal needs (such as the provision of life assurance)? This represents a problematic area faced by any existing flexible benefits scheme; for example, holiday choices for every employee will have an inevitable impact on others in the team, department or even on customers. It is simply not practical to allow every employee total freedom in relation to the choices available to them. Therefore some mechanism for putting boundaries around what is and is not permitted under the scheme is necessary but also difficult to achieve without giving the appearance that there is limited choice. Some would argue that there are aspects of the employee working experience that it is not appropriate to allow choice in: for example, how much freedom should be allowed in the choice of computer, office desk, chair, office space, office decor, and so on? There are natural limitations on the amount of money that any organisation has available to spend on business-related costs, such as desks and computers. Equally, in relation to such communal features of the working experience, some form of consensus is necessary but can be difficult to achieve. Trade-offs and compromises are inevitable and with such processes comes a degree of weakening of the original intention to provide choice and achieve the positive motivational outcome from it.

See also: *benchmarking; benefits; employee empowerment and engagement; employee relations and conflict; high performance working; incentive schemes; job evaluation; learning organisation; negotiation; performance management; quality of working life and the psychological contract; reward management; strategic HRM; trade union/employee representation; wage structure*

BIBLIOGRAPHY

Armstrong, M. and Stephens, T. (2005) *A Handbook of Employee Reward Management and Practice.* London: Kogan Page.

Brown, D. and Armstrong, M. (1999) *Paying for Contribution.* London: Kogan Page.

CIPD (2009a) 'Total reward'. *Factsheet* (revised June 2009). Available at www.cipd.co.uk

CIPD (2009b) *Reward Management: Annual Survey Report 2009.* London: CIPD. Available at http://www.cipd.co.uk/NR/rdonlyres/3ED186D0-CB5D-404B-951C-E330A0CA5852/0/reward_management_2009.pdf (last accessed June 2009).

Lawler, E.E. (1995) 'The new pay: a strategic approach', *Compensation & Benefits Review,* November.

Thompson, P. (2002) 'Total reward'. *Executive briefing.* Chartered Institute of Personnel and Development, London. Summary available at http://www.cipd.co.uk/subjects/pay/general/totrewd.htm (last accessed June 2009).

Trade Union/
Employee
Representation

Trade unions are organisations that represent people at work. Their purpose is to protect and improve people's pay and conditions of employment. They also campaign for laws and policies which will benefit working people. That makes no distinction between a trade union or an employee representative body made up of the employees within a particular company calling itself a staff association. For the purposes of being listed as a trade union by the Certification Officer, any such body has to be able to demonstrate that it meets the legal definition and requirements.

The factors used by the Certification Officer to determine whether or not a trade union satisfies the legal requirements for listing and independence include purpose, history, membership base, organisation and structure, finance, employer-provided facilities and negotiating record. The Certification Officer was created to enforce several aspects of trade union and employer association legislation and has the following responsibilities:

- Maintaining a list of trade unions and determining the independence of trade unions.
- Dealing with complaints by members that a trade union has failed to maintain an accurate register of members or failed to permit access to its accounting records; seeing that trade unions keep proper accounting records, have their accounts properly audited and submit annual returns; investigating the financial affairs of trade unions; ensuring that the statutory requirements concerning the actuarial examination of members' superannuation schemes are observed; and dealing with complaints that a trade union has failed in its duty to ensure that positions in the union are not held by certain offenders.
- Dealing with complaints by members that a trade union has failed to comply with one or more of the provisions of the Act which require a trade union to ensure that its president, general secretary and

members of its executive are elected to those positions in accordance with the Act.

- Ensuring observance by trade unions of the statutory procedures governing the setting up, operation and review of political funds, and dealing with complaints about breaches of political fund rules or the conduct of political fund ballots or the application of general funds for political objects.
- Seeing that the statutory procedures for amalgamations, transfers of engagements and changes of name are complied with, and dealing with complaints by members about the conduct of merger ballots.
- Dealing with complaints by members that there has been a breach or a threatened breach of the rules of a trade union relating to the appointment, election or removal of an office holder; disciplinary proceedings; ballots of members other than in respect of industrial action; or relating to the constitution or proceedings of an executive committee or decision-making meeting.
- Maintaining a list of employers' associations; ensuring compliance with the statutory requirements concerning accounting records, annual returns, financial affairs and political funds; ensuring that the statutory procedures applying to amalgamations and transfers of engagements in respect of employers' associations are followed.

The TUC (Trades Union Congress) is a body with the stated objectives of (TUC, 2009):

- Bringing Britain's unions together to draw up common policies.
- Lobbying the government to implement policies that will benefit people at work.
- Campaigning on economic and social issues.
- Representing working people on public bodies.
- Representing British workers in international bodies, in the European Union and at the UN employment body (the International Labour Organisation).
- Carrying out research on employment-related issues.
- Running an extensive training and education programme for union representatives.
- Helping unions to develop new services for their members.
- Helping unions to avoid clashes with each other.
- Building links with other trade union bodies worldwide.

The TUC grew out of a debating assembly and its first national congress was held in 1868. It represents a forum where trade unionists can discuss common problems and a shop window for trade unionism. Although a national body, it also has eight regional TUC groupings to interact with local issues and to be able to act as an effective conduit between national and local issues of interest to trade unions and their members.

There are different forms of recognition arrangement between management and a trade union that can exist in an organisation:

- *Multi-union recognition* This is likely where there is more than one trade union within the company each having 'recognition' rights covering a specific category of employees. With each union having rights based on separate recognition agreements this provides for a complex employee relations environment.
- *Single table bargaining* This approach represents an attempt to simplify and unify what would otherwise be a complex employee relations environment by providing a common (single table) approach for the unions to negotiate with management at the same time. High levels of trust and partnership between all the parties are required for this to work.
- *Single union recognition* This exists when a company recognises one union for all categories of employee. There would be one agreement and one set of procedures and negotiations involved.

There are occasions when derecognition of a recognised trade union takes place. This does not happen very often but if it does it could be for any of the following reasons:

- Management decide to adopt a 'macho' approach to employee relations for some reason and unilaterally terminate the recognition agreement.
- The number of employees in membership of the union falls to an unsustainable level, making representation impractical and not representative of a majority of employees.
- A majority of employees decide that they would prefer different representational arrangements.
- There is a planned change to recognition, perhaps introducing a single union agreement (with or without the support of the union(s) currently recognised).
- A reduction in the scope of rights provided to the union under an existing recognition agreement. If membership levels fall significantly, an employer might decide to withdraw collective bargaining rights and restrict recognition to individual rights issues.

There exists a complex legal framework surrounding trade union recognition. The Central Arbitration Committee (CAC) has a role in seeking to resolve disputes between employers and trade unions over recognition claims. For example, the CAC will:

- Encourage the creation of voluntary recognition agreement between a company and the trade union claiming recognition.
- Where that proves impossible to achieve, the CAC can either:

  o Require management to recognise the trade union (where it can be demonstrated that over 50 per cent of employees within the proposed bargaining group are already members), unless it can be shown that sufficient members do not wish the union to be recognised, or the panel can be persuaded that it would not be in the interests of good employee relations.

  Or:

  o Organise a ballot of the workforce within the proposed bargaining group to determine the level of desire for recognition. To succeed the result must achieve a positive response from a majority of those voting and at least 40 per cent support from those eligible to vote. The ballot would be paid for jointly by management and the trade union.

There are different levels of recognition that can be arranged between a trade union and an employer. At the lowest level of recognition individual rights would be the focus for any formal contact between management and unions. So for example that would involve representing individual members in disciplinary and grievance situations. At the other end of the spectrum recognition would involve the ability to negotiate over the terms and conditions of employment. However, taking precedence over such agreements is the legislative provision for consultation over redundancies and so on. In Britain collective agreements are usually binding 'in honour only' and don't therefore have a formal legal status. However, in the case of recognition awarded by the CAC a failure to implement a recognition agreement can result in legal action against the employer. Other rights conferred on the trade unions as a result of legislation include:

- Consultation over redundancy plans involving 20 or more people.
- Consultation over a transfer of business undertakings between employers.

- Consultation over health and safety matters.
- Consultation over pensions where the employer scheme would be 'contracted out' of the State Earnings Related Pension Scheme.
- To be involved in the European Works Councils required to be established for any business operating on a European scale. Also to be informed and consulted about plans and issues in relation to their employment as a result of the EU directive extending these original rights.
- Consultation over workplace agreements covering issues such as the Working Time Regulations and maternity and paternity rights.
- Individual representation covering representation at discipline type hearings, whether or not the trade union is formally recognised by the employer or not.

There are of course obligations placed on trade unions as a result of legislation including holding secret ballots before industrial action, conducting industrial action within the terms of the unions rule book, a union taking unjustified action against a member, or unlawful use of union funds or property by trustees. There are also individual rights that apply to employees in relation to trade union membership even if the trade union is not formally recognised, for example, the right to join and not to be disadvantaged (being refused employment, dismissed or selected for redundancy) as a result of being a trade union member (even if the union is not recognised). Where a trade union is recognised there is a right to be involved in trade union activities (some of which might be eligible for wages to be paid for a reasonable duration of the activity).

See also: discipline and grievance; downsizing, reorganisation, outsourcing and redundancy; employee communication and consultation; employee relations and conflict; Human Resource Management (HRM) and Personnel Management (PM); negotiation; statutory bodies; strategic HRM

BIBLIOGRAPHY

Certification Officer (2008) *Annual Report of the Certification Officer 2007–2008*. Certification Office for Trade Unions and Employers' Associations. London: HMSO.

CIPD (2009) 'Trade unions: A short history'. *Factsheet* (updated April 2009). Available at www.cipd.co.uk (last accessed July 2009).

Directgov (2009) *Introduction to Trade Unions*. Available at http://www.direct.gov.uk/en/Employment/TradeUnions/DG_10027544. (last accessed July 2009).

The Certification Officer official web site: http://www.certoffice.org/pages/index.cfm?pageID=home&CFID=204366&CFTOKEN=97f6b8900039cfcb-3AD2CC89-BDE4-DFC6-B57049C27D67479D (last accessed July 2009).

TUC (2009) http://www.tuc.org.uk/the_tuc/about_role.cfm (last accessed July 2009).

Wage Structure

> *A wage structure represents the arrangements within an organisation that structure the different wage levels, payment types and monitoring processes into an understandable system that offers a robust, defendable and consistent basis for the main elements within the reward package. There are various forms of wage structure that could be used within an organisation and this section will introduce the main variations.*

There are a number of wage structure possibilities and variables to consider. These include:

- *Salary bands*   This option represents a wage band with a maximum and a minimum, in other words a range. This approach has a number of advantages and disadvantages: for example, when designing a new pay structure and a need arises to correct previous anomalies. Such cases could be dealt with as so-called 'Red circles'. The use of a wage band for a new structure means that it is easier to accommodate changes to wage levels (both plus and minus) for individuals as an alignment within the correct wage band is more likely to occur, even if individual differences in pay exist. Another advantage in the use of salary bands is that it provides the opportunity to incorporate another element into the determination of wages – most usually performance. So differences in the level of pay of individuals can be justified on the basis of their contribution measured by performance. The disadvantage of such systems is that of a potential complexity in administration terms, but the availability of computer-based reward packages makes this largely irrelevant.

- *Spot rates*   These reflect the application of a single wage level to a particular job category or grade level. So, for example, all HR associates in Grade 5 will earn £30,000 per year. The advantages are simplicity and transparency in operation. Everyone knows what everyone else earns and there are no exceptions – unlike in salary band systems. The greatest weakness is the inability to differentiate the worth or value of individuals. As a system it relies on management being able to manage underperformance effectively through non-pay means.

- *Pay interval variations* These include being paid by the hour, week, every four weeks, or every calendar month. The issues involved in such decisions include traditions, employee expectation, cash flow, and administrative complexity.
- *Broad- or narrow banded structures* Narrow banded structures as the name implies are small with a relatively large number of grades within the pay structure. For example, the use of a points rating job evaluation scheme might result in the identification of eight grades with perhaps a pay difference between the top and bottom salary in each band being typically below 50 per cent. Broad-banded structures, by comparison, group jobs into about four or five wage bands with a pay difference between the top and bottom of the band being anything up to 100 per cent. The original idea here is to focus attention on the lateral job movement and work development rather than on a vertical points acquisition as a way of 'earning' more pay. However, that intention had proved difficult for managers in applying the guidelines fairly and consistently and also employees can become confused by the rules and procedures. Consequently the trend has been to drift back towards narrow bands in one form or another.
- *Skill based pay* Skill based pay is relatively simple in its arrangement. It can be based on a clear starting wage and then provide for additional payments to be made to an individual determined by the range of extra skills they acquire. It fundamentally changes the dynamic of work organisation. Most pay systems will pay for outputs in some way or another. This type of scheme pays for inputs i.e. capability. It rewards people as they become able to perform a wider range of tasks. It means that management become responsible for managing the range of skill development on offer and also the rate of acquisition. It also requires managers to ensure that they get value for money from the scheme by making actual use of the developing capabilities of employees.
- *Competency based pay* Among the potential benefits are that it can tie reward into the broader use of competency within HR management practice and it should focus attention on development issues rather than just work or task activity. However, the potential difficulties are many and include being able to manage the demand for development; the difficulty in defining and measuring competencies; and the difficulty of ensuring that it can actually use (or even need) the competencies that employees acquire.
- *Market price based pay* This is based on a company determining its wage structure based on market rates of pay. It is often aligned with job

family structures, for example the accountancy job family. The market would be surveyed for accountancy pay levels and in doing so it might be found that years of experience since qualification was the variable that determined pay magnitude. The company would then draw a pay curve with pay on one axis and length of post-qualification experience on the other. Thereafter, for any individual accountant the appropriate salary would be determined by identifying the point on the pay curve that reflected their years of experience. This approach has the advantage of locating company practice within market-based levels of competitiveness, but it has the disadvantage of ignoring internal implications and administrative complexity. For example, if every job family were treated in this way they could all be moving at different rates and in different directions which could result in a loss of internal coherence in the reward strategy and potential discrimination.

Then there are also issues associated with pay progression that need to be resolved, including:

- *No wage progression systems*   These are based on spot rate systems and the only changes to pay within such systems would be as the result of any scheme review or as a result of cost-of-living changes.
- *Incremental progression*   This option would be used in salary band systems where a number of steps or increments existed between the minimum and maximum within each wage band. Traditionally such schemes automatically paid one increment each year (usually on the anniversary of appointment to the job) until the individual reached the top of their salary band. This would be in addition to any pay review as a result of cost-of-living or annual reviews and would probably take place at a different time of the year. This approach is based on the assumption that each year (for a number of years) an individual will become more proficient at their job. As such it rewards service. It is transparent and understandable to individuals. However, there is no automatic link to performance and over time it can make the cost of labour relatively expensive.
- *Incre-merit progression*   This is a variant of the incremental approach in that rather than simply adopting the automatic award of annual increments, it bases the award on performance in some way or another. In its simplest form it allows for the award of an increment providing that the performance of the individual is judged to be satisfactory or above. Possible variations include the awarding of more than one increment for an excellent performance or the withholding of an increment for an

unsatisfactory performance. It is also possible to have the lower portions of a salary band with automatic increments and the higher portions to be performance-based.

- *Performance-based progression*   This approach does not use any increments within the salary band, perhaps with the exception of having a mid-point in the range. There are a number of variations possible in this type of arrangement including having some guidelines on rate of progress through the salary range based on performance markings, to combining current performance marking with current position within the grade and awarding a percentage rise depending on the pay matrix (Armstrong and Stephens, 2005: 237–8), or perhaps using a mixture of performance and competence in a matrix (Armstrong and Stephens, 2005: 242–3).

- *Skill or competency based progression*   These approaches pay additional money (which allows progress through a wage structure) based on the acquisition of additional skills or competencies. Naturally the acquisition needs to be demonstrated (perhaps through a skill test or a performance review) in order to qualify for the additional payment. The use of such approaches changes the dynamic of wage structure management from one of managing outputs to managing inputs, as employees will actively seek the additional skills or competencies in order to qualify for more pay.

Wage structure review processes also include:

- *Salary surveys*   The purpose here is to identify the market rate for particular jobs so that the company can assess how its wage rates compare. The difficulties include comparing like jobs – just because two organisations both employ an HR officer that does not mean that the two jobs are the same or even broadly similar. Appropriate organisations, industries, size of company, and locations should be surveyed in order to identify market comparisons, which gets back to the issue of what defines the labour market for the organisation and standardising the jobs in question can also be problematic. There is also the issue of the reward system design to take into account when comparing salary levels: some organisations will use low salary and high payments schemes and also the benefits package relative to the base pay needs to be considered. There are statistical issues associated with converting the range of salary information collected into usable data that can serve as the basis for meaningful interpretation and action planning in relation to pay and benefits.

wage structure

- *Pay curves*   The output from salary surveys is a series of pay curves or tables of salary data categorised by job level and pay. Pay curves are, as the name suggests, graphs usually with job magnitude along the X axis and money on the vertical Y axis. The actual curves would usually include decile curves (usually 10% and 90%) as well as the median (one measure of average or midpoint) and the quartile (25% and 75%) curves as well. These curves then provide the ability to map company intentions and plans on to the market data as part of its salary planning. The two most common internal company pay curves that would be included would be the pay policy line – representing the company intentions in relation to what it regards as the most appropriate 'intended' company pay line relative to the marketplace – and the pay practice line – the average actual pay for each wage band paid by the company (which may or may not be the same as the policy line per-haps because the company operates a performance-based salary system and the actual levels of pay may be higher or lower than the policy line). The implications arising from the range of pay curves charted can then be assessed and taken into account at the next pay round in terms of where money is targeted and distributed around the wage structure based on company intentions, market conditions, and other factors that need to be incorporated into such planning.
- *Equal value*   This aspect of wage structure planning is vital and in essence quite simple in its intention and approach. Legislation requires that pay systems should not discriminate on the basis of gender (Armstrong and Stephens, 2005: Chapters 11 and 12). Among the issues that do impact on wage systems is the need to demonstrate that pay, the basis of job measurement, and the salary management prac-tices operated by the company do not discriminate. It is suggested that organisations should carry out equal pay reviews of their reward systems regularly – perhaps every four years.

See also: benchmarking; benefits; competency; contract of employment; employee relations and conflict; expatriation and international management; Human Resource Management (HRM) and Personnel Management (PM); high performance working; incentive schemes; job, job analysis and job design; job evaluation; negotiation; performance appraisal; performance management; reward management; strategic HRM; total reward; trade union/employee representation

BIBLIOGRAPHY

Armstrong, M. and Stephens, T. (2005) *A Handbook of Employee Reward Management and Practice*. London: Kogan Page.

key concepts in human resource management

index

key concepts in human
resource management

index

285

key concepts in human
resource management